Kimbell Art Museum

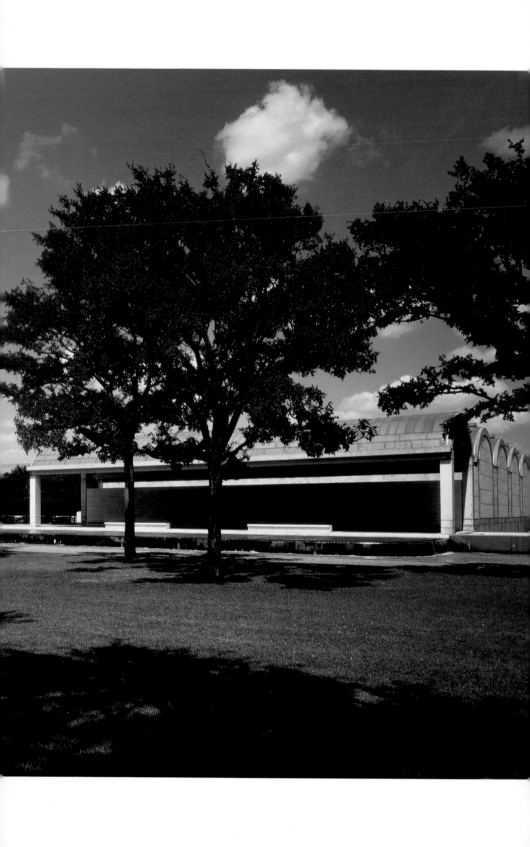

Kimbell Art Museum

HANDBOOK OF THE COLLECTION

Edited by
Timothy Potts

Kimbell Art Museum

Fort Worth

Distributed by
YALE UNIVERSITY PRESS
New Haven and London

Published by Kimbell Art Museum, Fort Worth
Distributed by Yale University Press, New Haven and London

© 2003 Kimbell Art Museum
3333 Camp Bowie Boulevard
Fort Worth, Texas 76107-2792

Produced by the publications department of the Kimbell Art Museum,
Wendy P. Gottlieb, manager of publications, and Anna Lazarus, publications assistant
Designed by Tom Dawson
Separations by CS Graphics, Inc., Singapore, and Studio 2000, Arlington, Texas
Printed by Authentic Press, LLC, Fort Worth
Bound by Universal Bookbindery, Inc., San Antonio

ISBN 0-912804-40-8 (cloth: alk. paper)
ISBN 0-300-10181-3 (Yale pbk.: alk. paper)
ISBN 0-912804-41-6 (Kimbell pbk.: alk. paper)

Library of Congress Control Number: 2002113168

On the cover: Georges de La Tour (French, 1593–1652), *The Cheat with the Ace of Clubs* (detail), late 1620s.
Oil on canvas, 38½ x 61½ in. (97.8 x 156.2 cm). Acquired in 1981 (see pages 68–69)

On the back cover: Southwest corner with reflecting pool and waterfall

Frontispiece: Southwest portico with reflecting pool, seen from the park (1992)

CONTENTS

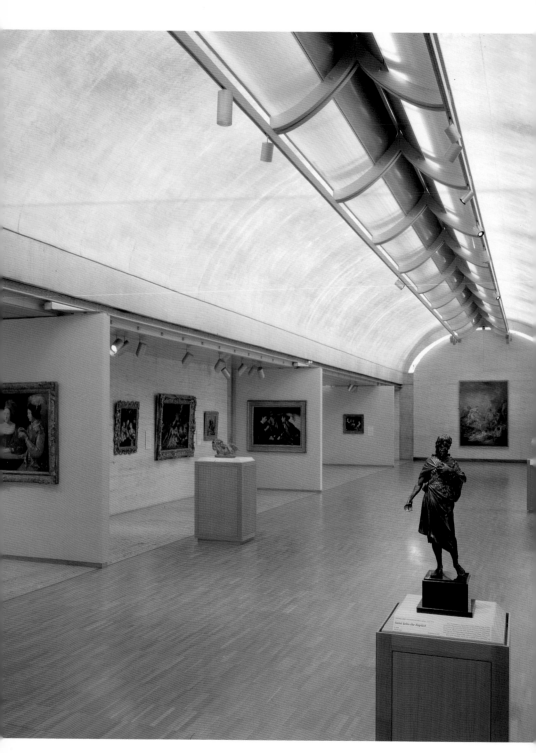

INTRODUCTION

Timothy Potts

Director

I n its short history of some thirty years, the Kimbell Art Museum has come to
occupy a distinctive place in the international community of museums. A small
collection of less than 350 works, acquired at a time when the supply of great
masterpieces was thought by many to be drying up, the Kimbell has nonetheless
become a byword for quality and importance at the very highest level. Particularly in
its holdings of European old- and modern-master painting—and more selectively in its
collections of ancient classical and Egyptian, Asian, African, and Precolumbian art—the
Kimbell possesses a core of works which not only epitomize their eras and styles, but
also touch individual high points of aesthetic beauty and historical importance that
assure them a place among the masterpieces of world art. Leaving to older and larger
institutions the role of collecting broadly and in depth, the Kimbell has chosen as its
primary collecting aspiration the pursuit of quality over quantity.

Enjoyment and admiration of the Kimbell's collection has, from its inception, been
wedded to the equal acclaim accorded the building in which it is housed. Working in
close collaboration with its first director, Richard F. Brown (1916–1979), the American
architect Louis I. Kahn (1901–1974) created for the Kimbell one of the purest and
most perfect statements of architectural modernism, one that is today regarded among
the finest of all twentieth-century museum designs. The signature cycloid-vaulted
ceilings; the restrained choice of complementary materials and minimalist interior
detailing; the careful articulation of open and enclosed spaces, mediated by the
reflecting pools and planted grove of the entrance; and, most of all, the famously
"silvery" light, diffused from slits in the cycloids and reflected off the gray concrete

South center gallery

vaults—all these together create what has seemed to many a close to perfect environment for viewing and contemplating art. The magic of the Kimbell's galleries has become a celebrated aspect of visiting the Museum and a touchstone for many subsequent museum architects, who pay homage to Kahn's design in their own work the world over (most recently in our new neighbor, the Modern Art Museum of Fort Worth, designed by Tadeo Ando). As the Kimbell's curator of architecture, Patricia Cummings Loud, has observed: "The unforeseen destiny of the Kimbell Art Museum is the high regard and admiration in which it is held internationally, as an ideal and inspirational museum building." It is this marriage of equals—collection and building—so beautifully attuned to each other that has come to represent the Kimbell's distinctive achievement.

North portico with reflecting pool and its waterfall (1987)

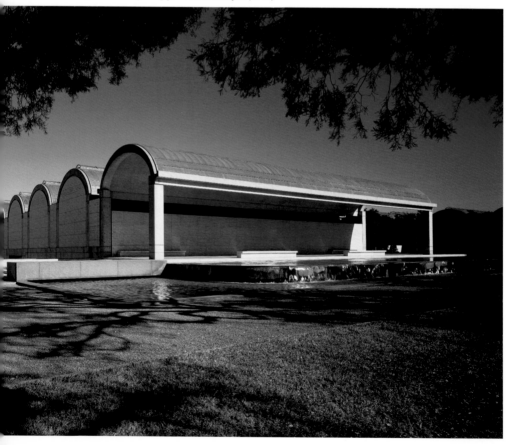

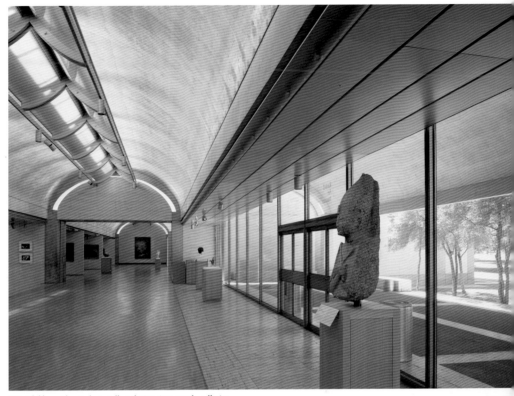

West lobby with window wall and view into south galleries

THE CREATION OF A MUSEUM

The "founding father" and chief benefactor of the future museum was Kay Kimbell (1887–1964), a successful Fort Worth businessman and art collector. Mr. Kimbell and his wife Velma had begun collecting paintings in 1935, favoring British portraits in the grand manner, especially the work of Gainsborough, Reynolds, Romney, and Lawrence, as well as a broader range of subjects by French and other European artists. The following year the Kimbells, together with Dr. and Mrs. Coleman Carter (Mrs. Carter was Mr. Kimbell's sister), formed the Kimbell Art Foundation to continue building the collection, which eventually grew by the time of Mr. Kimbell's death in April 1964 to 260 paintings and 86 other works of art. During his lifetime, works from the collection were regularly lent for public display to the Fort Worth Public Library and area colleges and universities. Thus from the beginning the Kimbells saw collecting and exhibiting as twin aspects of their overall mission to bring a greater awareness and appreciation of art to the people of their community.

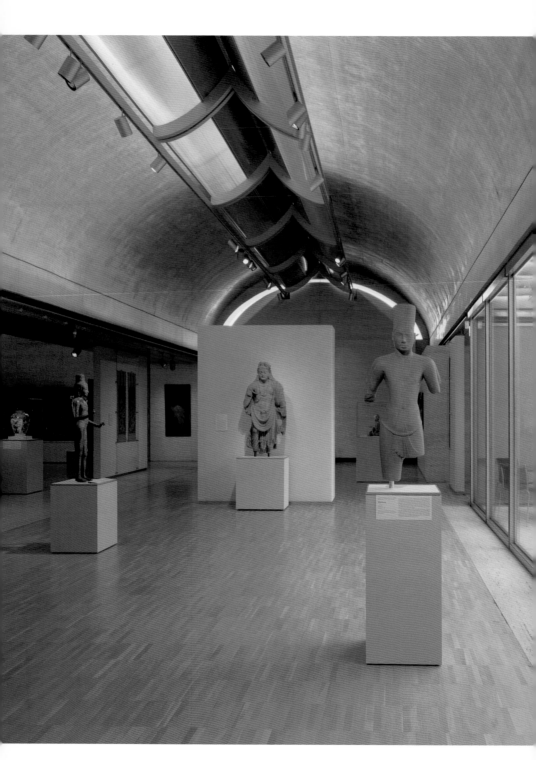

Mr. Kimbell did not himself wish to oversee the creation of a museum for his collection, assigning this charge through his will to the Kimbell Art Foundation, which continues to own and operate the Museum. Before his death Mr. Kimbell had made clear his desire that the future museum be "of the first class," and to further this aim, within a week, his widow Velma contributed her share of their community property to the Foundation. In 1965 Richard F. Brown, then director of the Los Angeles County Museum of Art, was hired to head the future museum, and Brown in turn proposed Louis Kahn to be the architect of a new building. A nine-and-one-third-acre plot of land had already been set aside for the project by the city of Fort Worth in November 1964, and Kahn was duly commissioned on 5 October 1966.

The design for the Museum went through three principal versions, eventually reducing the plan to a scale commensurate with the numerically modest collection.[1] Kahn often spoke about his work in poetic, even mystical terms, always returning to the interplay of light with architectural form and how they work together to create a spiritual experience of the built environment. Although his aesthetic remained at all times quintessentially modernist, Kahn had a profound interest in earlier periods of architecture, from ancient Rome and Egypt to nineteenth-century Beaux-Arts design. Some of these influences can be seen very tangibly in the Kimbell's design: the vaults of monuments like Caracalla's Baths (third century A.D.), and Boullée's proposed addition to the Bibliothèque Nationale in Paris (c. 1780), for example, were very much in Kahn's mind when he designed the distinctive cycloid-shaped, concrete-shell roofs. Each of these is supported solely at the four extremities (none of the travertine walls is load-bearing), which represented a significant engineering challenge. The final solution for their construction involved a novel system of post-tensioned steel cables that allows the hundred-foot-long cycloids to float above the four corner pillars. Construction of the Museum began in July 1969, and the building first opened its doors to the public on 4 October 1972.

THE GROWTH OF THE COLLECTION

With Richard F. Brown's appointment as director in 1965, the Foundation set about building a collection that would fulfill the aspirations of its founder. A policy was adopted "to form collections of the highest possible aesthetic quality, derived from any and all periods in man's history, and in any medium or style." In practice, however, in

North galleries with installation of Asian art

1. For a detailed account of the design process, and a discussion of the building generally, see Patricia Cummings Loud, "History of the Kimbell Art Museum," in *In Pursuit of Quality: The Kimbell Art Museum, An Illustrated History of the Art and Architecture* (Fort Worth, 1987), 1–95.

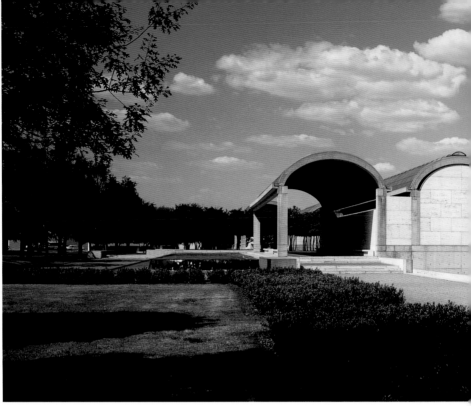

View from the southwest with the Noguchi sculpture garden and court of the myrtles in the right foreground (1987)

agreement with its neighbors, the Amon Carter Museum and the Fort Worth Art Center (now the Modern Art Museum of Fort Worth), the Kimbell did not collect the art of the Americas (except of the Precolumbian cultures) or more recent modern art. Initially, under Brown, the latest work acquired dated from 1922; under his successor, Edmund P. Pillsbury, this was extended to 1946. This left a potentially vast field to be covered, from antiquity to modernism, and ranging all over the globe. In seven years of vigorous collecting prior to the opening, Brown had laid out the broad parameters of the Museum with many significant acquisitions in European (ancient through early twentieth century) and Asian art, and smaller groups of African and Precolumbian works. European painting remained the heart of the collection, both in quantity and quality. A generous representation of British eighteenth- and nineteenth-century works continued to reflect Mr. Kimbell's legacy and taste, but the range of the European collection as a whole was extended back through the Baroque and Renaissance periods to late medieval times, and forward into modernism. Few European sculptures and decorative arts were acquired, in contrast to the non-Western collections, where a more inclusive approach to other media was adopted. Brown continued to build the collections after the opening until his death in 1979, at which point the Museum's holdings numbered 360 works, including 41 European prints and drawings.

Brown's unexpected passing was a serious blow to the institution but did not stop the quest for acquisitions. In 1980 the board acquired Cézanne's *Man in a Blue Smock*

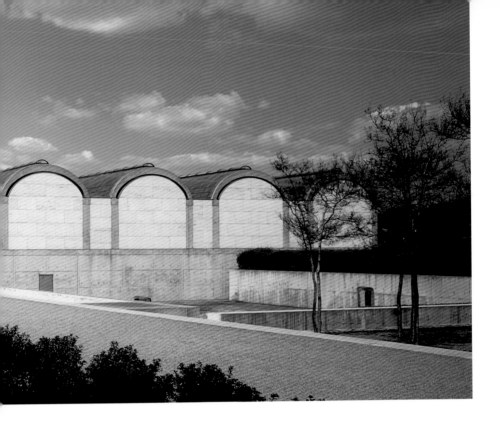

at auction, and some works already under consideration at the time of Brown's death were subsequently bought. Later in 1980, Edmund P. Pillsbury, then director of the Yale Center for British Art (another Kahn building), was appointed as Brown's successor and initiated a second very active period of acquisitions. A number of the Museum's most famous works—Fra Angelico's *The Apostle Saint James Freeing the Magician Hermogenes*, Caravaggio's *The Cardsharps*, La Tour's *Cheat with the Ace of Clubs*, Velázquez's *Don Pedro de Barberana*, Murillo's *Four Figures on a Step*, Caillebotte's *On the Pont de l'Europe*, as well as many Asian and Precolumbian works—all came into the collection between 1980 and 1987. These acquisitions were supported partly by selective deaccessioning of works, including all of the drawings and prints. Pillsbury also extended the Museum's coverage of modern art with paintings by Gauguin, Monet, Miró, Matisse, and Mondrian. Overall, by the end of his directorship in 1998, the collection had been reduced in size to some 316 works, but its quality had been notably enhanced.

Over the past five years the Kimbell has continued to pursue works of the highest aesthetic quality and historical importance. Sculpture—still a relatively small category within the European collections—has been enhanced by the addition of major works from ancient Greece *(Head of an Athlete)*, Renaissance Italy (Michelozzo, *Saint John the Baptist)* and Late Gothic Germany *(Virgin and Child)*. The Asian and other non-Western cultures have also continued to offer opportunities for major new additions, including the first works of Tibetan and Peruvian (Huari) art. The most recently acquired painting, Raeburn's *Allen Brothers*, takes us back to the grand British portraiture that was Mr. Kimbell's original enthusiasm, happily providing a new focus for this area of the collection. Malcolm Warner, senior curator since 2002, has played a crucial role in this and other acquisitions since his arrival, as have the other curatorial staff.

Throughout its history, the Kimbell's active program of visiting exhibitions has meant that much of the collection is often not on display. Fortunately digital technology has allowed us to alleviate this problem somewhat by posting images and descriptions of nearly all of the Museum's works on the Internet (www.kimbellart.org/collection). This *Handbook*, which includes all of the more important works, is the first such publication in more than fifteen years. We hope that it will serve not only as a convenient guide to the collection, bringing to bear the latest advances in scholarship, but also as the inspiration for further visits to the Museum, where alone the direct experience of art can work the magic that its creators intended.

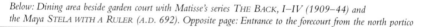

Below: Dining area beside garden court with Matisse's series THE BACK, I–IV *(1909–44) and the Maya* STELA WITH A RULER *(A.D. 692). Opposite page: Entrance to the forecourt from the north portico*

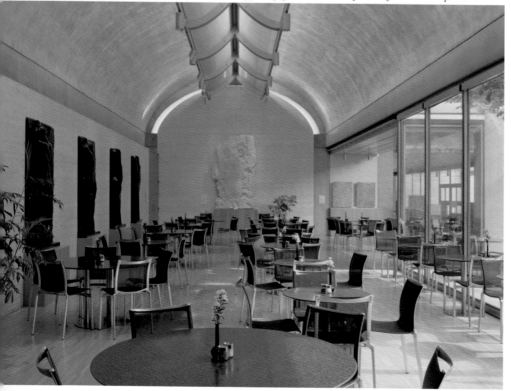

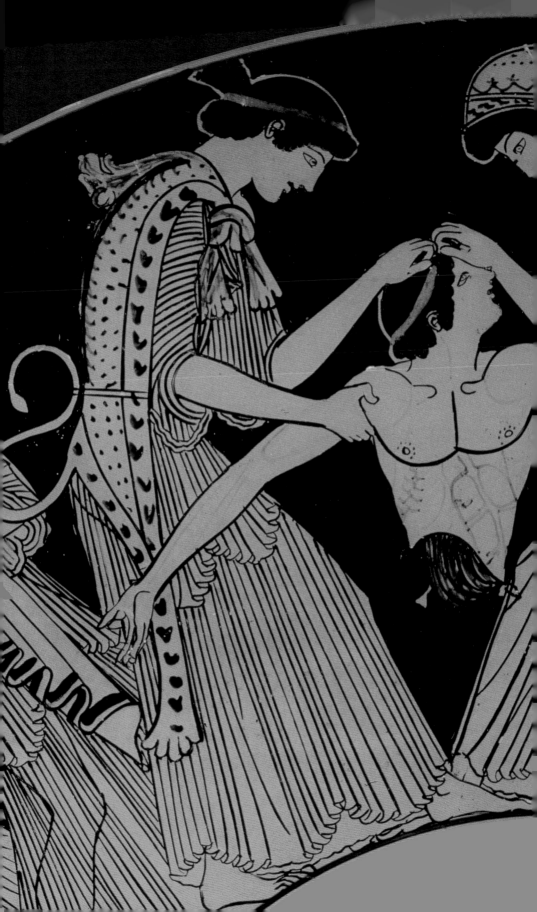

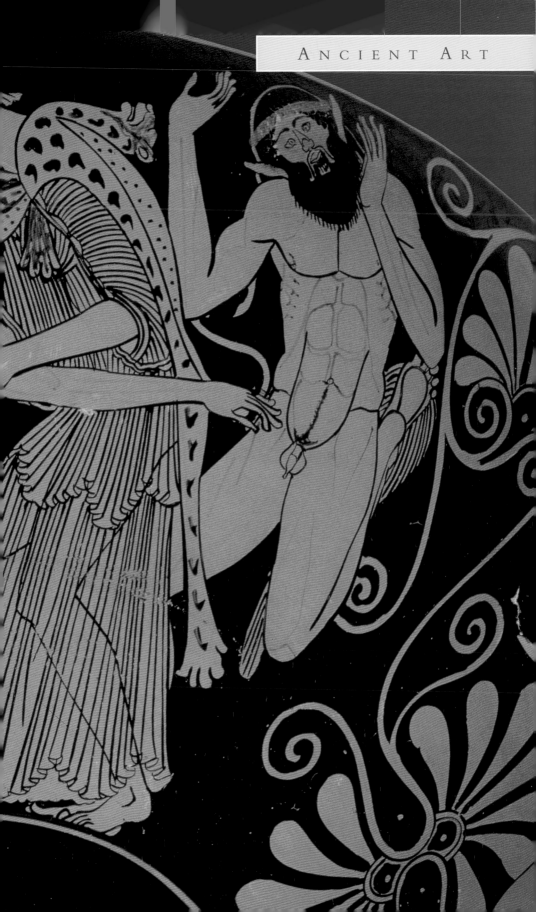

BASTIS MASTER
Cyclades Islands, Greece
Female Figure, c. 2500–2300 B.C.
Early Cycladic II phase

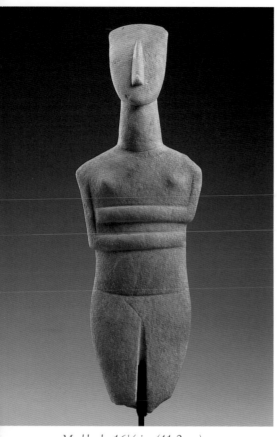

Marble; h. 16¼ in. (41.2 cm)
Acquired in 1970, Gift of Ben Heller

Characterized by its minimalist stylization, this marble statuette of a female figure was produced by the Early Bronze Age culture that flourished in the Cyclades Islands of Greece in the second half of the third millennium B.C. As well as standing (or lying) figures such as this, Cycladic artists also carved more complex figures playing the lyre, and a variety of elegantly shaped marble vessels.

The Kimbell sculpture belongs to what modern scholars have called the Late Spedos type of reclining, folded-arm figure. It has been attributed to the Bastis Master, so named after the previous owner of a work now in the Metropolitan Museum of Art, New York. The Kimbell's sculpture, whose legs are missing from the knees down, would originally have measured about fifty-five centimeters, placing it among the artist's larger and more developed works. The Bastis Master is known to have used a four-part canon of proportions, with divisions at the shoulders, pubic triangle, and knees, and, as can be seen here, modeled the undulating curves of the female anatomy with great sensitivity. Two red dots on the right cheek are all that remain of what would originally have been more extensive painted decoration. The artist follows a convention of separating the forearms by a clear space, which gives the figure an asymmetrical appearance. His style is typified by long, angular heads with a prominent, arching nose and rounded chin; curving incisions at the neck, hips, knees, and ankles; small, wide-spaced breasts; and clearly marked pubic triangle.

Figures of this kind were typically placed in burials, along with marble vessels and other funerary offerings. Because the original burial conditions of most folded-arm figurines were never recorded, their function remains a matter of speculation—perhaps magical representations of venerated ancestors, companions for the dead, cult images of a divinity, or even toys. The strikingly stylized quality of these figures made them a source of great interest to early modern sculptors in the first decades of the twentieth century.

Portrait Statue of Pharaoh Amenhotep II, c.1400 B.C.
Recarved for Ramesses II (the Great), c. 1250 B.C.; South Karnak, Egypt
Dynasty 18, reign of Amenhotep II, c. 1427–1400 B.C., and Dynasty 19,
reign of Ramesses II, c. 1279–1213 B.C.

This regal, life-size figure of Amenhotep II showed the king seated on a throne, holding the traditional insignia of kingship against his chest—the scepter in the form of a crook in his left hand and the flail or whip in his right. The king is depicted wearing Upper (southern) Egypt's distinctive white crown, embellished by the uraeus or royal cobra, and a broad collar composed of five bands. His body is enveloped in the jubilee *(Heb-Sed)* robe, worn by kings at festivals, particularly the Sed-festival, in which the king was physically and spiritually rejuvenated. Usually this festival was observed after thirty years on the throne; however, since most pharaohs never reached their thirtieth years, some, like Amenhotep II, celebrated it prematurely. Here, the back of the robe projects above the figure's shoulders, three incised lines marking the edge of its overlap down the front.

This sculpture was originally part of a seated figure excavated in 1896 at the Temple of Mut at South Karnak. The exact date of excavation of the Kimbell sculpture is recorded in a letter from the excavator, the semi-invalided pioneer archaeologist Margaret Benson, to her mother dated the following day, 9 February 1896.

Fragments of the king's throne found with this figure, but now lost, bore cartouches of Ramesses II ("the Great"), who lived more than a century after Amenhotep II. Ramesses is infamous today for having usurped statues of earlier kings, and this sculpture seems to be another such case. Careful examination of the face shows that Amenhotep's eyebrows

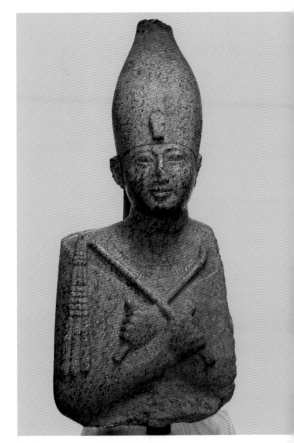

Red granite; h. 40½ (102.8 cm)
Acquired in 1982

were erased and his eyes, nose, and mouth slightly reshaped to make them resemble Ramesses' features. The bust leans against a pillar that still bears traces of the hammered original inscription, and signs of the new royal titulary, added when the statue was usurped. Ramesses must also have erased Amenhotep's name and replaced it with his own on the throne. Another clue to the statue's true identity is that Ramesses carried his scepter with the hook up and Amenhotep carried his with the hook down, as here.

Kneeling Statue of Senenmut, Chief Steward of Queen Hatshepsut, c. 1473–1458 B.C.
Temple of Montu (?), Armant, Egypt
New Kingdom, Dynasty 18, reign of Hatshepsut, c. 1473–1458 B.C.

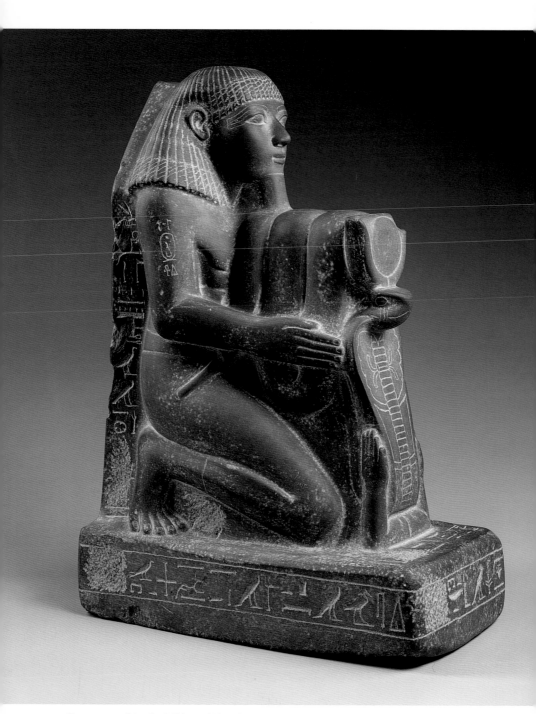

Gray green schist; h. 16⅛ in. (41 cm)
Acquired in 1985

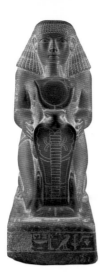

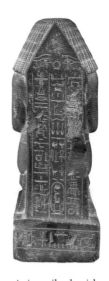

S enenmut was the favorite official of Queen Hatshepsut, one of only a handful of women in Egyptian history who reigned as pharaoh. As the queen's cherished advisor and tutor to her only daughter, Neferure, Senenmut was the first commoner since the Old Kingdom to enjoy a level of wealth, prestige, and privilege approaching that of royalty. He was also the chief royal architect, and is credited with the design of the splendid funerary temple of Queen Hatshepsut at Deir el-Bahri in western Thebes, Egypt's capital during Dynasty 18.

This votive statue, made of a prestigious hard stone, shows Senenmut presenting a statue of the cobra goddess Renenutet as a gift to a temple, in which it would originally have been placed. The cobra is crowned by a sun disk and cowhorns and rests on a base of two upraised arms (the hieroglyphic sign *ka*, meaning "spirit")—a magical gesture intended to preserve life and ward off evil. Together these iconographic elements spell Maat-ka-re, the throne name of Queen Hatshepsut, whose cartouche is inscribed on Senenmut's upper-right arm. This cartouche reads: "The good goddess, Maat-ka-re, granted life."

The statue is inscribed with a hieroglyphic text that runs in three columns down the back of the obelisk-shaped pillar behind the figure, and continues around the sides and front top of the base, and vertically on the sides of the pillar. The Kimbell statue, together with two other inscribed, kneeling statues of Senenmut (in Brooklyn and Munich), may be associated through its inscription with the temple of Montu, in Armant, a few miles south of Deir el-Bahri. The systematic erasure of Senenmut's name from these and other inscriptions (visible here as rough areas of pecked stone) has been the subject of extensive discussion, raising the issue of the courtier's fall from power. The traditional view links Senenmut's fate with that of Hatshepsut, whose memory was persecuted upon her death by her nephew, Tuthmosis III. More recently it has been suggested that Hatshepsut herself turned against her steward either in reaction to his usurpation of royal privileges or for switching political support to her rival. Interestingly, despite the intentional erasures of his name from the Kimbell inscription, the features of Senenmut have suffered no damage and the physical condition of the statue is excellent.

Pair of Winged Deities, 874–860 B.C.
Assyrian, reign of Ashurnasirpal II (883–859 B.C.)
Room L, Northwest Palace, Nimrud, Iraq

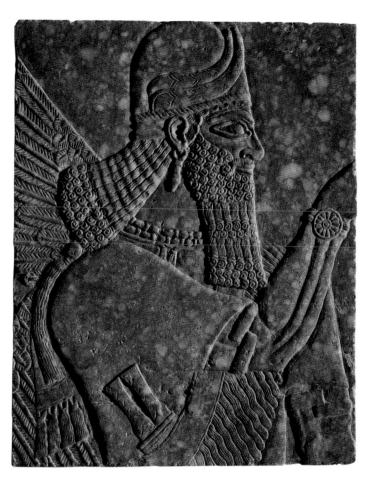

*Gypsum; left:
36¼ x 27⅝ in.
(92 x 70 cm);
right: 35¼ x 29 in.
(90.7 x 73.5 cm)
Acquired in 1981*

The Northwest Palace of Ashurnasirpal II (reigned 883–859 B.C.) at Nimrud (ancient Kalhu) is the earliest of the surviving royal residences of the Assyrian kings, lavishly decorated with monumental gateway figures and reliefs, whose discovery in the mid-nineteenth century created a sensation throughout the Western world. First uncovered by the pioneer British traveler and archaeologist Austen Henry Layard in 1845, the Northwest Palace consisted of a series of long, narrow rooms grouped around large courtyards. Seven-foot-high stone slabs that lined the walls of many of the rooms were carved with elaborate narrative, mythological, and ritual scenes in low-relief. The greatest and most original artistic achievement of the Assyrians, these images and accompanying inscriptions record the kings' military campaigns and testify to their prowess as warriors and hunters as well as their sanctity as the representatives of the Assyrian pantheon on earth.

One of the most recurrent and potent images on these reliefs is the depiction

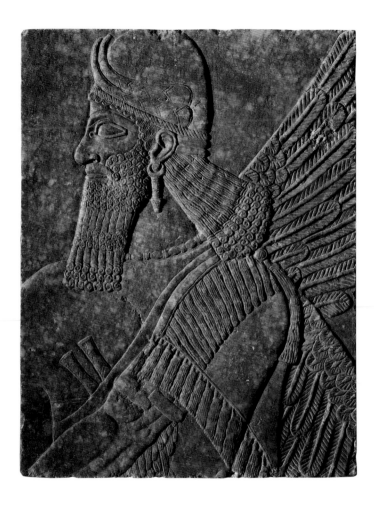

of a magic purification or protective ritual, in which winged griffin-demons (*apkallu*, "sages") or winged anthropomorphic deities, holding ritual "buckets" and pinecone-shaped objects, flank a "Sacred Tree" that they sprinkle with holy water or pollen. The Kimbell's pair of winged deities are fragments of two such full-length figures enacting this magic ritual, sprinkling or pollinating the central tree motif. As such, each figure would originally have held a bucket in his left hand and a cone in his right. The deities, marked as divine by their wings and horned helmets, are conceived in the image of the monarch, reflecting his facial features, stance, and physical strength. Their exaggerated musculature and luxuriant, tightly curled hair and beards suggest something of the king's vainglorious power and virility.

These reliefs come from a room that may have been used by the king for ritual ablution.

DOURIS (painter)
Greek (Athens), active c. 500–460 B.C.
Red-Figure Cup Showing the Death of Pentheus (exterior)
and a Maenad (interior), c. 480 B.C.
Late Archaic period

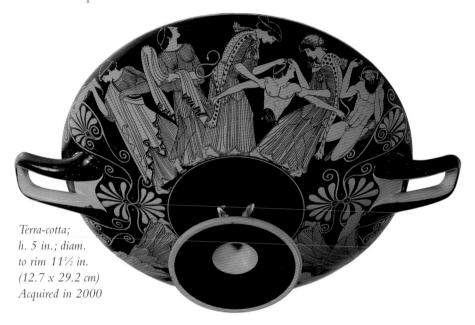

Terra-cotta;
h. 5 in.; diam.
to rim 11½ in.
(12.7 x 29.2 cm)
Acquired in 2000

This Attic red-figure wine cup *(kylix)* is one of the finest surviving works by Douris, a vase painter of exceptional talent and versatility of the late Archaic and early Classical period. The interior of the cup shows a maenad (female follower of the wine god, Dionysos) who glances back as she grasps a young leopard by the tail with one hand and holds a *thyrsos* (magic wand) with the other. An inscription praises her charms: "The girl is beautiful."

On the exterior of the cup, in two exceptionally rich and vivid scenes, we witness the gruesome death of Pentheus, a mythical king of Thebes who had offended the god Dionysos by denying his divinity and forbidding his worship. The vengeful god, shown seated with a *kantharos* (wine cup) in his hand and listening to a piping satyr (man-animal with horse's tail and ears, and snub nose), had caused the wretched

Pentheus to be attacked by a group of Theban women, who had been worked into an ecstatic frenzy by the god. Coming upon Pentheus in the woods, they mistook him for a wild beast and, as the god had willed, tore him limb from limb.

Two of the women are shown in the center of one scene grasping Pentheus's

Detail of interior

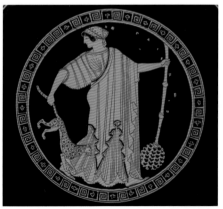

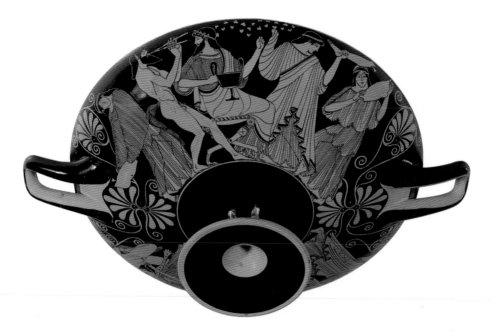

head and twisted torso, his guts hanging out, his eyes staring blankly in the knowledge of imminent death. Four other women wield aloft his dismembered legs, while a fifth, perhaps his mother Agave, holds the king's garment and gazes skyward, oblivious for now to the identity of her victim. Another satyr, shown kneeling and frontal-faced, completes the scene.

Painted at the beginning of the Classical period, when Greek artists were preoccupied above all else with the naturalistic representation of the human body, Douris is here seen grappling with many of the key developments that were to revolutionize European art. He uses the naked satyrs in particular to display his talent with difficult three-quarter and frontal poses. The bodies of the women, on the other hand, are rendered more economically in outline through their diaphanous garments, whose folds and hems are meticulously represented. One satyr and two of the women are shown with frontal faces, the most challenging and rarest of views. Great attention is given throughout to details of the facial features, hair, musculature, and subsidiary elements like furniture. One of the most precise and meticulous of draftsmen, Douris had first sketched in the figures with the blunt end of the brush and then painted them in with a steady, controlled hand. Thinned paint was used for internal details like the musculature of the satyrs and the leopard's pelt, and blobs of thick black paint, which stand out in relief, for patterns of hair. Red paint was added sparingly for hair bands and Pentheus's blood. Both for the quality of its conceptions and drawing, and for the exceptional state of its preservation, this cup ranks among the finest expressions of Douris's mature art, and as one of the masterpieces of early Classical vase painting.

Greek (Athens), active c. 490–470 B.C.
Red-Figure Lekythos Showing Eros in the Role of Archer, c. 490–480 B.C.
Late Archaic period

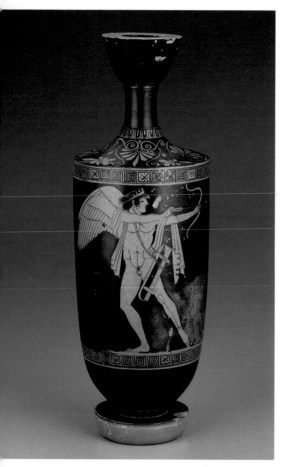

Terra-cotta; h. 13½ in. (34.3 cm)
Acquired in 1984

The image on this red-figure *lekythos* (one-handled oil jug) marks the earliest known appearance of Eros, the god of love, in Attic vase painting in his role of archer, predating by forty to fifty years the representation of this subject on one of the east metopes of the Parthenon. Prior to his acquiring the bow and arrow, Eros pursued lovers with cruder weapons, such as an ax, whip, or a pair of sandals. Arrows, however, became his more common attribute due to their literary association as shafts of desire, a notion that appears in a number of passages in the plays of Euripides.

The *lekythos* is attributed to the Brygos Painter, a second-generation master of the red-figure style, whose main production centers on the 480s and 470s. Dating from c. 490–480 B.C., this vase is among his early works, and epitomizes the freshness and vigor of Late Archaic art. Known primarily as a cup painter, the Brygos Painter also decorated a good number of *lekythoi*. An acute observer, the Brygos Painter's vases usually depict scenes from daily life: revels, symposia, athletes, warriors with horses, men and youths courting, and erotic scenes. Here the figure of Eros, nude but for the mantle draped over his shoulders, has the artist's typical poise and balance, while retaining the potentiality for sudden movement: the figure is set frontally, his weight on his right forward-moving foot, while his head turns back in profile as he draws his bow.

The *lekythos* dates to the time of the Persian Wars, when the Athenians saved Greece from Persian domination in battles on land and sea at Marathon (490 B.C.) and Salamis (480 B.C.). The repulse of the mighty Persians was interpreted by later generations as the triumph of Greek freedom and order over barbarian despotism—a divinely sanctioned justification of Hellenic culture. The sea victory also formed the springboard for Athens's maritime hegemony of the Aegean in the Classical period, laying the basis for the prosperity and power that would culminate in the age of Pericles.

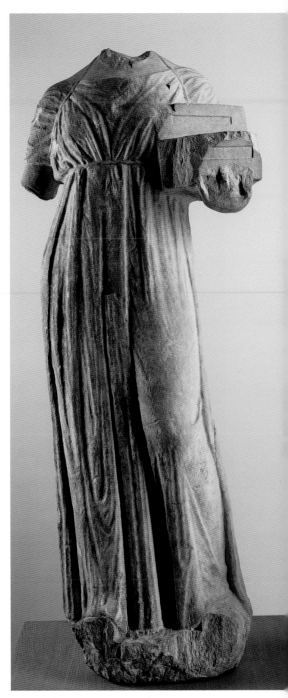

This sculpture of a young female attendant is probably one of a group of votary figures that originally accompanied the statue of a goddess in the performance of a ceremonial rite. Although it probably dates from a century later than the maidens from the famous frieze of the Parthenon in Athens, the attendant shares their ceremonious attitude of participating in a solemn ritual. New, however, are the ease and languid grace that were introduced into Attica sculpture by fourth-century-B.C. masters like Praxiteles and Lysippos. Her gown, held close to the body by a cord at the shoulder and waist, falls in soft folds over her weight-bearing right leg while revealing her flexed left leg underneath. Corresponding to similar objects preserved on funerary monuments, the jewelry box she bears may have been intended as an offering to the deity, as in the *Stele of Hegeso* (c. 400 B.C., Athens, National Museum), where a young girl presents an open box to her seated mistress.

Carved in the round, the Kimbell figure is less finished in the back, where the rough chisel marks left by the artist are still evident, indicating that she was intended to be viewed from the front.

Marble; h. 46 in. (116.9 cm)
Acquired in 1972

Head of an Athlete (Apoxyomenos), c. 2nd–1st century B.C.
Hellenistic or Roman, probably after Lysippos (Greek, c. 365–310 B.C.)

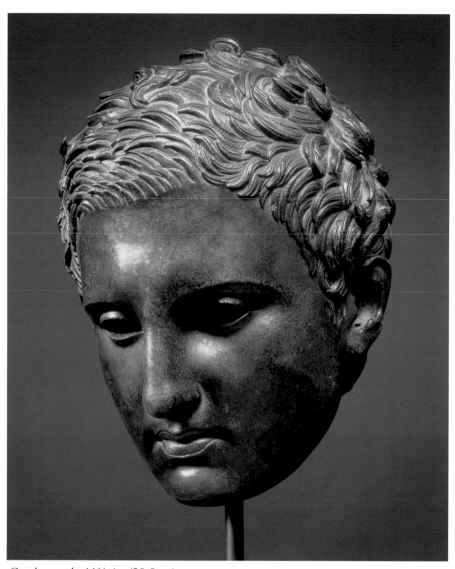

Cast bronze; h. 11¾ in. (29.9 cm)
Acquired in 2000

This exceptionally fine and rare head comes from the figure of an athlete, who was shown scraping oil from his naked body after exercising. Other more complete versions of this statue allow the full figure to be reconstructed, standing with his weight on the right leg, the head turning slightly to the left and down as the athlete scrapes the dirty oil from his left forearm with a *strigil*. The lips were originally overlaid with copper, and the eyes inlaid with stone, glass, and metal.

According to recent research, the lost original of this much-copied statue was probably the bronze *Apoxyomenos* ("Scraper") by Lysippos, the court sculptor of Alexander the Great, and may be dated on stylistic grounds around 340–330 B.C. (Other scholars identify that work with the type known from the marble copy in the Vatican Museum, showing an athlete scraping oil off his outstretched arm.) The Kimbell's thick-walled bronze is the finest of the surviving casts of the head of this popular subject, and fits well with what we know of Lysippos's distinctive style as described by Pliny in the first century A.D., particularly the emphasis on the athlete's carefully modeled hair—here shown radiating from the crown in short, overlapping locks merging into vigorously voluted curls above. Lysippos also introduced a new canon of proportions for the ideal male body, with slimmer limbs, smaller heads, and a more fluid musculature than his fifth-century-B.C. predecessors. According to Pliny, whereas other artists

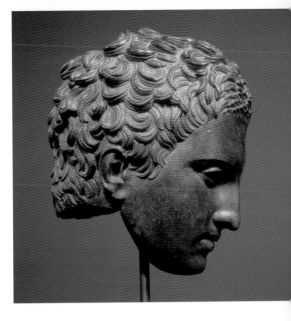

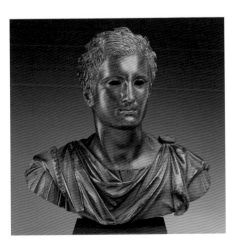

had depicted men as they really were, Lysippos claimed to show them as they appeared to be. Taking nature rather than other sculptors as his teacher, he was renowned for his fastidious attention to even the smallest details of his figures, which were later said to lack only movement and breath.

Lysippos's *Apoxyomenos* was one of the most celebrated sculptures of classical antiquity. Pliny relates that the Roman general Marcus Agrippa installed Lysippos's masterpiece in his public baths in Rome around 20 B.C. Later, the emperor Tiberius became so enamored of the figure that he had it removed to his bedroom. Such was the public outcry, however, that the emperor was shamed into putting it back on public view.

The Kimbell head must have been discovered by the early sixteenth century, when a draped bust was made for it, probably by a Venetian (Lombardo family?) workshop. In the eighteenth century the head and bust were acquired by the Venetian collector Bernardo Nani.

Head of Meleager, 50 B.C.–A.D. 100
Roman, after Skopas (Greek, c. 370–330 B.C.)
Late Republican–Early Imperial period

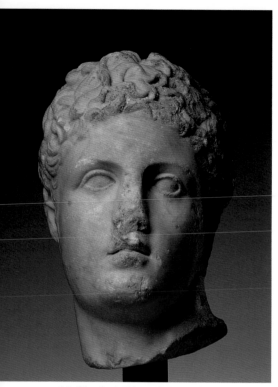

Marble; h. 11¾ in. (29.8 cm)
Acquired in 1967

This head is from a Roman copy of a full-length statue by the famed fourth-century-B.C. Greek sculptor Skopas, which showed the mythological hero Meleager with a hunting dog and the head of the Kalydonian boar. Along with Praxiteles and Lysippos, Skopas was one of the three great sculptors of his age, renowned especially for his depictions of gods. His style was notable for its introduction of an intense depiction of human emotion into the previously more reserved psychology of Greek classicism. Typical of Skopas's innovations

here are the slightly parted lips, the low forehead that protrudes over the bridge of the nose and eyes, and the heavy roll of flesh swelling over the outer corners of the eyes. These elements—all of which would be further exaggerated in Hellenistic sculpture—contribute to the quality of barely suppressed agitation.

According to Homer, the Kalydonian boar was sent by Artemis to ravage the countryside after Oeneus, king of Kalydon and Meleager's father, failed to sacrifice to the goddess. Meleager then led the hunt to kill the ferocious boar, but in its aftermath quarreled with his mother's two brothers and killed them. Learning of this, his mother, Althaea, set in motion the dire prophecy that the Fates had decreed soon after Meleager's birth, stating that he would die when a brand, then on the fire, had burned out. Althaea now took out the brand that she had secreted for years in a chest, and thus brought about her son's death. Fourth-century-B.C. artists favored themes such as this, which humanized the gods and depicted mythological heroes caught up in the suffering and imperfections of man.

Most of Skopas's works were in marble, like this Roman copy of the first century B.C./A.D. While no ancient author mentions a Meleager by Skopas, the many Roman copies of this subject must go back to a celebrated Greek original, which is plausibly attributed to Skopas on stylistic grounds. The identification as Meleager is established by the presence of a boar's head next to the figure in several copies.

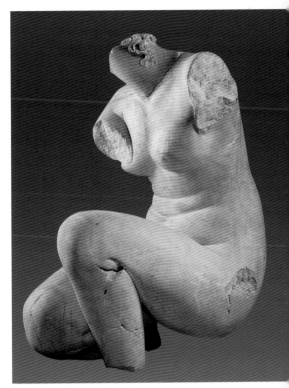

Marble; h. 25 in. (63.5 cm)
Acquired in 1967

According to the primal Greek myth recounted in Hesiod's *Theogony* (genealogy of the gods), Aphrodite, the goddess of love, was born of the *aphros*, the foam created when Kronos threw the genitals of his father, Uranos (Heaven), into the sea. The impregnated foam floated first to Kythera, then across the Mediterranean to Cyprus, where the goddess was born as she stepped ashore fully grown. Reflecting this aqueous origin, Aphrodite is frequently depicted in relation to water, bathing, or drying herself after her bath, sometimes accompanied by a seashell or dolphin.

Aphrodite was a highly popular subject in Greek art. The most famous sculptural representation, by Praxiteles in the fourth century B.C., showing the goddess unrobing to bathe, established the first ideal of nude female beauty that could stand alongside the canon of the athletic male. The theme of Aphrodite crouching in her bath also enjoyed great popularity, and was the subject of numerous sculptures known from ancient authors and Roman copies. The Kimbell version, one of many variations on a famous Hellenistic original, embodies the qualities of beauty and voluptuous sensuality that characterize the goddess of love. She is shown crouching to bathe, her head turned sharply to the right, her left arm (here lost) brought across the body to touch the right thigh, her right arm held up to near the left breast and shoulder. The somewhat spiral effect of her stance appealed to the Hellenistic taste for animated poses that embrace and engage with the space around them.

Based on an incorrectly emended text by Pliny, the figure of the crouching Aphrodite was previously traced back to a lost, third-century-B.C. original by the Greek sculptor Doidalsas. Recent scholarship, however, no longer accepts this attribution, and the authorship of this very famous and popular type remains unknown.

Mummy Mask, c. A.D. 120–70
Egypt
Roman period

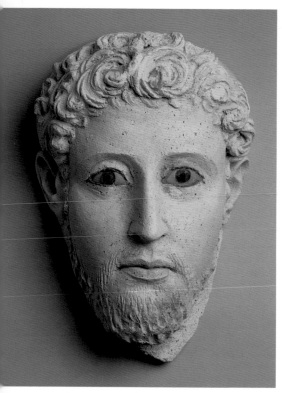

*Stucco/gesso with paint, gold leaf, and glass
inlays; h. 11⅝ in. (29.4 cm)*
Acquired in 1970

The most distinctive aspect of ancient Egyptian funerary practice was the ritual preservation of the body through mummification. For most of their history, the Egyptians also made likenesses of the deceased individual as a cover for the face, so that if the mummy should deteriorate or become damaged, the spirit—after its nightly wanderings—would recognize it and return. During the Old Kingdom, such masks took the form of wrapped linen with painted facial features. In the Middle Kingdom, shaped masks of plaster and linen were gessoed and painted with

relatively realistic portraits. These were called in ancient Egyptian *swht*, meaning "eggshell." The most famous mummy mask of all is the elaborate, gold-and-inlay mask of Tutankhamun.

During the Roman occupation of Egypt, this ancient practice continued but with a distinctly Italic accent. The Kimbell mask shows the melding of these two cultures. The materials are traditionally Egyptian: gesso, paint, gold leaf, and glass. Patches of gilding are still visible on the beard and hair, and there is reddish paint on the lips. The eyes are inlaid in green, black, and cream glass. The facial structure and fashion of the face, however, are not at all Egyptian or North African, but Roman. The hair and beard styles are typical of second-century Rome, where they were made fashionable by the emperor Hadrian.

Throughout Egyptian history, the use of mummy masks was restricted primarily to the wealthy and political elite. The process of mummification was complex and time-consuming, and all of the accouterments, including the mask, were expensive. During the later centuries, the family of the deceased also needed a large enough home to house the mummified loved one for a time, so that he could continue to participate in festivals and family activities before eventually being placed in a cemetery. We do not know the identity of the person who owned this mask. Perhaps he was a wealthy merchant or government official. His physiognomy suggests that he was at least partially European; yet he was Egyptian enough to give his remains and his soul to the ancient gods.

This life-size head of a young woman was originally part of a full-length, draped statue. Due to a generalized resemblance to Faustina the Younger and a similarity to her distinctive hairstyle, it was formerly identified as a portrait of that empress, who was the wife of Emperor Marcus Aurelius and daughter of Antoninus Pius. The features of Faustina the Younger are well documented from successive coin portraits that were produced to mark the births of her eleven children between the years A.D. 147 and 166, in her efforts to perpetuate her father's newly established Antonine dynasty.

Of the coin-portrait types, eight are extant in sculpture. However, the Kimbell head does not conform to any of Faustina's accepted numismatic or sculptural types, and it may more plausibly be identified as a priestess of the imperial cult. The work is datable on stylistic grounds to the period A.D. 170–80, suggesting that the three now-headless busts emerging from the headband represented Marcus Aurelius (reigned A.D. 161–80) and other members of the Antonine line— perhaps Hadrian and Antoninus Pius.

The face has many of the features that the ancient Romans prized in women: a wide smooth brow, wavy hair, softly modeled cheeks, small firm chin, and gentle smile. As in most Roman portraiture, these features are also intended to convey a sense of character, and we may see here something of the sitter's modesty, virtue, and harmony.

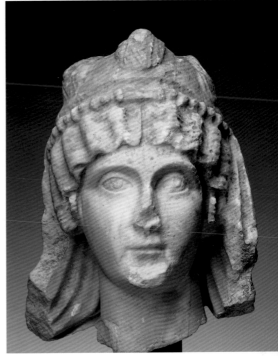

Marble; h. 13¼ in. (33.6 cm)
Acquired in 1969

Portrait of Emperor Marcus Aurelius
Roman, c. A.D. 210–25

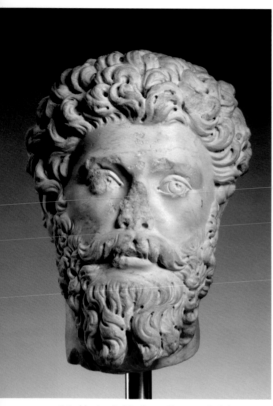

Marble (probably from Carrara, Italy);
h. 14⅛ in. (36.5 cm)
Acquired in 1967

This marble head portrays the Roman emperor Marcus Aurelius (reigned A.D. 161–80), the archetypal "philosopher-king," who is perhaps best known today as the author of the Stoic philosophical treatise *The Meditations.* Despite his nonroyal birth, Marcus gained the attention of the emperor Hadrian while still a child and was the subject of imperial portraiture from his youth. The ensuing corpus of official portraits records the emperor's changing facial features as well as his evolving hair and beard styles. The Kimbell head, which comes from a bust or full-length figure, is one of a group that replicates the fourth and last of Marcus's official portrait types, characterized by upswept curls above the forehead, a thick mustache covering the upper lip and partially overlapping the lower, and a full beard that falls in two main groups of curls.

The powerfully modeled features lend this portrait a quietly authoritative and intelligent air, the lofty upward gaze signifying the emperor's divine nature. Some features, especially the distinctive, drilled pupils of the eyes, find parallels in later portraits of the emperors Caracalla and Alexander Severus, suggesting that this may be a posthumous work made under the subsequent Severan dynasty. Septimius Severus, an army general who established a new dynasty in A.D. 193, claimed the deified Marcus Aurelius as his adoptive father to legitimize his claim to the throne.

Atypical features of this head are the lack of incisions to render the eyebrows, and the absence of a small tuft of beard below the lower lip.

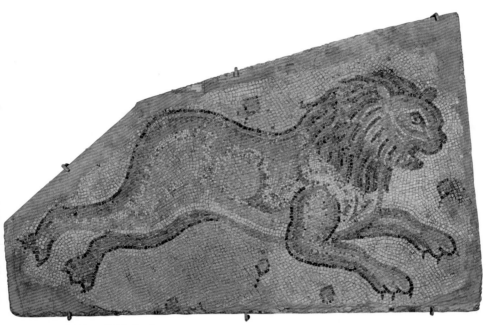

Mosaic; l. 77 in. (195.5 cm)
Acquired in 1972

This schematized image of a rampant lion probably came from a large mosaic floor in an early Christian church in Homs, Syria, dated by an inscription to a.d. 450–62. The other subjects in the floor included a leopard, a gazelle, and a griffin. Animals appear frequently in pavement art, where the use of sacred images and symbols had been prohibited in areas where worshipers would walk (an imperial decree of a.d. 427 forbade the representation of crosses on church floors). Narrative scenes from the Bible and various images of Christ were permitted on walls. These wall compositions came to be arranged in set programs and sequences, while floors tended to remain within the traditional secular repertory inherited from Roman times. Animal, marine, and pastoral subjects appeared in the nave of the church, which was associated with the

created world. Designs of a more abstract, metaphysical nature decorated the sanctuary, denoting the world of the spirit.

The lion of this fragment may represent part of a hunt scene or a motif in a religious narrative, or it might be purely symbolic. The subject of the hunt originated in Near Eastern royal hunt scenes, and was very popular in Roman pagan imagery. The flying gallop pose recalls numerous images of lions and other beasts found on Sasanian Persian silverware. Early Christians associated the symbol of the hunt with the concept of duality—the triumph of good over evil—and dangerous animals could be identified with irrational elements of the human soul. The lion, however, also stood as a royal emblem, and could therefore symbolize Christ. In this work the ferocity of this beast rather suggests a hunt scene.

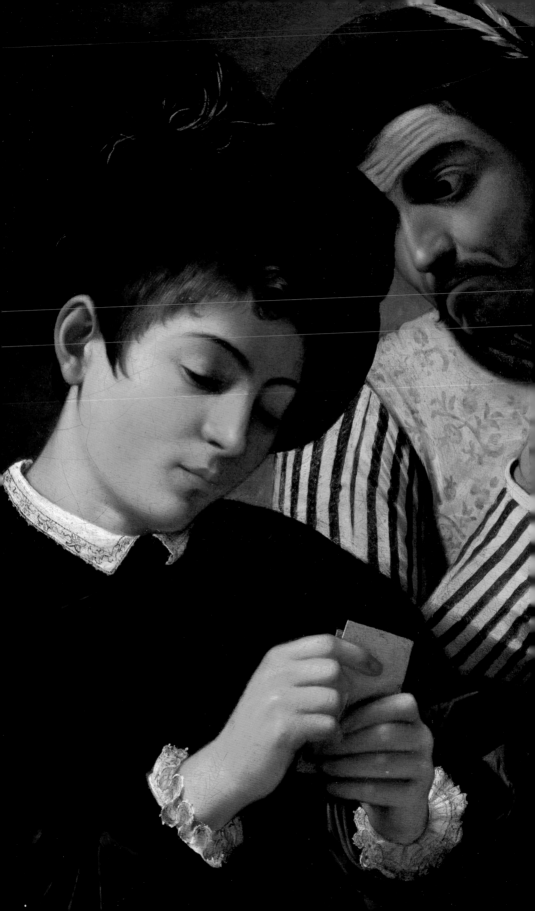

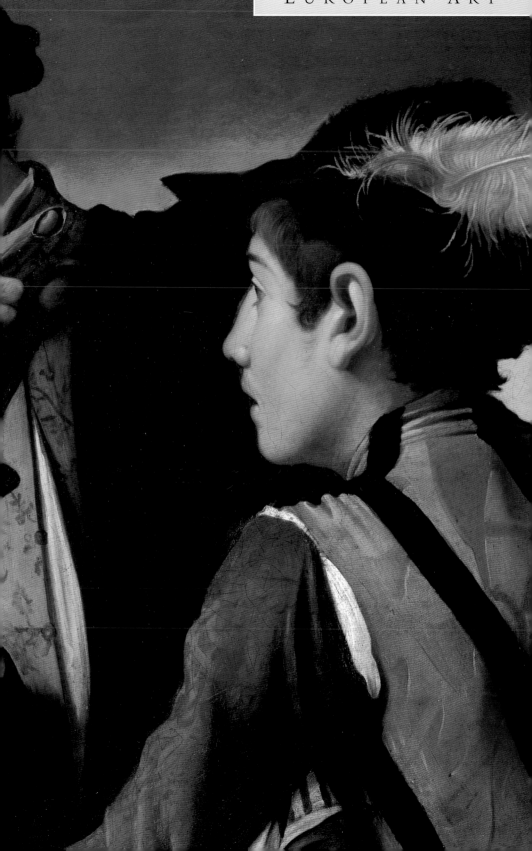
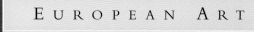

Reliquary Arm, c. 1150–1200 (crystal possibly added in the 15th century)
Mosan (Liège?)

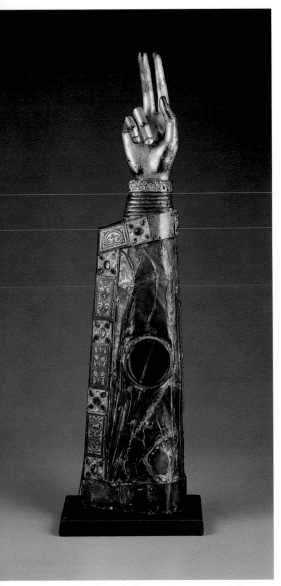

Silver, champlevé enamel on copper, gilt bronze,
wood core, glass cabochons, and crystal;
h. 24½ (62.1 cm)
Acquired in 1979

The veneration of the physical remains of saints—or objects with which they had come into contact—began to be practiced during the Early Christian era. In A.D. 393, the Church decreed that every altar must have a relic. Placed inside reliquaries and set on altars, these sacred objects soon became an essential part of Christian ceremony and were frequently ascribed miraculous powers. During the medieval era their numbers proliferated, and reliquaries were decorated with lavish and costly materials.

Apart from shrines, reliquaries often took the form of arms, hands, feet, or heads to house the bones of venerated saints. The Kimbell *Reliquary Arm*, with hand raised in the gesture of the Latin benediction, encased the bone fragment of an unknown saint. In this sumptuous display, precious materials are used to fashion the vestments; the folds of fine linen and embroidered cuff of the undersleeve are rendered with silver repoussé, and the wide sleeve of the dalmatic is bordered with champlevé enamel plaques. Many of the original gems, along with some of the plaques, have been lost. The beautiful enamel work, with intricate floral and heart motifs, is characteristic of Mosan art, which flourished during the twelfth and thirteenth centuries in the Meuse valley (today in Belgium and northeastern France). A crystal was set into the arm at a later date, probably the fifteenth century, transforming the reliquary into a monstrance so that the relic could be viewed by the faithful.

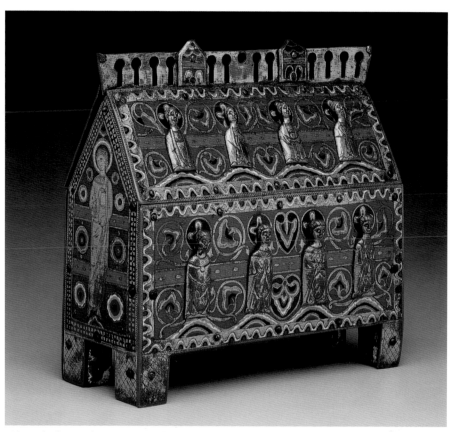

Champlevé enamel on copper, wood core; h. 9 in. (22.6 cm)
Acquired in 1979

A major center of the manufacture and export of exquisitely crafted reliquaries in the Middle Ages was Limoges, which was located in southwestern France along several ecclesiastical and pilgrimage routes. Limoges workshops producing liturgical objects employed the technique of champlevé enamel, whereby brilliantly colored, powdered glass was placed in cavities gouged into a copper plaque that was then fired at high temperatures.

The principal face of this *Reliquary Casket (châsse)*, which probably contained the relics of several saints, features eight half-length, raised, and gilded figures of saints against a richly enameled ground decorated with halos, scrolling floral motifs, and wavy cloudbanks. The appliqué relief figures, set in two rows, are portrayed with various liturgical gestures, such as upraised palms and arms crossed against the chest. In contrast to these *poupées* (dolls), which gained currency in Limoges enamels during

Miniature Casket, c. 1250–1300
French (Limoges)

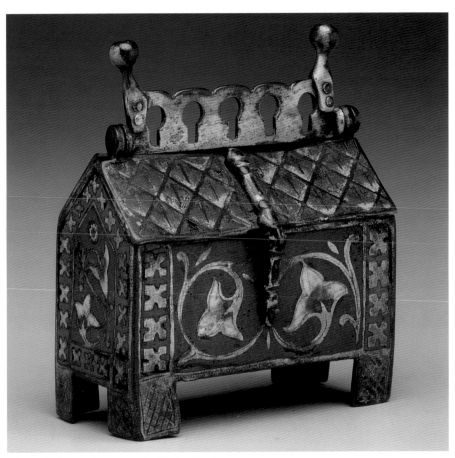

Champlevé enamel on copper; h. 3⅝ in. (9 cm)
Acquired in 1979

the thirteenth century, the full-length saints holding books on the gabled end panels are engraved in reserve on the enamel ground, their elegant figures revealing a lingering Byzantine influence. The casket, with its gabled roof and cresting, recalls not only a tomb enshrining the relics, but also the Church in the form of a cathedral that represents the Heavenly Jerusalem, where the saints eternally abide.

The enameled decoration of this fine _Miniature Casket_, produced in Limoges, features scrolling vines with fleurons on all four sides and tilelike lozenge patterns on the pitched roof, which is surmounted by a crest pierced with five keyholes and ending in two knoblike terminals. The enameled copper plaques of reliquaries are normally nailed to a wooden core; the absence of such a wooden carcass, along with the miniature scale of this casket, makes it difficult to ascertain its original function.

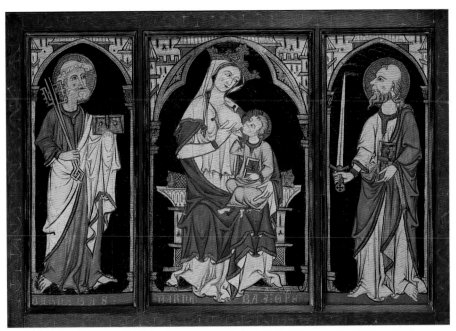

*Tempera and oil on panel; left panel: 35⅞ x 14⅜ in. (91 x 36.5 cm); central panel:
35⅞ x 22⁷⁄₁₆ in. (91 x 57 cm); right panel: 35⅞ x 14⁹⁄₁₆ in. (91 x 37 cm)
Acquired in 1969*

The place of origin and original function of *The Barnabas Altarpiece* are
unknown. It is named after the inscriptions on its lower border—*BARNABAS*
on the bottom of the Saint Peter panel,
BARNABAS: EPS: on the bottom of the
Virgin panel—although there is no corresponding figure to match these labels. The
identification of a Bishop Barnabas who
may have commissioned the altarpiece, or
a church or chapel dedicated to Saint
Barnabas, might aid in locating the origin
of this work.

Consisting of three separate panels, the
surviving ensemble is undoubtedly a fragment of a once-larger work. The central
panel is dominated by the image of the
enthroned Virgin as Queen of Heaven,
nursing the infant Christ Child. The nurs-

ing Virgin, an image of Mary's mercy and
intercession on behalf of humankind, is
flanked by Saints Peter and Paul, founders
of the Church, bearing their traditional
attributes, the keys and sword of martyrdom. The Child and saints also clasp holy
books—the Word of God made tangible.

Although the altarpiece shares stylistic
features with English manuscript illumination, it remains most likely that the painting originates from southwestern France
or northern Spain, where the influence of
itinerant English painters is attested during
the Gothic period. The date of the work
may most plausibly be placed on stylistic
and iconographic grounds in the third
quarter of the thirteenth century, although
its somewhat provincial character would
not rule out a date after 1300.

DUCCIO DI BUONINSEGNA
Italian, active 1278–1318
The Raising of Lazarus, 1310–11

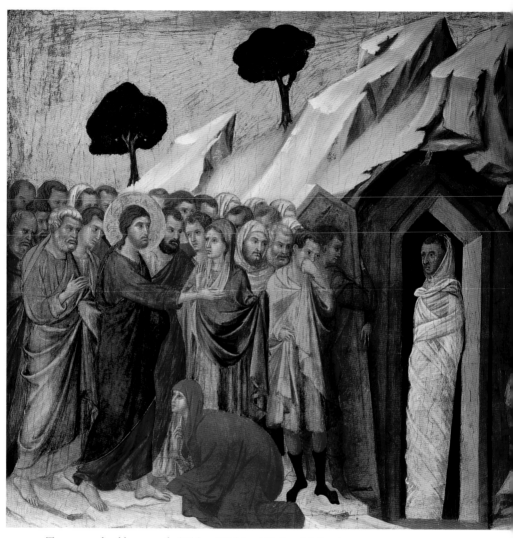

Tempera and gold on panel; 17⅛ x 18¼ in. (43.5 x 46.4 cm)
Acquired in 1975

Duccio di Buoninsegna was the preeminent Sienese painter in the early years of the fourteenth century—a crucial period of transition during which he infused the prevailing Byzantine style with a more naturalistic, narrative mode.

The Kimbell painting originally formed part of the acknowledged masterpiece of Duccio's maturity, the altarpiece known as the *Maestà* (Majesty), which was commissioned for the high altar of Siena Cathedral and carried from the artist's studio to the cathedral in solemn procession on 9 June 1311. In the *Maestà*, Duccio set forth a complex theological program tracing Christ's life and sacrificial death for mankind. Originally some sixteen feet high by fifteen feet wide, the *Maestà* was painted on both sides. Its main front panel depicted the enthroned Madonna and Child receiving the homage of her celestial court of saints and angels. Below the Madonna, the front *predella* (a boxlike base) recounted scenes from the childhood of Christ. The back side of the *Maestà* consisted of twenty-six episodes from Christ's Passion and Resurrection, the rear *predella* comprising nine stories from the ministry of Christ.

The Kimbell *Raising of Lazarus* was most likely the final scene of this back *predella*, providing the climactic proof of Christ's divinity, when he brings a man back from the dead. The Gospel of John (11:1–44) tells how Lazarus, a friend of Jesus, lived in Bethany with two sisters, Martha and Mary. When Lazarus fell ill, his sisters sent for Jesus, but by the time he arrived in Bethany, Lazarus was already dead four days. Here, Duccio shows the crucial moment when Christ extends his arm to call the resuscitated Lazarus forth from the tomb and restores the dead man, as their eyes lock together.

In many ways, Duccio follows Byzantine conventions in depicting this important subject, which prefigures Christ's own Resurrection after he was put to death on the cross. However, the narrative is made more compelling, the roles of the various protagonists sharpened, and the theological import highlighted in many details of the composition. Whereas Lazarus's sisters usually kneel together, here Mary— identified by her bright vermilion robe, a reference to her burning love for Christ—kneels, while Martha stands, raising her hand in acknowledgment of Christ's divine presence. Christ alone is haloed, the stark green tree above his head further emphasizing his divinity. Identified by his short beard and characteristic green mantle and blue robe, Saint Peter follows in Christ's footsteps, signaling his role as Christ's successor and founder of the Church. An attendant to the right holds his nose, a reminder that the corpse has been dead four days. Dramatic tension is created by the locked gazes of Christ and the risen Lazarus, and the gestures and expressions of the crowd that register their wonder upon witnessing the miracle.

A noteworthy compositional change is apparent at the lower right. The paint surface, thinned by age, now reveals an underlying paint layer showing a horizontally placed sarcophagus. Duccio's final solution, the upright tomb, supplies a more effective vertical stop for the last scene of the back *predella*.

The Kimbell panel, and several others, became separated from the *Maestà* after the altarpiece was dismantled in 1771 and later removed from Siena Cathedral; most panels are today in the cathedral museum.

FRA ANGELICO (FRA GIOVANNI DA FIESOLE)

Italian, c. 1395/1400–1455

The Apostle Saint James Freeing the Magician Hermogenes, c. 1426–29

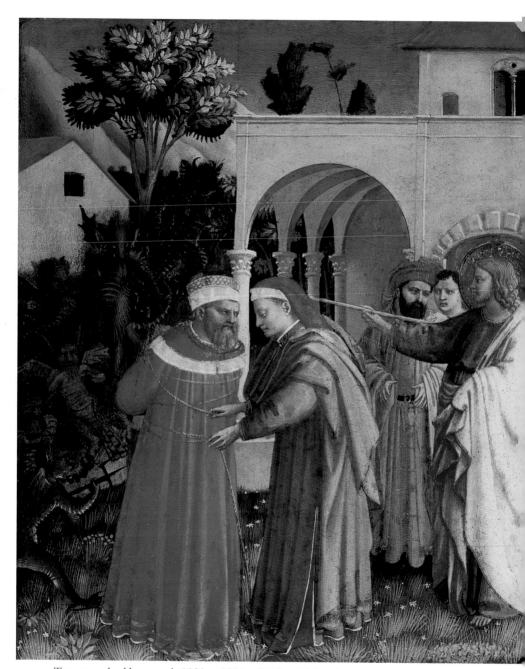

Tempera and gold on panel; 10⁹⁄₁₆ x 9⅜ in. (26.8 x 23.8 cm)
Acquired in 1986

Born Guido di Piero, the artist known as Fra Angelico acquired his nickname not long after his death, when he was referred to as "Angelicus" by a Dominican monk for his pious life and artworks. He was already an established painter and illuminator of manuscripts in Florence when he entered the Observant Dominican Order as Fra Giovanni sometime between 1418 and 1423. Since he joined the order later than the customary age of thirteen or fourteen, it has been suggested that some kind of spiritual conversion brought the painter into the monastic life.

The rare subject of the Kimbell panel is taken from the thirteenth-century *Golden Legend*, compiled by the Dominican friar Jacobus de Voragine. Here Saint James the Greater, set apart by his golden halo and an enframing archway, resembles Christ himself. The magician Hermogenes, at left, had objected to James's preaching the Gospel and summoned his devils to capture him in chains along with the magician's former disciple Philetus, whom James had converted. But the tables were turned, and the devils were empowered instead to seize Hermogenes and bring him to the saint. Fra Angelico deftly illustrates this lesson of Christian compassion, when James instructs Philetus: "Let us return good for evil, as Christ taught us to do. Hermogenes put you in bonds, now you unbind him." The power to bind (condemn) and to loose (absolve)

had been conferred upon James and the other Apostles by Christ (Matthew 18:18), and thus the saint not only releases Hermogenes physically, but also absolves Hermogenes metaphorically of his past sins. Rising above Hermogenes and the dark demons to the left, a tree's foliage catches the sunlight, hinting at the sorcerer's eventual conversion.

The Apostle Saint James Freeing the Magician Hermogenes originally formed part of the *predella* of an unidentified altarpiece. The four other extant panels are devoted to the lives of the Virgin, John the Baptist, and various saints. The style of these works reflects the influence of Masaccio's Brancacci Chapel in Santa Maria del Carmine, Florence, which was painted shortly before the artist's death in 1428. Fra Angelico was among the first Florentine artists to adopt this new Renaissance ideal, using rational perspective and lighting. The sensitivity to spatial intervals in the Kimbell painting, especially the receding columns of the loggia, shows the artist at the vanguard of pictorial innovation.

The panel has been slightly reduced at the left but is otherwise exceptionally well preserved. The refinement of Fra Angelico's technique is apparent in his use of pure pigments, such as brilliant vermilion and precious lapis lazuli, in the delicate hatched strokes modeling the forms, and in his masterful use of gilding in the decorative borders of the drapery.

MICHELOZZO DI BARTOLOMEO
Italian, 1396–1472
Saint John the Baptist, c. 1450–56

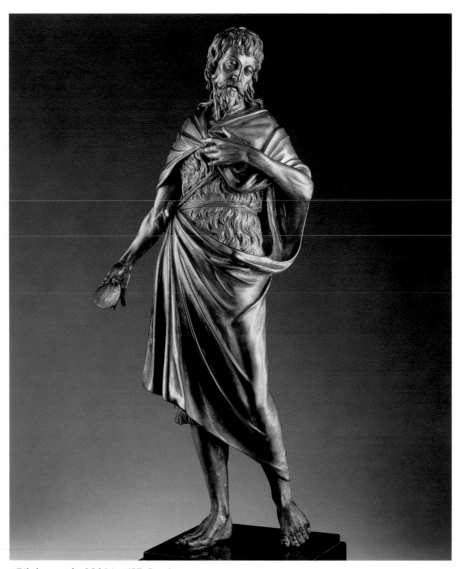

Gilt bronze; h. 22⅝ in. (57.5 cm)
Acquired in 1999

This masterpiece of early Renaissance sculpture was recently identified as the lost statue of Saint John the Baptist by Michelozzo from the church of Santa Maria dei Servi (known as the Santissima Annunziata), in Florence. Commissioned by Piero de' Medici around 1450, this work was much admired by contemporary and later critics, including Giorgio Vasari, who, in his *Lives of the Artists* (1550 and 1568), calls it "a most beautiful thing." The graceful figure is shown wearing his characteristic camel-pelt undergarment with a cape wrapped around his shoulders and fastened at his waist, and holding a shell-shaped baptismal bowl in his right hand. A document of 1476 records that a ring was given to the Santissima Annunziata in that year and sold to pay for the statue's repair and regilding, which survives in remarkably fine condition to this day.

The statue originally stood atop a marble stoup, or basin, of holy water placed just inside the entrance to the Annunziata, one of Florence's most popular pilgrim destinations. Light water corrosion around the lower parts of the statue attests to this usage, along with the pattern of wear to the gilding of the feet, where it was touched by the hands of the faithful. Subsequently moved into the church's atrium and eventually deposited in the church's museum, the statue was probably sold in the wake of Napoleon's invasion of Italy.

The lucid modeling of the Baptist's face, elegant handling of the folds of the mantle, and incisive articulation of his locks of hair and camel-pelt tunic all betray Michelozzo's characteristic manner, known from two other sculptures of Saint John the Baptist by the artist: a life-size terra-cotta (1444–45, Santissima Annunziata) and a silver statuette, of similar dimensions to the Kimbell bronze, which forms the centerpiece of the silver altar of the Florentine Baptistery (1452, today Museo dell'Opera del Duomo).

Originally apprenticed as a metalworker, Michelozzo became an expert in the art of casting, chasing, and finishing. His outstanding skill in bronze casting led

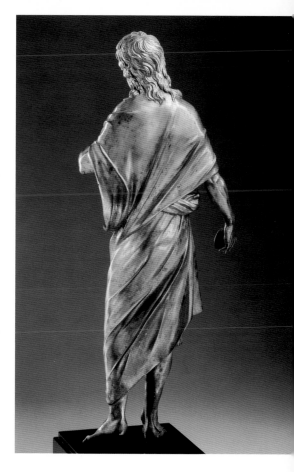

to his collaboration in many of the most significant sculptural projects of the era. He assisted Lorenzo Ghiberti on the north doors of the Baptistery of Florence Cathedral and successfully cast the large bronze *Saint Matthew* for the Orsanmichele after the failure of Ghiberti's initial casting. In 1425, Michelozzo formed a partnership on terms of equal status with Donatello, with whom he shared a studio until 1433, and collaborated on some of the most important funerary monuments of the Early Renaissance, pioneering the adoption of a classical idiom. Renowned equally as a sculptor and an architect, Michelozzo was charged with a number of architectural projects for Cosimo de' Medici, including convents, villas, and the Medici Palace on the via Larga (now via Cavour).

GIOVANNI BELLINI
Italian, c. 1438–1516
The Madonna and Child, c. 1465

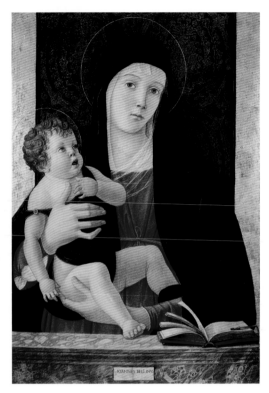

Tempera, possibly oil, and gold on panel;
32½ x 23 in. (82.5 x 58.4 cm)
Acquired in 1971

Giovanni Bellini's half-length devotional paintings of the Madonna and Child enjoyed great popularity in Venice, and later in his career he employed a large workshop to meet this demand. Giovanni's innovative father, Jacopo, with whom he trained, had introduced to Venice a more intimate type of devotional painting. Extending this approach, Giovanni's tender images appeal to the viewer's human sentiments, the many variations of pose and motif serving to remind the worshiper of Christ's redemptive role—that in time he will be sacrificed. They typically feature a sweet, wistful Virgin who signals her awareness and acceptance of the preordained fate of her Son.

In the Kimbell painting, Bellini's Madonna stands behind a veined marble parapet, in front of a cloth of honor brocaded with pomegranates to symbolize the Resurrection. The Child's mouth is open and his head tilted back as he sings, perhaps a verse from the book clipped open with a metal holder. The parapet demarcates the holy space reserved for the sacred figures, and recalls both Christ's tomb and the altar whereupon his sacrifice is reenacted in the Eucharistic offering. This meaning accounts for Mary's determined display of her Child, whom she presents to the devout viewer as the living Host. The illusionistic *cartellino* affixed to the parapet and inscribed with Bellini's name attests both to his identity as an artist and to his own religious devotion.

Although the head of the Christ Child and the book are well preserved, other parts of the composition, especially the face of the Virgin, have suffered abrasion. A related version of this subject, until recently in the church of Santa Maria dell'Orto, Venice, differs in its details, most notably the absence of the book and the inclusion of Greek inscriptions on either side of the Madonna's head.

An ingenious and versatile Renaissance artist, Ercole de' Roberti spent the latter half of his career at the court of Ercole I d'Este, Duke of Ferrara. In addition to painting altarpieces, small devotional works, portraits, and fresco cycles for the Este residences, Ercole performed a variety of tasks, such as producing beds and carriages for the weddings of the Este children. Portia's story, the rare subject depicted in this painting, is told by the first-century moralist Valerius Maximus in the widely read *Memorable Acts and Sayings of the Ancient Romans*, where she exemplifies fortitude and conjugal love. Portia pledges to take her own life if the secret plot of her husband, Brutus, to kill Julius Caesar fails. Here Portia reveals to her husband the self-inflicted cut on her right foot as evidence of her resolve. When Brutus was later slain, Portia carried out her vow by swallowing hot coals.

Ercole underscores Portia's feminine virtue by counterposing her open gesture and serene countenance to Brutus's guarded stance and reproachful expression. Celebrated for his use of color, Ercole clothes Portia in a light-catching blue drapery with an undergarment of iridescent plum and blue, complementing Brutus's orange and burgundy overcoat. The delicately hatched strokes that model the flesh tones are combined with new effects, like the transparent green glaze of the backdrop, to impart a jewel-like luminosity to the painting.

Portia and Brutus is one of three similar surviving panels by Ercole depicting illustrious women from ancient history, all

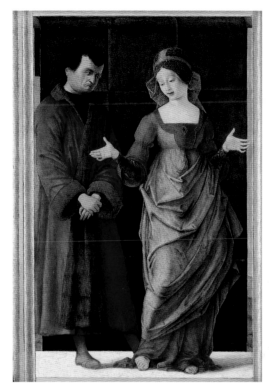

*Tempera, possibly oil, and gold on panel;
19³⁄₁₆ x 13½ in. (48.7 x 34.3 cm)
Acquired in 1986*

of whom resisted tyranny or subjugation and took their own lives to preserve their honor (the other two representing the wife of Hasdrubal, and Lucretia). In all likelihood, the paintings were commissioned by Eleonora of Aragon (died 1493), who married Ercole I d'Este and frequently ruled in his absence when he served as a *condottiere* (professional soldier). The high, humanistic ideals of these heroines illustrate the motto of Eleonora's father, the powerful King Ferrante of Naples: "I prefer death to dishonor."

ANDREA MANTEGNA
Italian, c. 1430/31–1506
**The Madonna and Child with Saints Joseph, Elizabeth,
and John the Baptist**, c. 1485–88

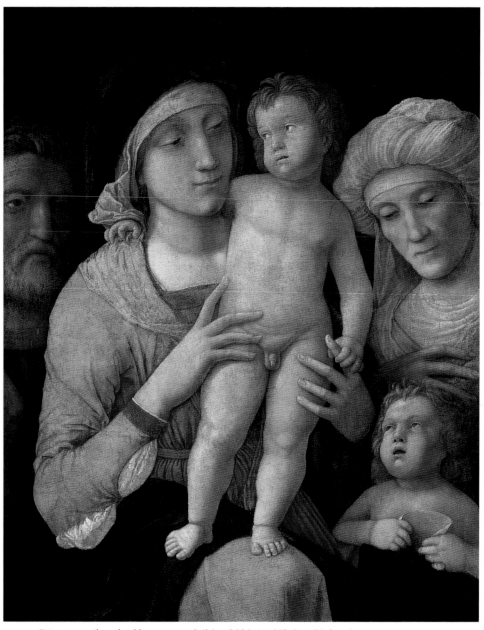

Distemper, oil, and gold on canvas; 24¾ x 20⅟₁₆ in. (62.9 x 51.3 cm)
Acquired in 1987

Trained in the humanist university town of Padua, Andrea Mantegna developed a lifelong passion for antiquity that profoundly informed his own work as an artist. His incisive drawing, brilliant coloring, and novel spatial effects soon established Mantegna's reputation as one of the major artists of his day and led to his appointment as court painter to the Gonzaga family in the duchy of Mantua. His famous, frescoed "Camera Picta" in the Ducal Palace was described by a contemporary as "the most beautiful room in the world." Both in his devotional paintings and in his historical subjects, Mantegna shows a remarkable capacity for invention, innovative composition, and emotional depth.

In the Kimbell's *Madonna and Child with Saints*, the five closely grouped figures press forward in the shallow space, a series of diagonals guiding the worshiper's eye to dwell on the mystery of the Incarnation: the Word made flesh. We see something of Mantegna's poetic mastery of paint in the undulating fall of the Virgin's veil over the Child's tiny hand, the crisp folds of Saint Elizabeth's golden yellow turban, and Saint John's rapt expression. The triumphant *contrapposto* pose and figural canon of the Christ Child, which recurs in other works by Mantegna, derives from antique Roman sculpture, which was then being ardently collected.

In this and other devotional paintings Mantegna seems to have experimented with distemper, a glue tempera, painted on a fine linen canvas. This delicate technique facilitates the great precision in handling for which the artist is renowned. Mantegna's thin and exquisitely rendered surfaces are very fragile, and some abrasion has occurred to this work in areas such as the Virgin's coral-colored robe, which was once embellished with a gold pattern. In some of the best-preserved areas of the painting, such as the head of the young Baptist, the wonder of Mantegna's extraordinary technique can still be appreciated.

Virgin and Child, 1486
South German

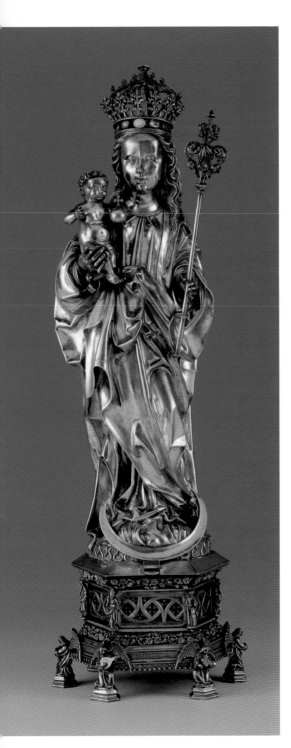

One of the finest known silver sculptures in the Late Gothic style, *Virgin and Child* is an extremely rare survival of pre-Reformation church sculpture. Created in southern Germany in 1486 (as indicated by an inscription under the base), the sculpture depicts the Queen of Heaven holding the infant Christ in her right hand and a scepter in her left. An elaborate crown of foliate design and stars is set with twelve stones. With one foot resting on an upturned crescent moon containing the profile of a vividly detailed face, the Virgin stands above a hexagonal plinth decorated with figures of saints and intricately cast grapevines, and supported by angels playing musical instruments.

The treatment of the drapery folds and the cascade of hair falling loosely down the Virgin's back reveals an exquisite sense of sculptural and pictorial design. On the back of the figure, four holes indicate where a burst of sunrays (or mandorla) was formerly attached. The figure of the Virgin was executed in repoussé (shaped by hammering from the reverse side). Her hair and dress, the borders of her mantle, as well as the crown, scepter, and moon, are all gilded, and there is much accomplished embossing and chasing throughout. Scholars have noted affinities between the statuette and the work of Michel Erhart (c. 1440/45–after 1522), the foremost sculptor working in Ulm. The identity

Silver, parcel-gilt, stones (opal, clear and pale sapphires, garnets, and pale emeralds);
h. 20 ⅞ in. (53 cm)
Acquired in 2002

of the goldsmith, who may have worked from another artist's model, is unknown.

The subject of the sculpture can be identified as the Virgin of the Apocalypse, whose imagery—the aureole of the sun, along with the twelve stars in her crown, and the crescent moon beneath her feet—is derived from the book of Revelation (12:1–5): "And there appeared a great wonder in heaven, a woman clothed with the sun, and the moon under her feet, and upon her head was a crown of twelve stars . . . And she brought forth a man-child, who was to rule all nations. . . ." The statue can be related to a particular devotional type widely diffused in Germany, the Virgin in the Sun, who is depicted surrounded by rays of light and standing on a crescent moon. The Virgin in the Sun represents a belief in Mary's purity and perpetual virginity, and is also associated with the Immaculate Conception (the belief that the Virgin was born without sin).

The plinth bears the heraldic shield of Wilhelm von Reichenau (c. 1426–1496), Bishop of Eichstätt, a small city located on the Altmühl River in Bavaria. A great patron of the arts, von Reichenau supported building projects in the Eichstätt Cathedral and at other religious institutions. It is likely that the silver *Virgin and Child* was a gift of von Reichenau to the cathedral. The inclusion of Eichstätt's popular saints on the base of the statue supports this hypothesis: Saint Richard and his children, Saint Willibald (first bishop of Eichstätt), Saint Winnibald, and Saint Walburga, eighth-

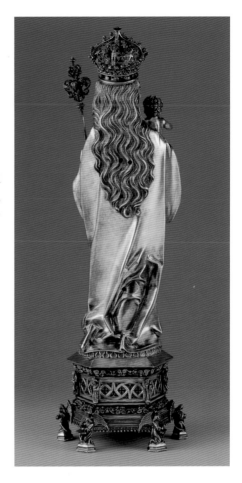

century Anglo-Saxon missionaries to the Diocese of Eichstätt, are shown with Saint James the Great (or Saint William of Maleval?) and Saint John the Evangelist.

The *Virgin and Child* was probably removed and sold following the secularization of the Diocese of Eichstätt at the beginning of the nineteenth century. It was later in the collection of Meyer Karl von Rothschild in Frankfurt, where it was published and illustrated in 1885.

GIOVANNI BELLINI
Italian, c. 1438–1516
Christ Blessing, c. 1500

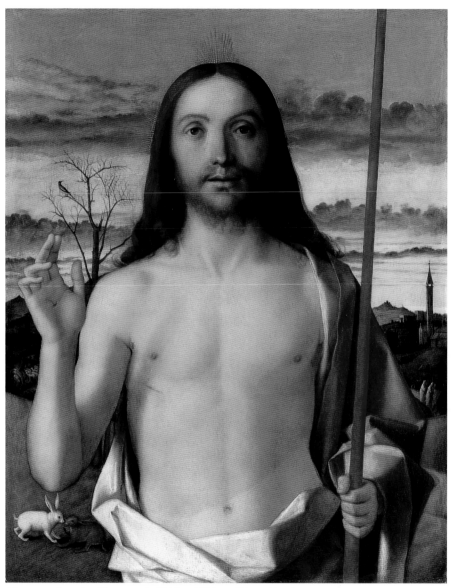

Tempera, oil, and gold on panel; 23¼ x 18½ in. (59 x 47 cm)
Acquired in 1967

Like Giovanni Bellini's half-length figures of the Madonna and Child, *Christ Blessing* vividly portrays the central mystery of the Christian faith: the incarnation, when Christ—fully human and fully divine—was sent to earth to redeem humankind. For greater immediacy, the devotional image is brought close to the picture plane as the Resurrected Savior faces the worshiper with a level gaze. Lips parted, he raises his right hand in blessing, and with his left grips the bright red staff of the banner of the Resurrection (the white flag with a red cross, denoting his triumph over death, is out of view). Golden rays of light emanate from the top and sides of his head, signaling his divinity. A cool, lavender white drapery encircles his warm exposed flesh, incandescent with a preternatural beauty. The message of Christian compassion is conveyed by his wounds of suffering, which are lightly visible on his hand and chest, while the shadow cast by his raised arm serves to confirm the reality of the Resurrection.

Various motifs in the distant landscape allude to the Resurrection theme. On the left side of the panel, the withered tree with the solitary bird probably stands for the Old Covenant, out of which the New Covenant would grow. The pair of rabbits signify regeneration, while the shepherd tending his flock is a reminder that Christ, himself, is the Good Shepherd (John 10:14). The three robed figures at the right edge of the picture are undoubtedly the three Marys, who are hurrying to tell the disciples of the empty tomb, and above them the distant bell tower denotes that salvation is found through Christ's sacrifice and the Church.

Since the early Christian era, Christ had been identified with the sun god, Apollo. Like "Sol Invictus," the never-vanquished Sun, the risen Savior is victorious over death. He presides here like a classical hero over the glowing landscape, where clouds are dappled by the dawning light. This poetic outdoor setting transfigures the painting and communicates Bellini's spiritual message of God's triumphant presence on earth and the life everlasting.

Jacob Obrecht, 1496
Netherlandish or French

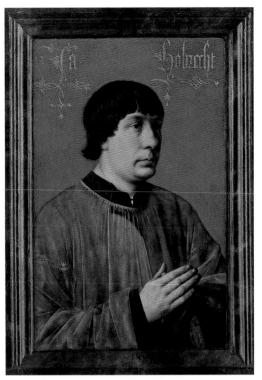

Tempera, oil, and gold on panel;
20¼ x 14¼ in. (51.4 x 36.2 cm)
Acquired in 1993

A masterpiece of northern Renaissance portraiture, this painting captures the solemn, plainspoken humanity of the sitter with a directness, clarity, and sympathy characteristic of the Netherlandish tradition. Hands clasped in devotion, he is shown wearing a dark clerical robe covered with a fine linen surplice. The gilt Gothic inscription identifies the subject as Jacob Obrecht (1457/58–1505), the renowned choirmaster, and one of the greatest composers of his age. On the engaged, marbled frame is inscribed both the date of the painting, *1496,* and the sitter's age, *38.* Born in Ghent, Obrecht led a peripatetic career, taking posts in Bergen op Zoom, Cambrai, Bruges, and Antwerp. Such was the musician's international standing that in August 1487 he was invited to the court of Ferrara by Duke Ercole I d'Este. He returned to that city in 1504, where he died from the plague in 1505, eulogized as "a most learned musician, second in the art to no one, in respect to either voice or cleverness of invention."

The Kimbell painting is probably the left-hand side of a diptych, or the left-hand wing of a triptych. As such, it would have been attached to a facing panel on the right showing the Madonna and Child, or a similar devotional subject. Preserved in exceptional condition, the painting is remarkable for the virtuosity of its details—the folds of Obrecht's translucent surplice, with its lace trim, and the soft gray fur of the almuce (the badge of office of a canon, including the choral clergy) draped over his left arm. The technical refinement of the paint layers, from the finely hatched brushstrokes in the hands to the smoothly blended flesh tones, suggests that the artist used a mixed medium of egg tempera and oil. Although some art historians have associated this painting with the Bruges master Hans Memling (c. 1435–1494), the evidence suggests another, yet unidentified painter.

JAN GOSSART, called MABUSE
Netherlandish, c. 1478–1532
Hendrik III, Count of Nassau-Breda, c. 1516–17

J an Gossart was one of the first artists to
disseminate the Italian style in the Low
Countries, an interest stimulated when he
accompanied his patron Philip of
Burgundy to Rome in 1508–9. The
subject of this portrait is Hendrik III,
Count of Nassau-Breda (1483–1538),
who instigated Philip's appointment as
Bishop of Utrecht in 1517. An esteemed
statesman and captain general, Hendrik
was entrusted with the education of
Emperor Maximilian's son, the future
Emperor Charles V, who appointed him
governor of Holland, Zeeland, and Fries-
land in 1515.

In keeping with the meticulous attention to detail of the northern schools,
Gossart takes particular care in rendering
the textures of the carpet, fur collar,
buttons, and checkered black-and-gold
doublet, creating an image of jewel-like
intensity. The sitter's features are finely
delineated (the underdrawing is visible
around the lips, nose, and chin) and the
flesh tones subtly modulated to achieve a
sympathetic likeness. The marked illusion-
ism of the work, with the fictive frame
and figure's shadow cast against the
feigned green marble backplate, derives
from the great Flemish master Jan van
Eyck. Gossart's close study of Italian art
is evident in the imposing bulk and
balanced composition of the figure. The
humanist pursuits of both sitter and
artist are reflected in the antique cameo
adorning the hat.

The painting is datable after 1516,
when knights of the Order of the Golden

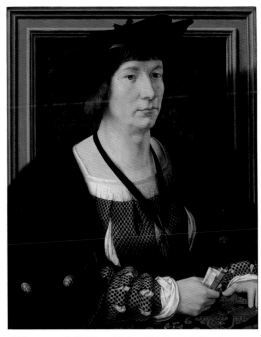

Oil on panel; 22⅝ x 18 in. (57.2 x 45.8 cm)
Acquired in 1979

Fleece were allowed to suspend their
pendants from a ribbon rather than a
collar. The faint inscription *DUX SAX*
at the top of the panel is a later addition.

Hendrik III was an adventuresome
and noteworthy art patron. An Italian
visitor's diary remarks on the beautiful
pictures he saw in Hendrik's palace in
Brussels in 1517, including Hieronymus
Bosch's *Garden of Earthly Delights* (Museo
del Prado, Madrid), which the count very
likely commissioned.

BAMBAIA (AGOSTINO BUSTI)
Italian, c. 1483–1548
Fortitude and ***Unidentified Virtue***, c. 1520–25

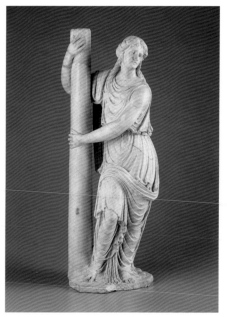 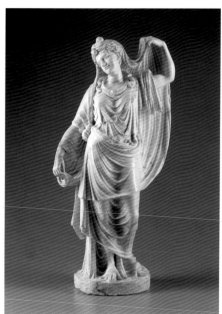

Marble; h. 23⅞ in. (60.5 cm); 26¼ (66.5 cm)
Acquired in 1981

Agostino Busti, known as Bambaia, was an important Lombard sculptor, notable for his refined technique and innovative classicism. First mentioned in 1512 in the workshop of Milan Cathedral, Bambaia created a number of major tomb and altar commissions, often in collaboration with other sculptors such as Cristoforo Lombardo. The two marble sculptures in the Kimbell collection represent Virtues: one, wearing a classical robe draped over one shoulder, is identifiable as *Fortitude* by her attribute, the column; the other figure is without an attribute and cannot be positively identified, but the exquisite sweep of its diaphanous drapery, with close pleats and rippling edges, exemplifies Bambaia's virtuoso carving technique. Its pose derives from the ancient Venus Genetrix

type, and the sweet and lyrical expression of the face was inspired by the work of Leonardo da Vinci, with whom Bambaia apparently traveled to Rome in 1513.

The *Virtues* may originally have adorned a tomb monument that was later dismantled and dispersed, such as the Birago family tomb, formerly in the church of San Francesco Grande, Milan, or the funerary monument of a humanist in Pavia, parts of which were taken as war loot between 1527 and 1528 by the *condottiere* Mercurio Bua for his own tomb in the church of Santa Maria Maggiore in Treviso. However, the original configuration of Bambaia's tomb monuments, for which the collaborative nature of Lombard workshops must be taken into consideration, remains difficult to reconstruct.

PARMIGIANINO (GIROLAMO FRANCESCO MARIA MAZZOLA)
Italian, 1503–1540
The Madonna and Child, c. 1527–30

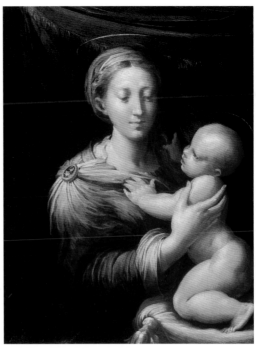

Oil on panel; 17⅝ x 13⅜ in. (44.8 x 34 cm)
Acquired in 1995

As a young artist, Francesco Mazzola, better known as Parmigianino, left his native Parma, where he had worked alongside Correggio at the monastery church of San Giovanni Evangelista, to seek his fortune in Rome. Hailed as the new Raphael, he was to become one of the most influential artists of the sixteenth century, cultivating a mannered gracefulness of pose and physiognomy combined with new and dramatic coloristic effects that transformed the classicism of his Renaissance predecessors. In his *Lives of the Artists* (1568), Giorgio Vasari observed that Parmigianino "gave to his figures . . . a certain loveliness, sweetness, and charm in their attitudes which were particularly his own."

Parmigianino spent the final years of his short career in Bologna (1527–30), and in this seminal period produced a number of small devotional works in the swift, assured manner that typifies his mature style. In the Kimbell panel, Parmigianino draws upon the work of Leonardo, Raphael, and Michelangelo in counterposing the serene Virgin with her active Son, who tugs at his pensive mother's veil, seeming to distract her from contemplation of his impending sacrifice. But the compressed pose of the dimpled Christ Child kneeling on a tasseled cushion, and the tall, sweeping foreheads of mother and child, introduce elements of Parmigianino's distinctive and idiosyn-cratic Mannerism. The Virgin's exquisite beauty is an outward sign of her inner grace, which Parmigianino reinforces through the golden strands of her ribboned hair and the fluid rhythms of her gossamer drapery, gathered at the shoulder with an antique cameo. The lovely color of her shot-silk dress is created by laying glazes of red lake, an organic pigment, over azurite blue.

SEBASTIANO DEL PIOMBO (SEBASTIANO LUCIANI)
Italian, c. 1485–1547
Head of a Woman, early 1530s

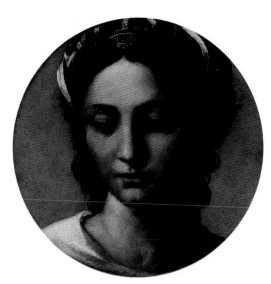

Oil on panel; diam. 10 in. (25.4 cm)
Acquired in 1985

Notable for the monumental grandeur of his religious paintings and portraits, Sebastiano del Piombo became the preeminent painter in Rome following Raphael's death in 1520. His Venetian training with Giovanni Bellini and later Giorgione is evident in Sebastiano's brilliant use of color and dramatic landscape backgrounds. The Sienese banker Agostino Chigi invited him to Rome in 1511 to fresco his villa, now known as the Farnesina, on the banks of the Tiber. An intense rivalry soon developed with Raphael, which was encouraged by Sebastiano's friend Michelangelo, who supplied him with drawings for some of his paintings.

Sebastiano produced some of the finest portraits of his day, a number of which were later mistakenly attributed to Raphael and Michelangelo. He pioneered the use of painting on stone, especially slate, and on dark grounds. In 1531, Pope Clement VII rewarded him with an appointment as Keeper of the Papal Seal *(piombo)*—the name by which he came to be known.

This majestic head is an essay in ideal beauty of the type known as a *testa ideale* (ideal head). Sebastiano has emulated the smooth and abstracted facial structure found in classical sculpture—here reflected in the high, straight bridge of the nose and the downcast, half-moon eyes—and employed soft tonal transitions in the woman's skin to achieve a correspondingly three-dimensional effect. Resembling the stately Virgins in Sebastiano's altarpieces of the 1530s, the Kimbell *Head of a Woman* may have been painted after he accompanied Clement VII to Bologna. The original context or purpose of this roundel has not been determined. While it cannot be ruled out that the painting might have formed part of a decorative ensemble or piece of furniture, it may also have been a presentation piece or gift, like Michelangelo's highly finished drawings of ideal heads. Whatever the case, Sebastiano has created an image of supreme physical and spiritual beauty that shows him the worthy rival of his competitors.

TITIAN (TIZIANO VECELLIO)
Italian, c. 1488–1576
The Madonna and Child with a Female Saint and
the Infant Saint John the Baptist, 1530s

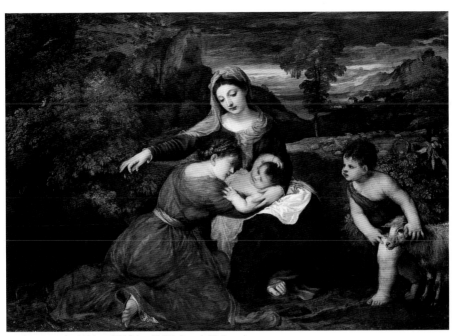

Oil on panel; 41½ x 58⅜ in. (105.4 x 148.3 cm)
Acquired in 1986

More than any other Renaissance master, Titian was acclaimed in his own lifetime and for centuries thereafter for his expressive handling of paint and rich use of color. Building upon the example of his teachers Giovanni Bellini and Giorgione, Titian set many of his religious subjects in a pastoral landscape. The Kimbell panel is closely related to a version of the composition in the National Gallery, London. In both works Mary cradles the Christ Child, who is embraced by a kneeling female saint. However, various aspects of the Kimbell painting have been reconceived to underscore its devotional theme of Christ's impending sacrifice. Christ's chubby arm is curled over his head in a pose used since antiquity to denote sleep as well as death. The white cloth that sets off his plump form foreshadows Christ's shroud and also recalls the cloth traditionally used to protect the host during the Mass. X-radiography reveals that, as in the London version, Titian initially painted a figure at the left (an angel in the Kimbell version) offering flowers to the Virgin. The artist later painted over this figure with a thicket and a finch, a symbol of Christ's Passion. Giving further emphasis to this sacrificial message, Titian introduced on the right the infant Saint John the Baptist gently leading a lamb by the ear.

Unlike the London canvas, the Kimbell painting is on panel, which results in more deeply saturated color. Some areas, such as the sky, the Virgin's mantle, and the saint's dress, have darkened in color and become more transparent with age.

JACOPO BASSANO (JACOPO DAL PONTE)
Italian, c. 1510–1592
The Supper at Emmaus, c. 1538

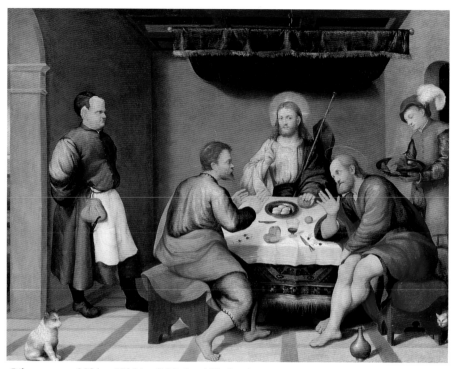

Oil on canvas; 39⅝ x 50⅝ in. (100.6 x 128.6 cm)
Acquired in 1989, with the generous assistance of a gift from Mildred Sterling Hedrick

In his lifetime Jacopo Bassano was one of the most famous and influential masters of the late Renaissance in Italy, admired for his luminous color and sensitively observed incidents from everyday life. Trained by his father in the north Italian town of Bassano del Grappa, he worked in neighboring Venice in the early 1530s. His youthful works reflect the influence of Titian and other north Italian masters, along with artists ranging from Raphael to Dürer, whose compositions he knew through prints. Already by the late 1530s his powers of invention rivaled those of his contemporaries Tintoretto and Veronese.

The Kimbell *Supper at Emmaus* depicts Christ's miraculous appearance after the Resurrection (Luke 24:30–31). In the act of blessing and breaking bread at the inn, Christ reveals himself to two of his disciples, who failed to recognize him as they traveled on the road to Emmaus. Christ is seated beneath a splendid velvet green canopy that delimits the sacred space. The sacramental message is elucidated in the finely executed still life of bread, wine, and eggs—the latter a traditional symbol of resurrection and immortality. Distinguished by their contemporary dress, the well-fed innkeeper with a large purse and the plumed serving boy—along with their visual counterparts, a wary dog and menacing cat—attend to mundane affairs, unaware of the divine mystery unfolding before them.

I n this imposing portrait, Jacopo
Bassano applies a vigorous and sharply
focused naturalism to convey the spiritual
temperament and preoccupations of a
Franciscan friar. The unidentified sitter
turns his head to look past the viewer, his
open left hand poised before a skull that
leans against a book at the lower right.
The simple habit of Saint Francis associates the sitter with the founder of his
mendicant order, whose exemplary life in
imitation of Christ he would have striven
to emulate. Portraits of Franciscans, who
avow humility in a life devoted to prayer
and penance, are not common.

Jacopo here portrays the distinctive
features of an individual with high cheek-
bones, a wandering eye, knit brow, and
animated mouth, which together convey
the impression of a serious but compas-
sionate man. The skull, a reminder of the
vanity of earthly life, supports the
contemplative aspect of the friar's piety,
and the pen holder that hangs from the
rope at his waist attests to his learning.
A sensitive colorist, Jacopo creates a rich
tonal range, contrasting the cool gray
of the wool habit with the warm flesh
areas, which derive luminosity from the
reflection of the white ground through
the glazes.

After the early 1530s, a period during
which Jacopo studied and worked in
Venice, he returned to spend the rest of
his long career in his hometown, Bassano
del Grappa, where he continued to
receive Venetian commissions. This early
work is datable to around the time that

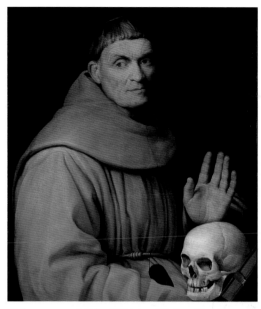

Oil on canvas; 31¼ x 27³⁄₁₆ in. (80.5 x 69 cm)
Acquired in 1997

Jacopo painted the Saint Anne altarpiece
(1541, Gallerie dell'Accademia, Venice, on
deposit in the Museo Civico, Bassano del
Grappa) for the church of the reformed
Franciscans in Asolo; possibly the artist
depicts one of its members.

Portrait of a Franciscan Friar, which
once belonged to the Marquess of Lansdowne, is one of three works from the
Earl of Shelburne's historic collection
in Bowood House, Wiltshire, in the
Kimbell's permanent collection: the
others are Domenichino's *Abraham
Leading Isaac to Sacrifice* and Jacob van
Ruisdael's *Rough Sea at a Jetty*.

JACOPO BASSANO (JACOPO DAL PONTE)
Italian, c. 1510–1592
The Adoration of the Magi, after 1555

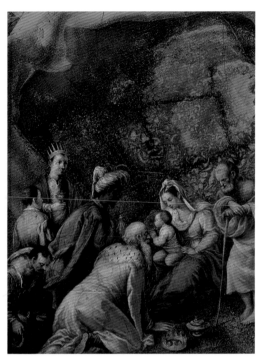

Oil on jasper; 7¼ x 5½ in. (18.4 x 14 cm)
Acquired in 1990, Bequest of Hedy Maria
Allen, New York

A long with the Adoration of the Shepherds, the subject of the Adoration of the Magi occupies pride of place in Jacopo Bassano's repertory. There exist a number of variants of the composition of this miniature painting, both on canvas (most notably in the Galleria Borghese, Rome, and a private collection, Bassano del Grappa, both datable to the mid-1550s) and stone,

and their attribution to Jacopo remains the subject of scholarly debate. The popularity of the composition is further attested by a 1598 engraving by Raphael Sadeler, after a work that was in the collection of Padre Caggioli, prior of the monastery of Santi Giovanni e Paolo, Venice. In the Kimbell painting, the yellow-veined, green jasper background that serves as the picture's support has been deftly integrated into the painted image to suggest an outcrop of rocks instead of the more traditional landscape setting with architectural ruins found in versions of the subject on canvas.

Small paintings on stone produced by Jacopo, or under his supervision in the prolific workshop he operated in conjunction with his four sons, reveal a little-known aspect of the family's output. Several of Jacopo's contemporaries praise his skill in painting night scenes on small black stones, and a painting on slate is listed in the inventory of the artist's studio after his death. Whereas a few Renaissance artists such as Sebastiano del Piombo experimented with stone for large-scale works, such supports became more common for miniature paintings during the Baroque period. In the Kimbell *Adoration*, the rare stone would have been valued as a precious specimen of nature, and for its smooth and durable surface, ideally suited for the detailed brushwork of this delicately painted work.

A prolific master of religious and historical works, as well as portraits, Tintoretto developed a rapid, often impetuous manner of painting that was both expressive and expedient. Here he captures the dignity, prudence, and calm equanimity befitting "the most serene prince" of the Venetian Republic. In 1567, the eighty-five-year old Pietro Loredan (1482–1570) had been elected doge by his fellow councillors to break a deadlock. Tintoretto portrays him in his ceremonial dress, every adornment dictated by protocol and decree: the gold brocade, fur-trimmed robe; the ermine cape with golden harness-bell buttons; and the distinctive *corno dogale* (doge's hat) worn over a white linen cap.

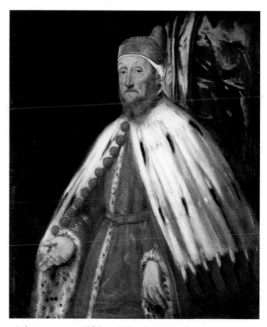

Oil on canvas; 49⅝ x 42 in. (126 x 106.6 cm)
Acquired in 1986

Loredan's gesture and countenance are receptive yet guarded, conveying the dutiful service of this reluctant doge who, during his brief three-year reign, presided over famine, pestilence, a great fire at the Arsenal, and the onset of war with the Turks over the possession of Cyprus. Tintoretto shows his subject ruddy-faced and world-weary, giving physical expression to the weight of his obligations and vulnerability, as well as tempering the formality of an official portrait.

Tintoretto's technical facility, his varied and fluent handling of paint, is evident especially in the vigorously modeled face and the swift, sure strokes of the cape. This proficient style recommended Tintoretto to the Republic's officials, who typically commissioned a number of portraits upon their election. Another version of this portrait, now in the National Gallery of Victoria, Melbourne—which shows alterations to the figure worked out on the canvas—may be the first version, painted from life, from which was derived the official portrait displayed in the Doge's Palace and destroyed in a disastrous fire in 1577. The portrait by Tintoretto in the Kimbell is possibly the painting that belonged to the Loredan family, mentioned in the will of the doge's son Alvise.

ANNIBALE CARRACCI
Italian, 1560–1609
The Butcher's Shop, early 1580s

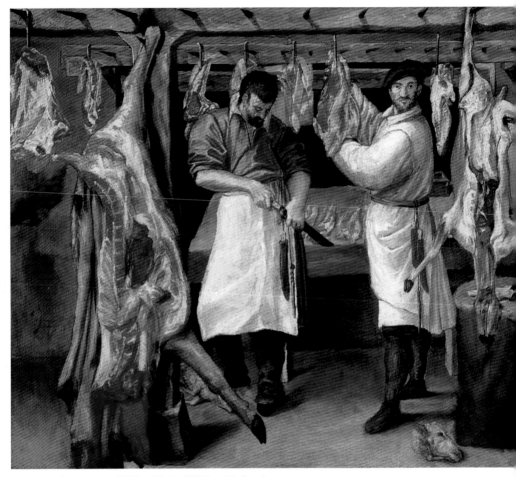

Oil on canvas; 23½ x 28 in. (59.7 x 71.0 cm)
Acquired in 1980

Around the time that he painted *The Butcher's Shop*, about 1582, Annibale Carracci, together with his older cousin Ludovico and his brother Agostino, co-founded the Carracci Academy in Bologna. This teaching academy not only trained the next generation of Bolognese painters, but also altered the future course of Italian art. In particular, the Carracci's radically new way of teaching and making art played a seminal role in the foundation of the Baroque style that would soon dominate Italy and Europe. Stressing the direct observation of nature, Annibale's "reform" of painting swept away the then-current Mannerism that he perceived as stultifying and affected. Aiming at a more honest, emotional expression of reality, Annibale drew incessantly from life, honing his genius for capturing fleeting visual effects. In 1594, he went to Rome to work for the powerful Farnese family, developing a grand and classicizing style that drew upon his study of antiquity, as well as the Renaissance masters of Venice and central Italy.

The Butcher's Shop, which was painted in the early, formative period of Annibale's career, is executed with a vitality and immediacy that heralds the artist's bold new mode of pictorial representation. Employing a limited palette of earthen colors—browns, reds, white, and black—unlike the unnatural hues of the prevailing Mannerist style, Annibale candidly describes the butchers and the cuts of meat displayed on hooks and the table. He applies the paint directly and spontaneously, with loose brushstrokes that reveal the texture of the loosely woven canvas, which is unconventionally stretched on the diagonal. The composition was developed as he worked, so that some forms—most significantly the man at the left—were painted on top of completed passages, such as the table. The interior of the shop is rationally defined by the recession of the floor, the wooden ceiling beams, and the foreshortened spikes. Likewise, Annibale's natural treatment of light, casting shadows across the floor and beams, lends a palpable sense of reality to the scene.

Also notable is Annibale's forthright portrayal of the tradesmen, with their sober, ceremonious demeanor and clean white aprons. Such sympathetic treatment distinguishes it from earlier, more humorous, low-life subjects, such as his teacher Bartolomeo Passarotti's *Butcher Shop* (Galleria Nazionale, Rome). In fact, Annibale's uncle and cousins were butchers, and he would have been intimately familiar with the trade. Annibale painted another, larger picture of a butcher's shop that is now in Christ Church, Oxford.

MICHELANGELO MERISI DA CARAVAGGIO
Italian, 1571–1610
The Cardsharps, c. 1594

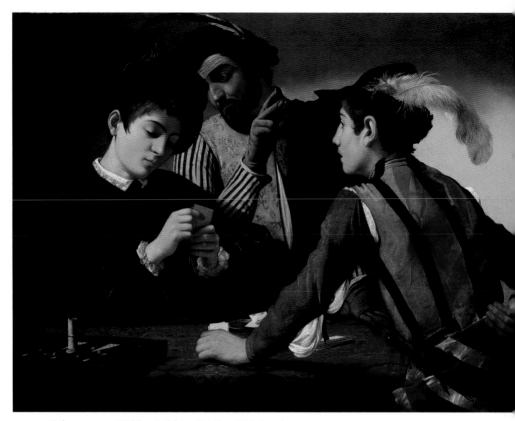

Oil on canvas; 37⅛ x 51⅝ in. (94.2 x 130.9 cm)
Acquired in 1987

Renowned for his robust realism based on the use of live models, and for his interest in low-life subjects, Caravaggio stands at the head of a major stream of Baroque art that reacted against the high artificiality of much late-Renaissance art. One of Caravaggio's early masterpieces, *The Cardsharps* was immensely influential in the development of genre painting in Italy and beyond, as illustrated by the Kimbell's *Cheat with the Ace of Clubs* by Georges de La Tour.

Caravaggio here presents a universal parable of innocence and corruption, staged with three dramatically character-ized cardplayers engaged in a game of *primero*, a forerunner of poker. Engrossed in his cards at left is the dupe—a smooth-cheeked boy wearing a plum-colored velvet jacket offset with a dainty white collar and cuffs. Sporting more flamboyant attire, the older cardsharp signals his accomplice with his raised, gloved hand (the fingertips exposed, better to feel marked cards). At right, the young cheat with traces of down on his upper lip looks expectantly toward the boy and reaches behind his back to pull a hidden card from his breeches. The composition is rigorously structured to pull the viewer's eye toward the crucial play of cards. Bold foreshortenings—the backgammon board poised at the edge of the carpeted table and the dagger tucked in the young cheat's belt—direct attention toward the unfolding drama.

The art of Caravaggio, who served his apprenticeship in Milan, is grounded in the realist traditions of northern Italy. Upon arriving in Rome in the early 1590s, Caravaggio painted a range of works, most notably still lifes and genre pictures, including *The Cardsharps*. According to the artist's earliest biographers, Cardinal Francesco Maria del Monte purchased this work from a dealer and then invited Caravaggio to live and work in his palace; Del Monte subsequently became one of Caravaggio's most important patrons. Spared from his former hand-to-mouth existence, Caravaggio thereby came to the attention of a circle of prominent clients, and soon received coveted commissions for altarpieces.

Ironically, the perils of gaming are well illustrated in Caravaggio's own violent and tragic life: in 1606 he killed a man over a disputed wager on a game of tennis and was forced to flee Rome.

In the short, peripatetic career that followed, Caravaggio continued to produce religious paintings that have come to be recognized as among the most affecting works of the Catholic Counter-Reformation.

Caravaggio's novel subject matter and style of painting, with its insistent naturalism and dramatic light effects, proved seductive to the younger generations of painters that flocked to Rome, and his influence spread throughout Italy and beyond to France and the Netherlands. *The Cardsharps* alone inspired dozens of copies, beginning as early as 1621. Since the 1890s, however, the location of Caravaggio's original painting was unknown until it was rediscovered in a European private collection in 1987, and acquired by the Kimbell. During conservation of the painting, a stamped seal was revealed on the reverse of the canvas. This stamp, identifying works from Cardinal del Monte's collection, is also found on Caravaggio's *Gypsy Fortune Teller* in the Capitoline Museum, Rome, which formerly hung next to *The Cardsharps* in the Del Monte palace.

The Cardsharps is among the best preserved works by Caravaggio, retaining even the delicate red lake glazes over the vermilion red hearts. Caravaggio composed the work from individually posed figures painted directly on the canvas without the aid of preparatory drawings, making several changes as he worked that survive as *pentimenti*— notably, the positions of the hand, cards, and belt of the cheat on the far right and of the stripes on his doublet.

ADAM ELSHEIMER
German, 1578–1610
The Flight into Egypt, c. 1605

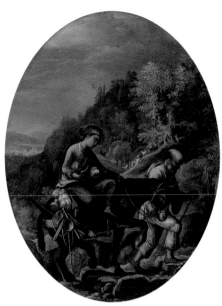

Oil on silvered copper;
3⅞ x 3 in. (oval) (9.8 x 7.6 cm)
Acquired in 1994

Elsheimer's directness of vision placed him, along with Caravaggio and Annibale Carracci, in the vanguard of reforming artists working in Rome in the first decade of the seventeenth century. He was a pioneer in the development of naturalistic landscape, whose influence extended to Claude and Rembrandt. Here he portrays the Holy Family in rustic apparel, taking an arduous path through rocky terrain. Devotional literature interpreted their difficult and dangerous journey to Egypt as a pilgrimage of life toward salvation, necessary to redeem humankind. This essential message is reinforced in the details of Elsheimer's miniature panel. The broad-brimmed hats that ward off the searing sun are the traditional attributes of pilgrims. The tiny, vulnerable Child

raises his arms to the weary Virgin, who wilts like a flower. The carpenter's tools, water gourd, and cup, and the rustic harness and saddle with its trapezelike stirrup, show the humility and poverty of the family. A goat, noted for its libidinous nature, nibbles foliage from a mighty oak in the middle distance behind Joseph— an allusion to the sins of the world that will be redeemed by the Savior. Singled out by a divine light, the oak suggests the Tree of Life—from whose wood the cross of Christ was made—which bestowed immortality on earthly sinners.

On receiving news of Elsheimer's premature death, the young Peter Paul Rubens wrote that "after such a loss, our entire profession ought to clothe itself in mourning. . . . In my opinion he had no equal in small figures, in landscapes, and in many other subjects." Elsheimer left his native Frankfurt for Venice at the age of twenty, stopping en route in Munich, where he studied the altarpieces of Albrecht Altdorfer. In 1600 he arrived in Rome, where he remained until his death ten years later. A member of the Academy of Saint Luke, he was part of a circle of northerners in Rome that also included Rubens.

According to contemporary accounts, Elsheimer worked slowly and thoughtfully, producing a relatively small number of finished works. He died in poverty, although his works were coveted; according to his contemporary Giulio Mancini, they were "in the hands of princes and those persons who, in order that they should not be taken from them, keep them hidden." No more than thirty finished paintings on copper, all diminutive in size, have survived.

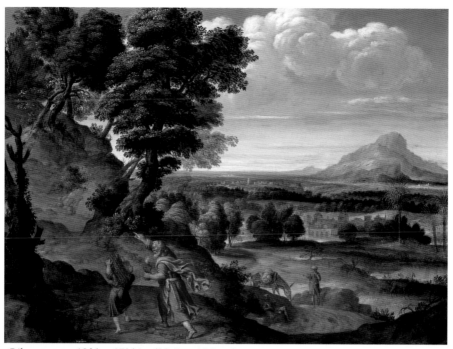

DOMENICHINO (DOMENICO ZAMPIERI)
Italian, 1581–1641
Abraham Leading Isaac to Sacrifice, 1602

Oil on copper; 12⅝ x 17½ in. (32.5 x 44.3 cm)
Acquired in 1982

Domenichino, who is renowned for his large-scale frescoes, history paintings, and altarpieces, became Italy's leading classical painter in the first half of the seventeenth century. Trained at the Carracci Academy in his native city of Bologna, Domenichino came to Rome in 1602 to work under Annibale Carracci at the Farnese Palace. *Abraham Leading Isaac to Sacrifice*, which appears in the January 1603 inventory of the collection of Cardinal Pietro Aldobrandini, the powerful nephew of Pope Clement VIII, was inspired by the naturalistic and carefully constructed landscapes of Annibale. Its composition and refined technique also recall the panoramic landscapes of Flemish artists like Paul Bril, who had settled in Rome a generation earlier, and anticipate the classical land-

scapes of masters like Claude Lorrain and Nicolas Poussin. Landscapes, largely painted for sophisticated patrons who valued the concept of nature as a blissful, Arcadian retreat, formed a small but significant part of Domenichino's oeuvre.

Domenichino depicts Abraham leading his beloved son Isaac to be sacrificed, as God commanded (Genesis 22:1–14) — a subject regarded as a prefiguration of God's sacrifice of Christ. Later, when Abraham took up his sword to kill his son, an angel stopped him, indicating a ram as a substitute.

The low-lying countryside records the topography of the Roman country-side with Mount Soracte in the distance; the tiny camel, palms, and ancient towns evoke the biblical past.

EL GRECO (DOMENIKOS THEOTOKOPOULOS)
Spanish, 1541–1614
Portrait of Dr. Francisco de Pisa, c. 1610–14

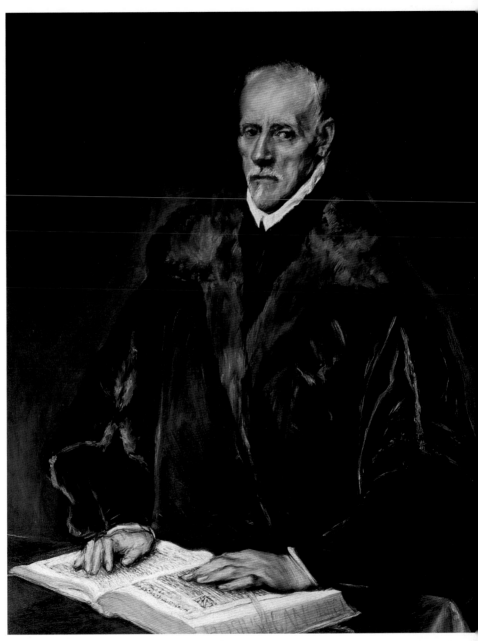

Oil on canvas; 42⅛ x 35½ in. (107 x 90 cm)
Acquired in 1977

The painter known as El Greco ("the Greek") was born Domenikos Theotokopoulos in Crete, then a territory of the Venetian Republic, where he trained as an icon painter. Talented and ambitious, he left Crete around 1568 for Venice, and later Rome. In Italy he studied the coloring and light of the Venetian masters, the figures of Michelangelo, as well as the grace and dynamism of the Emilian artists, all of which informed his own highly original style. In 1577, El Greco departed for Spain, and settled in the city of Toledo. He was patronized there by members of the city's wealthy and educated elite, who valued the presence of an intellectual artist trained in Italy. This portrait, which dates from the last period of El Greco's career, attests to the artist's profound gifts as a portraitist, which were praised since his years in Italy and remained undiminished in old age.

Because of the inscription on the book—*Bosius Canonici*—this portrait was formerly identified as a likeness of Giacomo Bosio, an Italian cleric who had no apparent connection with the city of Toledo, where El Greco lived and worked when this painting was made. Archival evidence, however, confirms the likelihood that the sitter is Dr. Francisco de Pisa (1534–1616), an important Toledan cleric and official historian of the city, who in 1610 expressed the intention to endow the Convent of the Purísima Concepción de Nuestra Señora, also known as the Convent of the Benitas. A portrait of Pisa approximately this size was bequeathed by him to the convent and was recorded there in 1616 and 1623, along with other paintings by El Greco. A miniature portrait of Pisa, traditionally attributed to El Greco, further supports the identification.

El Greco aptly characterizes the rectitude of Pisa, who was professor of Holy Scripture at the University of Santa Catalina. At an Inquisitional meeting, the conservative churchman argued against permission to publish a new edition of Saint Theresa of Avila's writings, citing "many things that appear to contradict true and correct doctrine as well as the good use of mental prayer." Pisa appears absorbed in thoughts that, despite his fixed gaze, surpass the scope of the viewer. This intensity of expression is heightened by the deep, faceted hollows of his temples and cheeks. Dressed in scholar's robes, his hands rest upon the large open tome. The bulk of his voluminous mantle, in contrast to the small head set off by the crisp white clerical collar, enhances the authority of the upright sitter as a model of probity. Despite the restricted palette, every part of the canvas is active; white highlights are boldly laid over the dark paint of the mantle, whose fur collar and lining take on sumptuous warmth, suggested by the reddish brown ground visible beneath the variegated brushstrokes.

PETER PAUL RUBENS
Flemish, 1577–1640
The Martyrdom of Saint Ursula and the Eleven Thousand Maidens, c. 1615–20

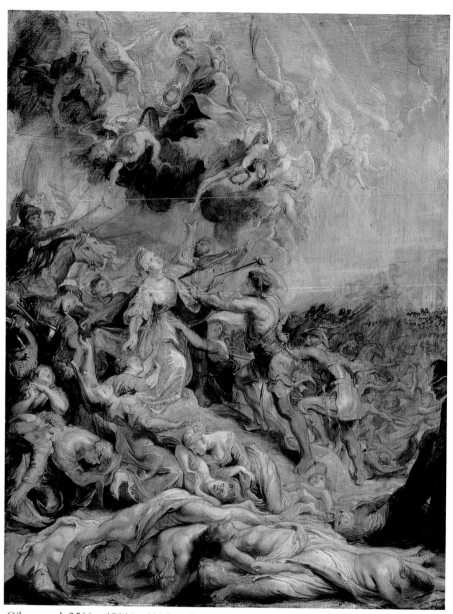

Oil on panel; 25⅜ x 19½ in. (64.5 x 49.5 cm)
Acquired in 1986

Peter Paul Rubens confessed that "My talent is such that no undertaking in size, or how varied in subject, has ever exceeded my confidence and courage." His monumental works exalting the Church and royal families of Europe are among the grandest accomplishments of the seventeenth century. As part of his preparatory process, it was Rubens's practice to make oil sketches for his compositions. With their inspired brushwork and fluid execution, the Flemish master's sketches have long been collected and acclaimed among the supreme masterpieces of this genre—not least for the process of creative genius that they reveal on such an intimate scale.

The Martyrdom of Saint Ursula and the Eleven Thousand Maidens is an oil sketch for an unidentified altarpiece. The legend of Saint Ursula recounts how the virtuous daughter of a British Christian king, having reached Cologne on her return from a pilgrimage to Rome, was slaughtered by Huns along with her entourage of eleven thousand companions. Rubens orchestrates the throng of figures—maidens, soldiers, and angels—into a series of thrusting diagonals bridging heaven and earth. At the calm center of this maelstrom is Saint Ursula, portrayed as a princess with her tiara and pearl necklace. She stands on the brink of martyrdom, as her tormenters prepare to impale her with spear and sword. Above, a flight of angels ardently dispenses wreaths and palms as Ursula prepares to be united with the Madonna and Child in heaven. Heaped up in the foreground is a horrific tangle of opalescent flesh and pearly white drapery. The pathos of the scene is heightened by motifs like the maiden in a yellow gown, whose long hair is yanked backward by a soldier on horseback. Touches of lemon, rose red, and sky blue brushed on the light buff ground lend the work an otherworldly beauty.

FRANS HALS
Dutch, 1581/83–1666
The Rommel-Pot Player, c. 1618–22

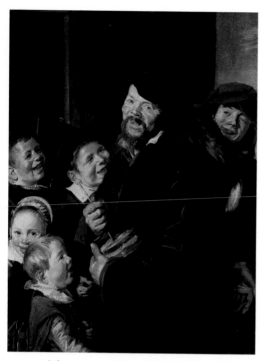

Oil on canvas; 41¾ x 31⅝ in. (106 x 80.3 cm)
Acquired in 1951

The smiling rommel-pot player in this painting by Frans Hals has gathered around him an audience of amused children offering him coins. The children delight in the appalling sounds emitted by this lowly instrument, which is made of a pig's bladder stretched over an earthenware jug half-filled with water. A reed is bound in a small pocket in the middle of the bladder and moved up and down with a wet hand to produce a growling or rumbling sound. Played by impoverished street musicians, rommel pots were particularly associated with the pre-Lenten celebration of Shrovetide, here indicated by the fool's foxtail worn by the bearded man. Hals's musician may depict a contemporary figure. The figure in David Bailly's drawing dated 1624, apparently copied from this painting, is identified in an eighteenth-century sales catalogue as "Boontje . . . in those days a well-known fool of Haarlem, playing on the rommel pot."

The Rommel-Pot Player is one of the earliest paintings to portray convincingly the vivacious and joyful expressions of children, here conveyed with Hals's distinctive brisk brushstrokes. This composition—associated with the idea of folly—was one of the artist's most popular subjects, and a number of versions and variants survive. The best of these is the Kimbell painting, a work with numerous revisions and bravura handling of the light, which apparently served as the prototype for the others.

Frans Hals was the leading painter in the Dutch town of Haarlem, where he spent most of his life. Although he received many commissions from wealthy burghers for individual and group portraits, he also produced religious paintings and genre scenes from everyday life. He was especially famed in his lifetime, as today, for the spontaneity of his brushwork.

GOFFREDO (GOTTFRIED) WALS
German, c. 1595/1600–1638/40
A Country Road by a House, 1620s

An early example of pure landscape, this rare painting on copper by Goffredo Wals records the effects of warm light bathing a country road at the close of day. Wals was born in Cologne, and after an initial stay in Naples joined the Roman studio of Agostino Tassi. Wals later returned to Naples, where he was an early teacher of Claude Lorrain. He was influenced by the work of the Flemish painter Paul Bril and Wals's fellow German Adam Elsheimer, who produced jewel-like landscapes on copper, including the Kimbell's *Flight into Egypt*. Wals, whose oeuvre has only recently been reconstructed, died in an earthquake in Calabria.

As a group, Wals's paintings—of which some thirty have been identified to date—show a radically fresh approach to nature and coloring; most are without prominent figures and employ strong contrasts of light and shade. The simplified settings that the artist often placed in a round format, with an emphasis on straight and circular forms, have an air of serenity and contemplation that finds beauty in the quotidian and the mundane.

A Country Road by a House, the first work by Wals to enter an American public collection, is the prototype for a slightly larger variant in the Fitzwilliam Museum, Cambridge. Unlike Claude and other painters of classical landscapes, Wals forsakes framing elements, such as trees, to lead the viewer into the scene, whose bold composition exploits a number of novel means of achieving spatial depth.

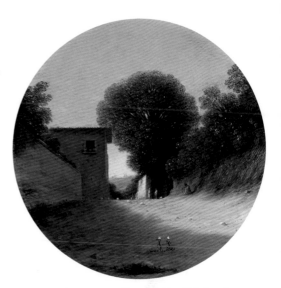

Oil on copper; diam. 9¼ in. (23.5 cm)
Acquired in 1991

From the daring empty foreground occupying the bottom third of the composition, whose distance is measured in blades of grass and small stones, the eye is channeled by strong foreshortening to the middle distance, marked by a spheroid tree that echoes the shape of the painting. Wals manipulates the receding elements of the wall and thatch beside the road to form a single horizontal that bisects the composition and thus continues the horizon line in the distance. This abstraction of form and sensitivity to atmospheric effects look beyond the seventeenth century to the work of Corot two centuries later.

PETER PAUL RUBENS
Flemish, 1577–1640
The Duke of Buckingham, 1625

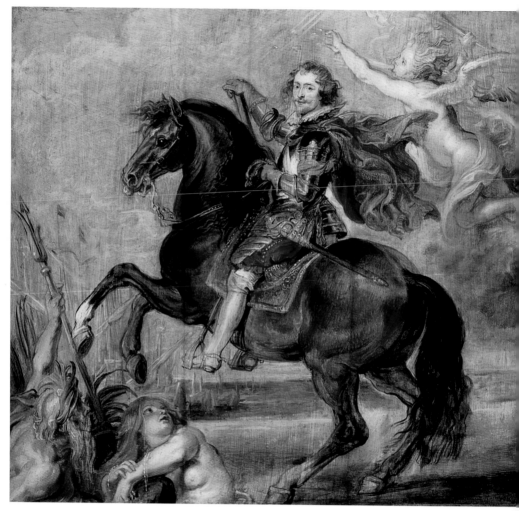

Oil on panel; 18⅜ x 20⅜ in. (46.6 x 51.7 cm)
Acquired in 1976

Peter Paul Rubens was a towering figure in the age of the Baroque, and his influence on later generations of artists was immense. Rubens's outstanding and wide-ranging talents—his deep knowledge of the classics and command of languages, his prodigious memory, affability, and unsurpassed productivity—recommended him to the courts of Europe not only as an artist of incomparable invention, but also as a diplomat who could be entrusted with delicate political negotiations.

In 1625, Rubens was summoned to Paris to install the magnificent cycle of paintings on the life of Marie de' Medici made for the Palace of Luxembourg, where the Queen Mother's daughter Henrietta Maria (sister of King Louis XIII) was to be married by proxy to Charles I of England. In Paris, Rubens met George Villiers (1592–1628), the Duke of Buckingham, who had helped to negotiate the royal match and would escort the new queen to England. Buckingham commissioned Rubens to paint an equestrian portrait, and it is likely that the Flemish master presented the Kimbell oil sketch to Villiers when they met later that year at the painter's studio in Antwerp. The duke, who within a decade had amassed a remarkable art collection, also purchased Rubens's own collection of antiquities for a great sum. Their cordial relations laid crucial groundwork for Rubens's diplomatic mission on behalf of the Spanish Netherlands to negotiate peace with England.

Described as "the handsomest bodied man in all of England," Villiers had a meteoric rise to power and wealth. Introduced to the court as a cupbearer in 1614, he quickly became the favorite of James I, who soon named him master of the horse and a member of the privy council. In 1619 he was made lord high admiral of the navy, and in 1623 he was created first Duke of Buckingham. After James's death in 1625, Villiers retained his influence with Charles I.

The elegance and bravura that captivated Buckingham's admirers—and inspired Alexander Dumas's romantic depiction of him in *The Three Musketeers*— are evident in Rubens's portrait. Wearing light armor with the blue sash and medal of the Order of the Garter and a billowing red cape, the duke holds a baton of command as his handsome bay horse rears on command. While the equestrian portrait has precedents in English engravings of aristocratic commanders, Rubens invested the genre with a new vitality that would be highly influential into the nineteenth century. Overhead, a winged allegory of Fame signals victory with a trumpet in hand as he tosses flowers and blows a propitious wind. Neptune bearing his trident and a naiad adorned with pearls, along with the impressive fleet of ships that looms on the horizon, indicate the duke's dominion over the sea. The full-scale painting (formerly at Osterley Park and destroyed by fire in 1949) was elaborated with additional allegorical figures, likely added at Buckingham's request.

Rubens privately noted Buckingham's "arrogance and caprice" and predicted that he was "heading for the precipice." The duke's audacious and unsuccessful military campaigns against Spain and then France were much resented, and in 1628 he was assassinated. Two years later, Rubens succeeded in facilitating the peace treaty between England and Spain, and was knighted by Charles I.

GUERCINO (GIOVANNI FRANCESCO BARBIERI)
Italian, 1591–1666
Portrait of a Lawyer, Probably the Doctor of Laws Francesco Righetti, c. 1626–28

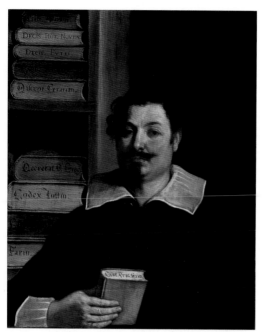

Oil on canvas; 32¼ x 26¼ in. (83.2 x 66.7 cm)
Acquired in 1991, Gift (partial and promised)
of Edmund P. Pillsbury in honor of the
Kimbell Art Museum's twentieth anniversary

The subject of this portrait by Guercino, one of the leading members of
the Bolognese school of painters in the
seventeenth century, has been identified as
Francesco Righetti (1595–1673), a patron
of the artist and the most eminent lawyer
in Cento, the artist's birthplace. Righetti

published widely and served as a member
of the city council of Cento. The books
that are prominently displayed on the
shelves behind Righetti characterize him
as a practicing lawyer rather than a theo-
retician. In addition to basic texts of
Roman and canon law, such as the *Codex
Justiniani* and the *Decretales* of Gregory IX
(1234) that remained fundamental for
legal practice, Righetti's library includes
modern manuals, commentaries, and
court decisions. In his right hand, for
example, Righetti holds a popular
modern text on criminal law by Julius
Clarus (c. 1575).

Guercino's portraits, although few in
number, are noted for their humanity and
immediacy. Placing the sitter directly in
the foreground, Guercino conveys the
robust self-confidence of Righetti as a
man of action. The background—one
side dark, the other with neatly stacked
tomes—offsets the frontal disposition of
the figure, as Righetti's unruly dark curls
are silhouetted against the blond book-
shelf at center. Guercino's supreme gifts as
a painter of texture and light are displayed
in the silvery sheen of the smooth collar
and cuff against the luxurious softness of
the dark robe. The rosy fleshiness of the
face and hand becomes a counterpoint to
the toughened surface of the calfskin
binding of the book he holds.

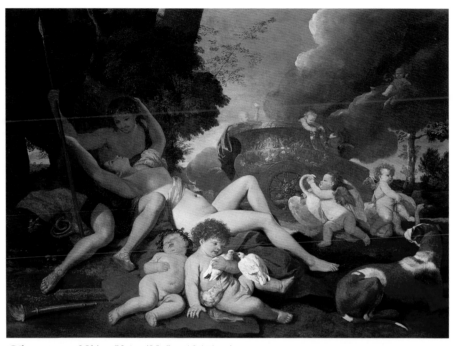

Oil on canvas; 38¾ x 53 in. (98.5 x 134.6 cm)
Acquired in 1985

Early in his career Poussin traveled to Italy and was introduced to a circle of important Roman patrons including the antiquarian Cassiano dal Pozzo. Poussin's classicism, nurtured by his knowledge of antique literature and art, was warmed by his study of Venetian art. *Venus and Adonis* reveals the influence of Titian in composition, coloration, and mood. The composition is built in a series of opposing diagonals, highlighting Venus's shapely limbs and soft belly and casting the lovers into shadow, foreboding Adonis's imminent doom.

According to Book X of Ovid's *Metamorphoses*, Venus and her mortal lover Adonis sought the shade of a poplar tree during an interlude from the hunt. The goddess mingled kisses and words, telling Adonis why she forbade him to pursue dangerous, wild animals—her mortal enemies. The lovers are attended by a host of putti who prepare Venus's golden chariot. A pair of reclining putti, along with a couple of billing doves, mimic the lovers' postures. Lance in hand and helical horn and dog nearby, Adonis is ready to disobey Venus and heed the call of the hunt. The tragic outcome—for Adonis is killed by a wild boar—can be inferred by the sleeping putto, unattended torch, and menacing clouds. Adonis wears a wreath of anemones, the flower that Venus created in his memory by sprinkling his blood with nectar.

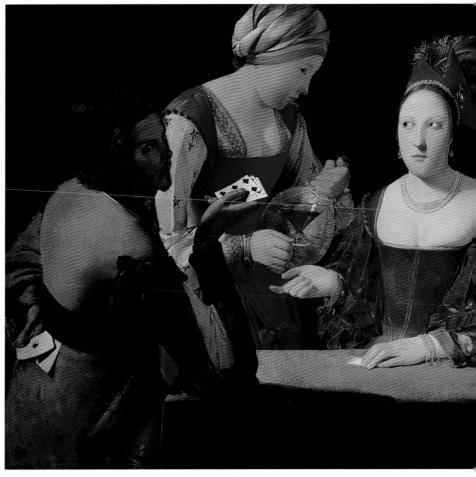

Oil on canvas; 38½ x 61½ in. (97.8 x 156.2 cm)
Acquired in 1981

One of the greatest masterpieces of seventeenth-century French art, Georges de La Tour's *Cheat with the Ace of Clubs* takes as its subject the danger of indulgence in wine, women, and gambling. While the theme harks back to Caravaggio's influential *Cardsharps*, also in the Kimbell, the roots of this engaging morality play can be traced to earlier representations of the subject of the prodigal son in paintings and prints.

A master of dramatic, candlelit scenes, La Tour here chooses a more even light that sets off the dazzling colors and elaborate decoration of the players' costumes. This brilliant decorative tableau, however, is only the stage setting for the psychological drama that is, as always in La Tour's work, his true subject. The players are subtly but unmistakably characterized: the snub-nosed, small-eyed young dupe at right; the cheat at left, with his foxy coun-

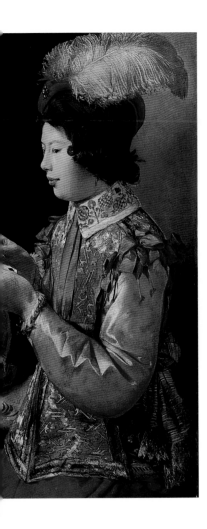

bodice) will prevail. The maid creates a diversion by serving the wine, and the stage is set: to the young victim's astonishment, the ace of clubs concealed by the cheat will be laid on the table to trump his anticipated win, and his pile of coins will join the cache hidden under the cheat's right arm.

La Tour offers a banquet of color, with an especially rich range of reds, from raspberry to watermelon. Striking passages of paint delineate the fanciful costumes—a drizzle of yellow edging the courtesan's russet velvet dress, and impastoed threads of colorful embroidery of the dupe's collar. La Tour's evocation of light, revealing the varied textures of ostrich plumes, pearls, and a wicker flask, and the shadows cast across the players' faces, is remarkable.

Another autograph version of this subject, *Cheat with the Ace of Diamonds* (Musée du Louvre, Paris), displays abundant variations in details of color, clothing, and accessories. La Tour appears to have used the same set of cartoons of individual figures for both the Kimbell and Louvre paintings, although the three figures at left are more tightly placed in the latter.

For most of his life, La Tour remained in his native duchy of Lorraine, remote from Paris and the mainstream of French art. Although he created some of the most visually compelling images of his age, and Louis XIII and Cardinal Richelieu owned several of his paintings, soon after his death he fell into obscurity. It was only in the early twentieth century that La Tour's oeuvre began to be rediscovered with the aid of archival research and connoisseurship.

tenance; and the ovoid-faced woman at center, who is both a cipher and key to the action that will ensue. The drama unfolds through the cues of the players' sidelong gazes and the measured gestures of hands that signal their next moves. The cheat tips his cards toward the viewer, who thereby becomes complicit in the scheme, knowing that in the next moment, the conniving trio of cheat, maidservant, and courtesan (identified by her low-cut

ATTRIBUTED TO GEORGES DE LA TOUR
French, 1593–1652
Saint Sebastian Tended by Irene, early 1630s

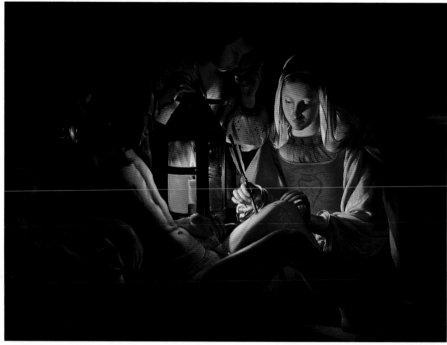

Oil on canvas; 41¼ x 54⅞ in. (104.8 x 139.4 cm)
Acquired in 1993

Saint Sebastian—a Roman soldier who suffered martyrdom around A.D. 300—was nursed by the pious Irene, who, upon discovering him still alive, tenderly removed the arrows that pierced his body. Saint Sebastian was a protector against the epidemics that plagued the artist's native Lorraine, and La Tour's various versions of this scene were by far the most copied of his works in the seventeenth century. In 1751 a local historian made reference to two paintings of Sebastian, the first of which La Tour presented to Duke Charles IV of Lorraine, and the second to King Louis XIII of France, who admired it so much that he "had all the other paintings removed from his room in order to leave only this one."

Today more than ten versions are known in horizontal format, differing widely in quality and condition. While most scholars consider the Kimbell *Saint Sebastian* to be a copy, it may be one of the two works painted by La Tour himself, possibly the first version given to Charles IV. The painting has suffered damage (especially in the darkest passages) from the transfer of the paint layer to a new canvas, rendering connoisseurship difficult. Nevertheless, it exhibits evidence of reworking or *pentimenti* during its creation, as well as the use of preliminary markings and incisions to establish the contours, a distinctive feature of La Tour's working method. Most important, the palette, modeling, and brushwork in the better-preserved passages are of a quality approaching La Tour's autograph works.

Jusepe de Ribera, whose earliest training remains undocumented, left his native Spain for Italy sometime before he turned twenty. Following a sojourn in Parma, he is recorded living in Rome by 1615, one of many talented young artists who were held in thrall by Caravaggio's revolutionary paintings. Ribera's considerable and precocious talents caught the eye of both his fellow painters and well-connected patrons, and the following year he settled into a highly productive career in Naples. Ribera was soon employed by the Spanish viceroys who governed Naples, and also enjoyed the patronage of the most important religious houses.

In this devotional painting, Ribera has created a believable and deeply affecting image that conveys the semblance both of a living being, and of an apostle who knew the Lord and his Word. Although the identity of the saint is not certain, the book he holds accounts for his traditional identification as Matthew, author of the gospel. Such paintings often formed part of an *Apostolado*, or series of portraitlike images of Christ's apostles. Here the influence of Caravaggio—the stark placement of the intensely lit figure against a dark background, the unrelenting naturalism, and the strength of characterization—is tempered by a classicism that reveals Ribera's study of the Renaissance masters and contemporary Bolognese painters. The noble pose of the figure, head slightly turned to counterbalance the placement of the body in space, recalls the artist's reputed admiration for Raphael.

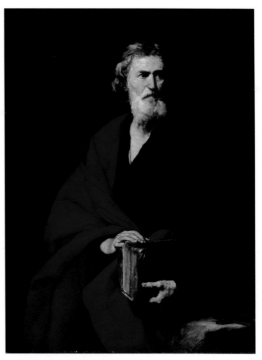

*Oil on canvas; 50½ x 38½ in.
(128.2 x 97.8 cm)
Acquired in 1966*

A technically brilliant artist, Ribera varies the texture of his paint, employing thin layers to describe the wooly, red brown cloak and a rich impasto for the deep furrows in the saint's brow. Warm underpainting can be seen through the flesh tones of the saint's hands, lending them greater depth and vitality. The artist, also known in Naples as "Lo Spagnoletto," neatly paints his signature on the rock at lower right: *Jusepe de Ribera español.*

DIEGO VELÁZQUEZ
Spanish, 1599–1660
Don Pedro de Barberana, c. 1631–33

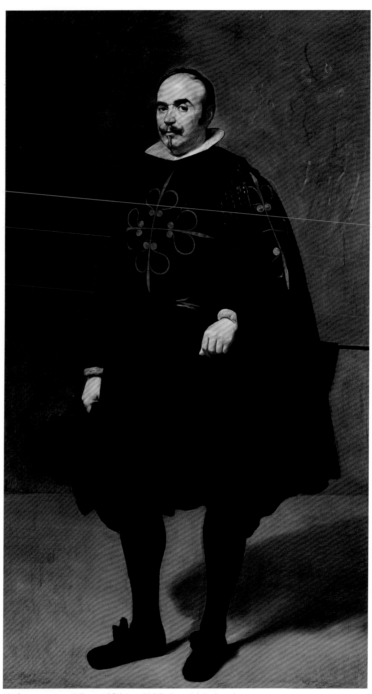

Oil on canvas; 78 x 43⅞ in. (198.1 x 111.4 cm)
Acquired in 1981

Born and trained in Seville, Velázquez moved to Madrid, where he served King Philip IV from 1623. As court painter, his main responsibility was to produce portraits of the royal family and their circle. These portraits, a major part of his legacy, remain unsurpassed in their depth of conception and extraordinary painterly technique. Velázquez worked tirelessly to raise the status of the artist in Spain, and he was rewarded shortly before his death with his induction as a knight of the Order of Santiago.

Identified by an inscription found on the painting's old relining canvas, Don Pedro de Barberana y Aparregui (1579–1649) was a member of Philip IV's privy council. He was named honorary postmaster of the realm and, by royal decree, governor of his native town of Briones. Prominently displayed on his doublet and cape is the red cross of the Order of Calatrava, founded in the Middle Ages as a defense against the Moors and subsequently a privilege of the aristocracy. Don Pedro was knighted in 1630, and Velázquez must have painted the portrait soon after he returned from his first trip to Italy in 1631.

Although he follows earlier prototypes for full-length portraits developed by Habsburg court artists such as Anthonis Mor, Velázquez devises new ways of heightening the illusion of the sitter's physical presence. Don Pedro commands the entire pictorial space, which is stripped of architectural elements and enlivened by his cast shadow and the soft, ambient light of the indeterminate background. His left brow raised with a pronounced asymmetry, Don Pedro looks out with cool, confident aplomb, seeming to scrutinize and appraise the viewer, rather than the reverse. Much of the force of the portrait derives from the tension between the evocation of a forthright personality and the refinement and elegance of the knight's costume. Especially noteworthy is Velázquez's ability to create palpable volumes, particularly in the subtle gradations of blacks in the sitter's clothing.

Velázquez utilizes an economy of means and variety of painterly techniques, no doubt encouraged by his studies during a recent trip to Italy, such as scraping through the wet paint to suggest the gray hairs of the goatee. Throughout the portrait, he alternates hard and soft contours to enliven the figure. With its soft edges, the thinly painted ear appears slightly out of focus, helping it to recede behind the sharply defined eyes and nose. In the background, to the right of the figure, can be seen the characteristic brush marks where Velázquez seems to have tested his colors or cleaned the paint off his brush.

CLAUDE LORRAIN
French, c. 1604/5–1682
Coast Scene with Europa and the Bull, 1634

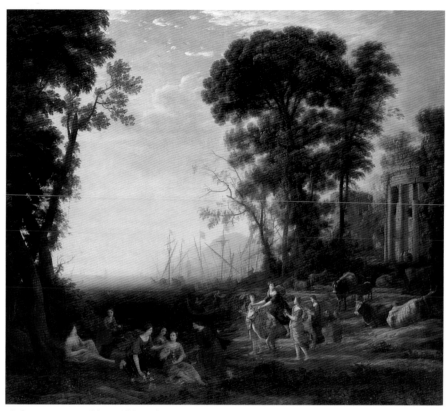

Oil on canvas; 67¼ x 78⅝ in. (170.8 x 199.7 cm)
Acquired in 1981

Claude Lorrain, the greatest artist of the classical school of European landscape painting, raised this previously secondary genre to a new level of sophistication and prestige. Characterized by the balanced arrangement of ideal landscape motifs and classical ruins, his works often introduce complementary mythological or pastoral elements that evoke a timeless, poetic world.

Claude left his native Lorraine as a young man and settled in Rome, where he remained for the rest of his career. This majestic and important work, apparently painted for the French ambassador to

Rome, helped to establish Claude as the city's most successful landscape painter. Following Ovid's *Metamorphoses,* Claude depicts Zeus as a divinely beautiful snow-white bull. In this guise the supreme god has enticed the princess Europa onto his back; he edges toward the water, across which lies the isle of Crete, to which he will abduct her. Claude includes a ruin inspired by the ancient temple at Tivoli, which he had studied during frequent excursions to the Roman countryside. The enchanting atmosphere of the landscape depends on carefully modulated effects of light.

I n this devotional painting, Saint Martina, a third-century martyr who was put to death for refusing to worship idols, gazes fervently at the Christ Child while holding the forked iron hook with which she was tortured, and accepting the palm of martyrdom. Cortona's use of strong colors, agitated drapery, and the dynamic play of light and shadow enhances the image's spiritual intensity.

Saint Martina held great personal significance for Pietro da Cortona, who painted her image numerous times. Elected president of the Academy of Saint Luke in 1634, Cortona proposed to rebuild the academy's church in the Roman Forum. During excavations in the crypt, where the artist planned to be buried, the remains of Saint Martina were discovered. Pope Urban VIII came to view them, and his nephew Cardinal Francesco Barberini financed the rebuilding of the church—now rededicated to Saints Luke and Martina—with Cortona as architect. Cortona bequeathed a considerable sum from his own fortune for the refurbishment of the lower church with its altar to Saint Martina.

In 1644, Cortona wrote to Cardinal Barberini expressing hope that the cardinal was pleased with his painting of the Madonna with Saint Martina. This was probably the Kimbell painting: of Cortona's known versions of the subject, only the Kimbell's accords with the dimensions recorded in the Barberini inventories. A painting of these same dimensions, presumably the Kimbell work, can later be traced to the

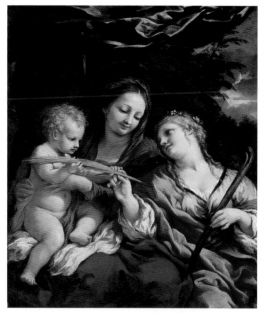

Oil on canvas; 27 9/16 x 22 13/16 in. (70 x 58 cm)
Acquired in 1984

collection of Cardinal Pietro Ottoboni (1667–1740), who inherited it from his great-uncle, Pope Alexander VIII.

The preeminent painter in Rome of his day and an architect of considerable invention, Pietro da Cortona developed a robust style, informed by his study of antiquity and the Venetian and Bolognese masters, that was ideally suited to the glorification of the Church and prominent patrons. Cortona painted a number of grand frescoes for princely patrons in Rome and Florence, as well as altarpieces, history paintings, and designs for tombs and other projects.

LOUIS(?) LE NAIN
French, c. 1600/1610–1648
Peasant Interior with an Old Flute Player, c. 1642

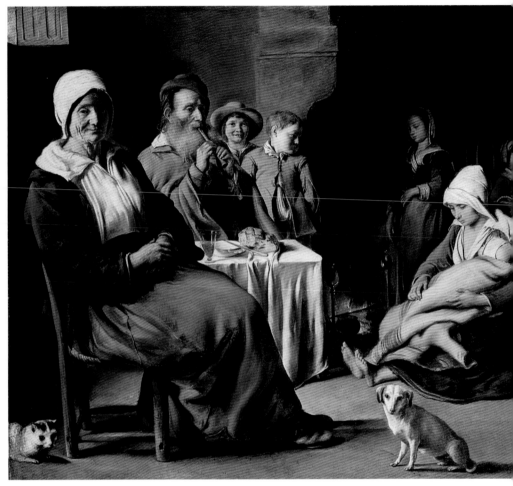

Oil on canvas; 21¼ x 24½ in. (54.1 x 62.1 cm)
Acquired in 1984

The Le Nain brothers—Antoine, Louis, and Mathieu—were born in Laon, in the region of Picardy, and settled in the artist's community of Saint-Germain-des-Prés, in Paris, by 1629. The brothers were founding members of the newly created Royal Academy of Painting and Sculpture in 1648. Antoine and Louis died that same year, presumably of the plague, while the youngest, Mathieu, survived. The Le Nain studio produced portraits and religious works as well as mythological and genre scenes. Some of their work, which was signed simply Le Nain, was undoubtedly collaborative. In the absence of documentation, a group of peasant scenes characterized by their sensitive, subdued palette and emotional solemnity has traditionally been assigned to Louis, who has been regarded as the "genius of the family."

In the *Peasant Interior with an Old Flute Player*, an air of serenity surrounds the dignified group, still and silent but for the sound of the flute. The eyes of the older woman, smiling boy, and docile dog and cat seem to invite the viewer's appraisal of the family gathering. A strong light throws shadows across the room, a harmony of grays and ochers, warmed by the claret color of wine and fire. Despite the artist's clear sympathy with humble values, however, this scene is an idealized portrayal of peasant life. Garments with bright white collars are neatly patched and clean. Wine in a crystal glass was not peasant fare and, together with the bread placed on the white tablecloth, evidently alludes to the Eucharistic meal and Christian charity, exemplified by this humble household.

Much remains to be learned about the Le Nains' patrons, who may have included members of the pious religious groups in Paris and the outlying regions where the brothers worked. Religious leaders such as Saint Francis de Sales (1567–1622) and Saint Vincent de Paul (1581–1660) encouraged the devout to emulate the virtues of the idealized poor, such as simplicity, humility, and patience. The clergy of lay religious groups such as the Daughters of Charity and the Company of the Holy Sacrament that flourished around Paris between 1630 and 1650 called upon their members to practice charity and compassion toward the poor, to visit them and receive them in their own homes.

Pictures such as *Peasant Interior with an Old Flute Player* may have helped their owners in their own pious meditations. The Christlike quietude, endurance, and humility of these simple peasants would have served as a worthy spiritual example for the faithful, in accord with the spiritual goals of the reforming clergy.

PIETER JANSZ. SAENREDAM
Dutch, 1597–1665
Interior of the Buurkerk, Utrecht, 1645

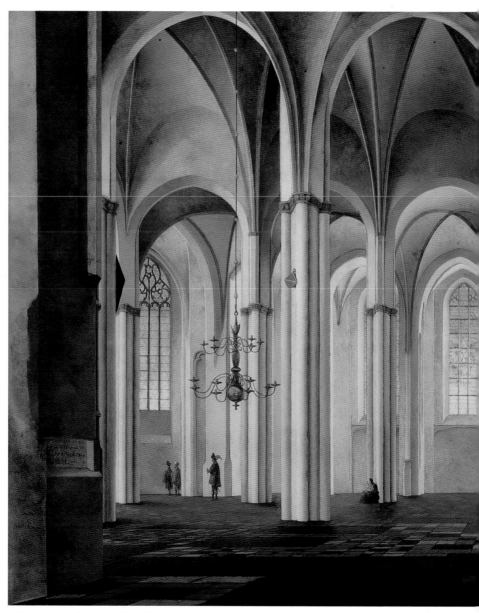

Oil on panel; 22⅞ x 20 in. (58.1 x 50.8 cm)
Acquired in 1986

Following a lengthy apprenticeship with a local Haarlem painter, Pieter Saenredam made a career specializing in what might be termed architectural portraiture. His powerfully descriptive views of churches in Haarlem, Utrecht, Amsterdam, and other Dutch towns also convey the sensation of entering these soaring, light-filled spaces. The clarity and harmony of the interiors, stripped of earlier Catholic furnishings by the Calvinists, is underscored by Saenredam's subtle manipulation of line and color. In the Kimbell painting, a crisp, cool light floods the interior space, enlivening it with blue and pink tones as it strikes the varied surfaces of the vaults and floor tiles, the thinly painted figures providing a sense of scale. To the right of the delicate chandelier, an armorial tablet hangs on the cluster of pillars, marking gravesites in the pavings below. During Saenredam's five-month sojourn in Utrecht in 1636, the town was beset by an epidemic of the plague, and hundreds of victims were interred in the city churches. On the niche of the pillar at the left, the artist neatly inscribed his name and the date that he painted this view of the Buurkerk.

While an inventory of his unusually large library shows that he owned theoretical treatises on perspective, optics, and mathematics, Saenredam's skill in the art of perspective was arguably gained from practical experience learnt from a Haarlem surveyor. His known oeuvre— some sixty paintings—is small, owing to his meticulous working methods. Saenredam made detailed freehand sketches on the site, and construction drawings based on his measurements and notes were often employed years later to create his paintings. The left half of a pen-and-chalk site sketch, inscribed 16 August 1636 (Municipal Archives of Utrecht), served as the preliminary drawing for the 1645 Kimbell panel; its right half corresponds to a painting now in the National Gallery, London, which is dated a year earlier. The underdrawing of *Interior of the Buurkerk, Utrecht*—visible with infrared light—reveals that Saenredam, following his usual practice, painstakingly traced the outlines from a measured construction drawing, which is now lost, onto the panel. The perspective in the Kimbell painting is exactingly calculated, the vanishing point marked by a pinhole in the far right pier, near where the floor meets the far wall. However, Saenredam has made subtle adjustments to his initial site drawing, heightening the elevation and maximizing the vertical thrust of the architecture to convey the church's lofty interior.

BERNARDO CAVALLINO
Italian, 1616–c. 1656
Mucius Scaevola Confronting King Porsenna, c. 1650

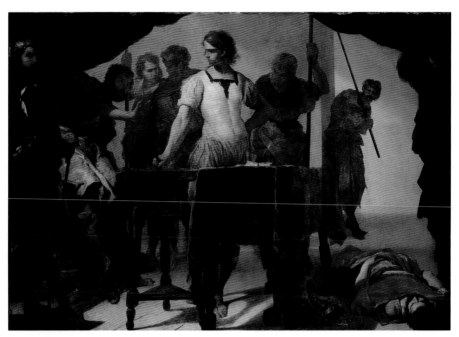

Oil on copper; 24⅛ x 35⅛ in. (61.2 x 89.2 cm)
Acquired in 1981

One of the leading painters of Baroque Naples, Bernardo Cavallino was influenced by masters as diverse as Caravaggio and Rubens, and developed a distinctive manner marked by the dramatic play of light and action. The subject of this painting is taken from Livy's account of the Etruscan siege of Rome. Gaius Mucius, a young Roman nobleman, infiltrated the enemy camp in an attempt to slay the Etruscan king Porsenna, but mistakenly killed the king's treasurer.

At center stage is Gaius, who defiantly turns his head and dagger toward Porsenna, warning him that he is one of many youths sworn to assassinate him. Demonstrating his resolve, Gaius unflinchingly holds his hand in the hot embers until it is burned away. Porsenna was so impressed by this action that he freed the young hero and concluded peace with Rome. Gaius Mucius was thereafter known as Mucius Scaevola (the left-handed).

The Kimbell painting comes from a Spanish collection that also included *The Shade of Samuel Invoked by Saul* by Cavallino (J. Paul Getty Museum, Los Angeles), and *Jonah Preaching to the People at Nineveh* by Andrea Vaccaro (location unknown). All share narratives in which a king is threatened with death unless he withdraws from warfare against a virtuous people. Another Cavallino, *The Expulsion of Heliodorus from the Temple* (Pushkin State Museum of Fine Arts, Moscow), concerning a warning against taxation by foreign rulers, may also belong to the group. These themes were of topical interest in Naples, which witnessed revolts against Spanish domination during this period.

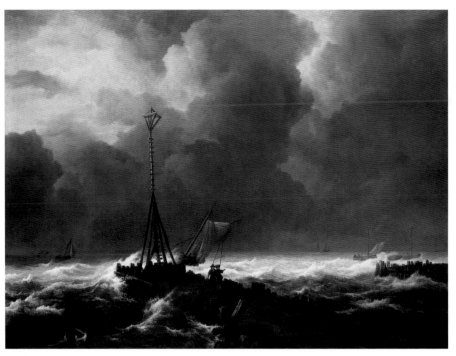

Oil on canvas; 38¾ x 51¼ in. (98.5 x 131.4 cm)
Acquired in 1989

Jacob van Ruisdael, the most influential and inventive painter of landscapes of the Dutch golden age, endowed the native tradition of realism with a newfound dramatic force. With extraordinary powers of observation, Ruisdael went beyond the topographic accuracy of earlier generations to portray nature in its various moods.

Ruisdael's seascapes are among his rarest and most highly valued works. *A Rough Sea at a Jetty* reveals the full scope of his genius for conveying the transitory and changeable face of nature. A violent storm approaching, the rustic beacon at the end of a long jetty guides distressed ships into harbor while two men with long poles stand nearby,

ready to come to the aid of a vessel striving to make port through the tempestuous winds that whip the waves into frothy caps. A dramatic light breaks through the clouds beyond the beacon, suggesting the power and grandeur of nature, and perhaps alluding to the salvation that greets those who steer the proper course.

A coveted work in the eighteenth and early nineteenth centuries, *A Rough Sea at a Jetty* was acquired in 1829 by the Marquess of Lansdowne and remained for the next 120 years at Bowood, in Wiltshire, where it was admired in 1850 by the historian Gustaav Waagen, who wrote: "In point of grandeur of conception and astonishing truth [it] is one of the finest."

BARTOLOMÉ ESTEBAN MURILLO
Spanish, 1617–1682
Four Figures on a Step, c. 1655–60

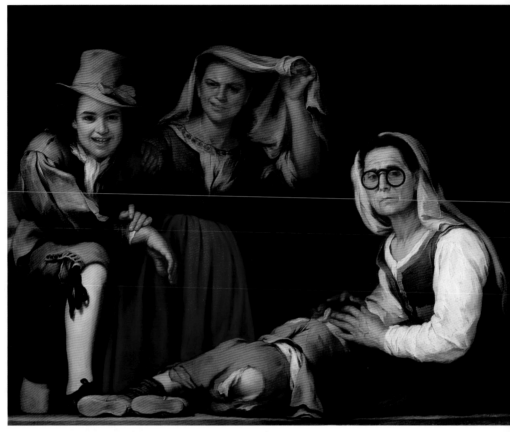

Oil on canvas; 43¼ x 56½ in. (109.9 x 143.5 cm)
Acquired in 1984

The leading religious painter of Seville and one of the great masters of Spain's golden age, Murillo was also for two centuries one of the most celebrated of all European artists, until his reputation was eclipsed by those of Velázquez and El Greco in the late nineteenth century. The many paintings that he created for Seville's churches, religious institutions, and private patrons remain unrivaled in their capacity to arouse the empathy of the faithful, and to assist in their pious devotions.

Murillo's rare and unusual genre scenes, which have always enjoyed great popularity, have no real precedent in Spain. Many of those that feature appealing street urchins seem to be sympathetic portrayals of poverty and privation, subjects sure to have brought to mind acts of charity encouraged by the Church. Other scenes of contemporary street life introduce novel subjects and striking attitudes that suggest multiple layers of meaning and have given rise to a variety of modern interpretations.

Four Figures on a Step, like Murillo's *Two Women at a Window* (National Gallery of Art, Washington), accosts the viewer, who is insinuated into a scene with an unsettling cast of characters. The large scale of the painting magnifies the illusion of direct confrontation with the figures represented. A jaunty young man, who sports a red bow on his hat and blue slashed sleeves, leans forward to engage the viewer with a broad smile. In contrast, the young woman beside him twists her face into a coarse, quizzical wink as she lifts the scarf over her head. While this latter gesture had alluded to marital fidelity since classical times, in this context it may instead signal her availability. Taking their cue from these suggestive elements, some scholars have interpreted the Kimbell picture as a scene of procurement, with the older woman identified as a procuress, the *celestina* of Spanish picaresque literature, who is often represented as a crone wearing glasses and a headscarf. She protectively cradles the head of a boy whose torn breeches reveal his backside—a detail that had twice been covered with repaint but is now restored to its original state.

On the other hand, the mature woman also resembles the respectable, bespectacled women in Netherlandish genre paintings, among them virtuous women inspecting the heads of children for lice. Interrupted in her task, which is facilitated by her huge glasses, she here trains a penetrating gaze on the viewer, who thereby "becomes" the Sevillian passerby. In Netherlandish art, which Murillo knew through prints, delousing a child served as a metaphor for cleansing the soul, as well as the body. Such works undoubtedly influenced Murillo's *Old Woman Delousing a Boy* (Alte Pinakothek, Munich), which features this domestic duty. If not simply a portrayal of the colorful characters to be found in the streets of Seville, *Four Figures on a Step* may carry an admonitory, moralizing message, urging the viewer to lead a virtuous life, and to avoid the temptations of worldly pleasures.

When exhibited in New York at the American Academy of Fine Arts in 1830, this painting was greatly admired for its force, vigor, and beauty of coloring. It remains today one of Murillo's most arresting and intriguing images.

GERRIT DOU
Dutch, 1613–1675
A Dentist by Candlelight, c. 1660–65

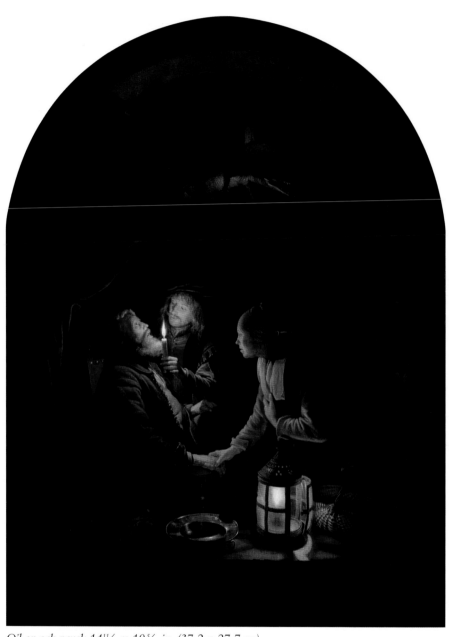

Oil on oak panel; 14¹¹⁄₁₆ x 10⁵⁄₁₆ in. (37.2 x 27.7 cm)
Acquired in 2001

A contemporary of Rembrandt, Vermeer, and Pieter de Hooch, Gerrit Dou was the founder of the so-called *fijnschilders* ("fine painters") of his native Leiden, admired for the miniaturistic detail and exquisitely "polished" surfaces of their work. He specialized in genre paintings of doctors, shopkeepers, schoolmasters, and other everyday scenes, often viewed through an arched window.

In *A Dentist by Candlelight*, Dou displays his legendary virtuosity in rendering still-life objects, the effects of artificial light, and the nuances of emotional states. He pays particular attention to the play of light and shadow from the lantern onto the textures of the other objects resting on the stone ledge: the liquid in the translucent flask; the soft, rumpled cloth; the gleaming barber's basin; and the weave of the wicker basket. Close examination affirms the assured quality of Dou's brushstrokes and his delicate use of color. The spectrum of tones in the illuminated hands and faces, and the delineation of veins and wrinkled, sagging, or smooth flesh, is remarkable.

The tooth-puller is a frequently depicted subject in Dutch and Flemish art from the seventeenth century. Dou incorporates the familiar components of the scene, including the long-suffering patient and concerned onlooker, here no doubt his wife. A crocodile was commonly displayed on the premises of barber-surgeons, along with other rare specimens of the natural world and sundry medications. Dou's visual wit is evident as the anxious, open-mouthed patient rolls his eyes upward to meet the sharp-toothed creature suspended above him.

By 1660, Dou's reputation surpassed those of all other Dutch painters, including that of his former teacher, Rembrandt. After visiting Dou's studio in 1662, the Danish scholar Ole Borch proclaimed the painter to be "unequaled in the Netherlands and even in all other countries in the world."

Dou's small-scale paintings commanded extremely high prices. Although Charles II of England invited Dou to his court, the artist chose to stay in Leiden, remaining his own master and dying a wealthy man. Archduke Leopold Wilhelm of Austria owned work by Dou, and Cosimo III de' Medici visited his studio in 1669. Soon after Dou's death, prominent patrons including Catherine the Great and Louis XIV acquired his paintings, and his work continued to be highly sought after in the next century.

The Kimbell painting was owned by Willem Six (1662–1733), burgomaster of Amsterdam and nephew of Rembrandt's patron Jan Six. Listed as "The famous dentist (tooth-puller) by candlelight by Gerard Douw, so splendidly painted, neat and naturalistic," it was sold at auction in 1734 after Willem's death to a Six relative for the substantial sum of 1,005 guilders.

SALVATOR ROSA
Italian, 1615–1673
Pythagoras Emerging from the Underworld, 1662

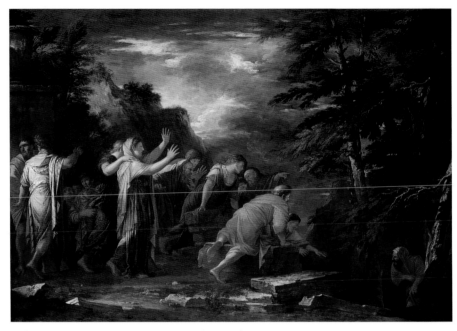

Oil on canvas; 51⅝ x 74⅜ in. (131.2 x 189 cm)
Acquired in 1970

Salvator Rosa was fascinated by obscure subjects, particularly those featuring the occult practices of ancient philosophers. In a letter of 1662, he expressed great satisfaction with two pictures he had just finished whose subjects "have never been touched by anyone." One of these, *Pythagoras Emerging from the Underworld*, which follows the literary account of Diogenes Laertius, shows the Greek philosopher leaving his underground dwelling, where he had spent some time in isolation. Here, Pythagoras's stunned and credulous followers react to his claim that he has witnessed the torture of the souls of Hesiod and Homer during his descent into Hades.

As part of his early training in his native Naples, Rosa was among the first artists to paint landscapes out of doors,

adopting a bold, naturalistic manner. Here, Rosa's distinctive landscape—with its jagged rocks, bowed trees, and livid skies—lends the painting a dramatic, otherworldly mood. In Florence and in Rome, where he eventually settled, Rosa also gained a considerable reputation as a satirical poet and actor—and as an impetuous, individualistic personality. He was among the first artists to express a passionate appreciation for the awe-inspiring beauty of untamed nature, and his landscapes were invoked by later generations of admirers as expressions of the "sublime."

When the Kimbell painting and its pendant were purchased by the important Sicilian collector Antonio Ruffo, Rosa demanded a considerable sum, telling Ruffo's agent he "would rather die of hunger than reduce his price."

Rembrandt van Rijn is recognized as the greatest Dutch painter of the seventeenth century, famed for his versatility in all genres: portraits, landscapes, and history painting, including secular, religious, and mythological subjects. In his maturity he developed a loose, highly expressive brushwork, combined with a psychological intensity in his sitters, that sets his work apart from all his contemporaries. Rembrandt was the most prolific portraitist of his time; in addition to commissioned works, he produced an unrivaled series of self-portraits.

Bust of a Young Jew may have been painted as a character study, rather than as a portrait commissioned by an individual, who would probably have chosen more fashionable dress and assumed a more formal pose. The dramatic lighting, which focuses attention on the subtly rendered face, achieves nonetheless many of the effects of a true portrait, and was probably painted from the live model. The sitter's modest apparel, full beard and curly hairstyle, and black skullcap—which was not, however, worn only by Jews at the time— identify him as a member of the Polish- or German-Jewish community in Amsterdam.

Bust of a Young Jew shows a subtlety of characterization surpassing the more overt expressions of his early picturesque paintings of heads, and bringing to mind the single-figure biblical subjects of his late years that explore tragic and conflicted emotions. Rembrandt's evident sympathy with his subject may be considered in the context of philosemitism, an ecumenical Protestant movement that advocated compassion toward Jews as part of a messianic belief in universal salvation.

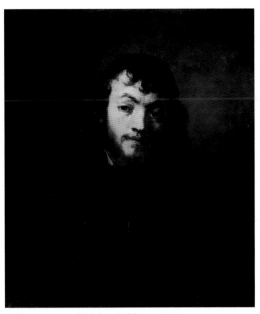

Oil on canvas; 25⅞ x 22⅝ in. (65.8 x 57.5 cm) Acquired in 1977

Rembrandt's penetration of outward likeness to suggest the temperament and mood of the sitter is conveyed with his typically deft and economic brushwork. Animated by the strong light that casts one side of his face into deep shadow, the compelling figure is painted in the "rough manner" of Rembrandt's late style, with a limited palette of earth colors. Rembrandt defines the form with assured, vigorous brushstrokes. The broadly rendered clothing blends smoothly into the dark background, beard, hair, and skullcap, focusing all attention on the thoughtful, sensitively rendered face. As with Rembrandt's finest portraits, the deep humanity of this image is anchored in the compelling engagement of the eyes.

GIANLORENZO BERNINI
Italian, 1598–1680
Angel with the Superscription and *Angel with the Crown of Thorns*
(two *bozzetti* for angels on the Ponte Sant'Angelo, Rome), 1668

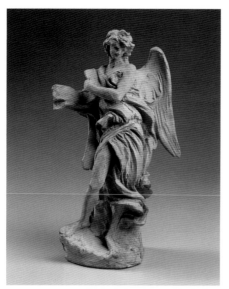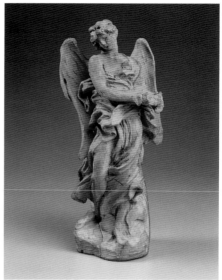

Terra-cotta; h. 11½ in. (29.2 cm); 11⅞ in. (30.2 cm)
Acquired in 1987

More than any other artist, it was Gianlorenzo Bernini, the leading sculptor of Baroque Italy, who reshaped the ancient city of Rome in a series of brilliant architectural and sculptural projects that affirmed its identity as the seat of the Roman Catholic Church. In 1667, Pope Clement IX appointed Bernini to supervise the renovation of the Ponte Sant'Angelo, the ancient bridge linking the city of Rome to the Vatican. Bernini designed ten angels, each carrying an instrument of Christ's Passion, to alight on the bridge's balustrades and guide the pilgrims' approach, physically and spiritually, toward Saint Peter's. Eight of the over-life-size angels were assigned to other sculptors, while the master himself made two: *Angel with the Superscription* and *Angel with the Crown of Thorns*. The pope deemed that the angels carved by the septuagenarian Bernini with his own hand were too

beautiful to be exposed to the elements, and copies were created for the bridge, which was completed in 1672. The original pair of angels remained in Bernini's studio and were eventually bequeathed to Sant'Andrea delle Fratte, in Rome.

The lively terra-cotta angels in the Kimbell collection, conceived as a complementary pair, are among the surviving *bozzetti* (quick sketches) that trace Bernini's successive ideas for the compositions. Leaving the imprint of his fingertips and toolmarks in the clay, Bernini modeled the figures in a rough, highly expressive manner, pinching and smoothing the forms into place. He arranged the components—long legs, arched wings, and swirling drapery—into a dynamic series of curves and counter-curves about the central axis so that each angel could be viewed from several directions.

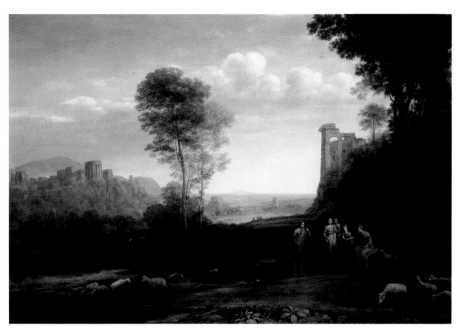

Oil on canvas; 22½ x 32⅜ in. (57.2 x 82.2 cm)
Acquired in 1967

This *Pastoral Landscape* is one of at least nine paintings that Claude created for Prince Lorenzo Onofrio Colonna, a great connoisseur and collector, between 1663 and 1682. The prince, whose family had its origins in the countryside outside of Rome, undoubtedly shared Claude's pleasure in hilly sites such as Tivoli and Nemi, adorned with ancient temples, bridges, and other reminders of the Arcadian delights celebrated by Virgil in ancient times. Although the other works Claude painted for Colonna have mythological and literary subjects, the group of shepherds engaged in conversation in the Kimbell painting cannot be associated with any particular narrative.

This ideal landscape view from late in Claude's career, when he often looked back to his earlier compositions, is pervaded by a sense of nostalgia. With its classical ruins and carefully calibrated landscape elements, it features many of the hallmarks for which he was celebrated and widely imitated. Claude developed the composition in a series of drawings in which he modulated tonalities and balanced proportions, dividing the width and height into fifths. (For example, the round temple is one-fifth from the left edge, and the horizon is at two fifths of the height of the canvas.) The cool, blue green palette and the clear articulation of spatial intervals are characteristic of the artist's late work. The massing of buildings on the hilltop is balanced by the gathering of shepherds and musicians, whose long, lean forms—a figural type favored by Claude—find counterparts in the stately trees.

JEAN-ANTOINE WATTEAU
French, 1684–1721
Heureux age! Age d'or (Happy Age! Golden Age), c. 1716–20

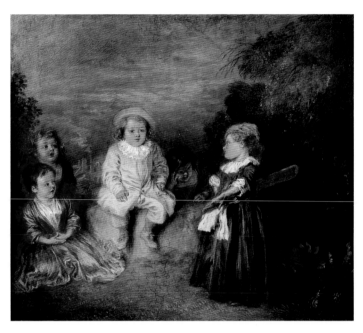

Oil on panel;
8 x 9⁵⁄₁₆ in.
(20.3 x 23.6 cm)
Acquired in 1981

As a young man, Watteau came to Paris from Valenciennes, a Flemish town that had recently come under French rule. In the French capital he painted decorative and theatrical subjects, and soon made his mark as the inventor of the *fête galante*, in which fashionable figures engaged in the rituals of love in a verdant parkland setting. Watteau continued to paint figures in theatrical dress throughout his short life. The little boy seated at the center of the Kimbell painting shares something of the inscrutable, poignant aspect of his grown-up counterpart in Watteau's celebrated *Pierrot* (called *Gilles*) in the Louvre. He is dressed in the cream costume with white ruff, shoes with satin bows, and brimmed hat that was worn by Pierrot, the tragicomic clown of the commedia dell'arte. The boy's outward, unfocused gaze contrasts with the animated figures around him,

who may all be girls, although little boys also wore dresses during this period. Pierrot avoids the steady stare of the little girl with one arm akimbo who grips Harlequin's bat, known as a slapstick. Resting on the ground behind her is a ribboned tambourine, an instrument that connotes love and folly. The delicately painted scene is set in a misty landscape whose sky is streaked with the icy blue and rose hues of the children's costumes.

The title of this picture derives from the verses accompanying Nicolas Tardieu's engraving of the painting, published some years after Watteau's death, which begins "Happy Age! Golden Age, where without tribulation / The heart knows to surrender to innocent pleasures." The painting's composition recalls *Jealousy* (untraced), which was one of the paintings that earned Watteau provisional acceptance to the French Academy in July 1712.

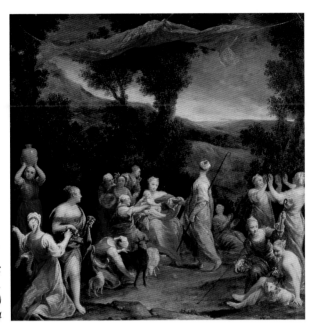

*Oil on copper;
26¼ x 26¼ in.
(66.7 x 66.7 cm)
Acquired in 1984*

Giuseppe Maria Crespi, the most innovative Bolognese painter of his day, was especially acclaimed for his intimate genre scenes. This fresh approach also infuses his more traditional subjects, which draw primarily upon his northern Italian predecessors. A blissful idyll evoking a golden age, *Jupiter Among the Corybantes* is possibly the work painted for the auditor Mansanti, mentioned by the artist's biographer, Zanotti. The classical subject, which allowed Crespi to paint a bevy of young women in graceful attitudes, is the upbringing of the god Jupiter. To avert the oracle that a son would succeed him, Saturn habitually devoured his male children, and so his wife took the infant Jupiter to Crete to be reared by the Corybantes. In Crespi's own words, the nymphs, "thinking that his cries might reveal him, as is usual with babies, devised a plan to beat out

a certain cadence, which they called Bactili, and so in unison they clanged little cymbals made of bronze, so that the cries of the infant Jupiter could not reach the ears of Saturn."

Painted on copper, the painting retains its delicate, transparent glazes and vibrant colors, especially in the apricot and cherry draperies of the figures and the canopy billowing overhead, perhaps intended to shield Jupiter from Saturn's Olympian gaze. The infant god's good fortune to be entertained by lovely nymphs reminds the viewer also that, as an adult, Jupiter would avail himself of the nubile beauties he henceforth considered his birthright. The melodious composition is arranged like musical notes, the dainty, ovoid heads of the maidens echoing the forms of the diminutive cymbals, vessels, and floral wreaths they hold.

JEAN SIMÉON CHARDIN
French, 1699–1779
Young Student Drawing, c. 1738

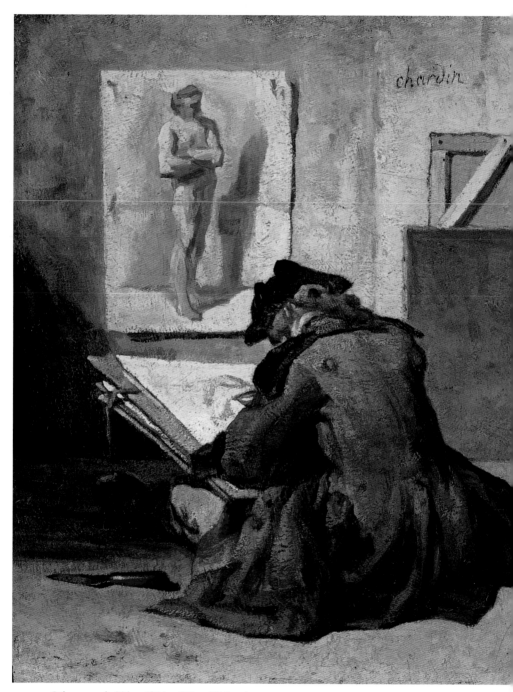

Oil on panel; 8¼ x 6¾ in. (21 x 17.1 cm)
Acquired in 1982

Chardin's masterful depiction of a *Young Student Drawing* comments upon the artist's own course of artistic study and hard-won success. His admirer Denis Diderot recorded the artist's recollection of his early training: "At age seven or eight, they put the crayon in our hand. . . . Our back has been bent over the sketchbook for a long time. . . . After spending days without end and lamplit nights before immobile and inanimate nature, we are presented with the living reality, and suddenly the work of all the preceding years seems to come to nothing."

After studying with the history painters Pierre-Jean Cazes and Noël-Nicolas Coypel, where he would have copied his instructors' *académies* (life drawings)—rather as the young draftsman is doing—Chardin was admitted as a member of the Academy of Saint Luke, the painter's guild. Such was his extraordinary talent as a still-life painter that in September 1728 he was made a full member of the more prestigious Royal Academy, into which he was received as a painter of "animals and fruits." Excelling in genre painting as well, Chardin became a devoted member of the Academy, and later in life served as its treasurer, as well as being entrusted with the installation of the biennial Salon, where members exhibited their works.

A tenacious draftsman, Chardin worked directly on his canvas or panel, applying the essential lesson of drawing—to "teach the eye to see nature." Here he calibrates his composition to harmonize with the pyramidal figure of the young artist. His muted palette of beiges, ocher, and umber is enlivened with touches of color—the student's blue legging and a sheet of blue paper slipped into his portfolio, the red lining of his coat, also revealed in the hole on his left shoulder. The layered, textured quality of Chardin's paint, which he seems to have bulked up by adding chalk, lends a strong tactile quality to the work, as does the complex play of light and shadow.

Chardin's works were avidly collected by European royalty, and were also engraved for a wider public. Another version of *Young Student Drawing* was exhibited at the 1738 Salon with its pendant, *The Embroiderer*, featuring a young woman likewise industriously engaged in her work. The early versions may be identified with the panels now in the Nationalmuseum, Stockholm. The virtually identical Kimbell panel is one of numerous autograph repetitions, most of which have been lost, that Chardin made of these popular compositions. Both subjects had been popularized by Dutch artists of the previous century, whose works were much admired in France during Chardin's time. Like his Dutch predecessors, Chardin alludes to the value of proper education. Only persistent, diligent training prepares the young artist for his next challenge—the canvases set against the wall that will ultimately test his genius.

CANALETTO (GIOVANNI ANTONIO CANALE)
Italian, 1697–1768
***The Molo, Venice**, c. 1735*

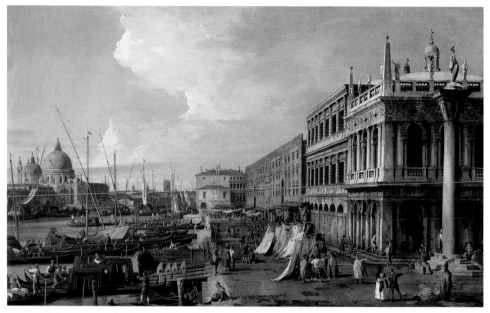

Oil on canvas; 24½ x 39⅞ in. (62.3 x 101.3 cm)
Acquired in 1969

Trained by his father as a painter of theatrical scenery, Canaletto gained international renown painting scenes of his native Venice. These vivid and compelling cityscapes were much sought after by British aristocrats who traveled to Italy on the Grand Tour. In this painting from the collection of the Earl of Rosebery, Mentmore, Canaletto depicts one of his most popular views of Venice—the Molo, the wharf just west of the Doge's Palace. At the far right is the column of Saint Theodore, set before the ornate library, which is next to the Zecca (the mint where the Republic's gold ducats, or *zecchini*, were coined) and the terra-cotta-colored public granaries. Across the water at the far left, marking the opening of the Grand Canal, is the church of Santa Maria della Salute.

Canaletto imposes order and balance on the busy scene, observed from an ideally high viewpoint, omitting or adjusting architectural motifs and bringing them into alignment. The sun-drenched scene of crowded gondolas and market stalls against a grand architectural facade, with its sweeping perspective and linear precision, is enlivened with engaging details of the figures' costumes and gestures. Canaletto synchronizes the view with touches of sky blue, bright and dull red, and crisp white—from the bright sleeves of the gondoliers, to the bell-shaped cloaks and skirts worn by the picturesque Venetians, and the feathered hat of the figure in Eastern dress at the far right.

A long with his contemporary Joshua
Reynolds, Gainsborough was one
of the leading figures in the glamorous
"golden age" of British portraiture. *Miss
Lloyd* is an early work, painted soon after
Gainsborough's return to his native Suffolk
from London, where he trained with the
French engraver Hubert Gravelot. It has
been traditionally identified as a member
of the Lloyd family of Ipswich.

Gainsborough's early, small-scale
pictures of figures in a parkland setting
with ornamental statuary show the influence of his mentor Francis Hayman, and
ultimately the example of the *fêtes galantes*
of Jean-Antoine Watteau. In contrast to
the rod-stiff posture of many of his early
female sitters, here Gainsborough has
adopted the informal cross-legged pose
favored by Hayman. In a series of preliminary drawings, he worked out the
relationship of the figure to the outdoor
setting. The landscape accommodates
the sitter's gangling, languid form, seated
on a grassy bank and propped against a
tree trunk, a branch offering a convenient
armrest. The twined trees at the right
mimic her crossed limbs, and draw the
eye to her blue silk dress with side hoops
and the gauzy fabric surrounding the
fashionable straw hat nestled in her lap.
The feathery brushwork and cool tonality
of the background reflect the influence

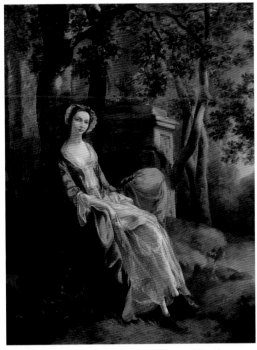

Oil on canvas; 27⅜ x 20⅞ in. (69.6 x 53 cm)
Acquired in 1946

of French painting, while the more
carefully delineated burdock plant in the
foreground was a motif Gainsborough
knew from Dutch landscapes, and also
sketched from life. The charm and unaf-
fected elegance of this early portrait, with
its dazzling costume, owes much to
Gainsborough's mastery of fluidly applied
paint and brilliant effects of light.

GIOVANNI BATTISTA TIEPOLO
Italian, 1696–1770
Apollo and the Continents, c. 1739

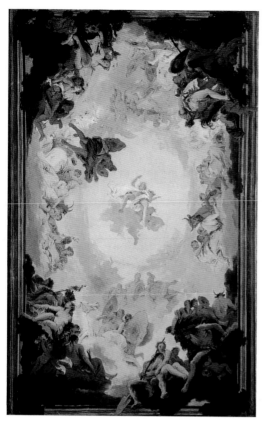

Oil on canvas; 39 x 25 in. (99.1 x 63.5 cm)
Acquired in 1985

This exquisitely prepared oil sketch served as Giovanni Battista Tiepolo's model for a frescoed vault in the Palazzo Clerici in Milan, commissioned by Marquess Antonio Giorgio Clerici. Clerici married Fulvia Visconti in 1741, uniting two of the most powerful families in Milan, and Tiepolo's sketch depicting *Apollo and the Continents* commemorates the impending nuptials. At the center of the sketch the sun god, Apollo, emanates a brilliant, yellow light. Nearby, nestled in the cloudbanks, are six planetary deities— Diana, Mercury, and Jupiter above Apollo, and Saturn, Venus, and Mars at his feet. In the four corners of the vault, whose fictive cornice is finished in gold, are personifications of the seasons and river gods, including Milan's river Po, identifiable by his bull's horns. Conspicuously silhouetted against the heavenly light are two embracing figures: Cupid, reunited with his beloved Psyche, bears her to Mount Olympus, where an assembly of gods will celebrate their marriage. The auspicious nuptial imagery of the sketch, with its allusions to abundance and fertility, speaks to the dynastic aspirations of Antonio Clerici and his new bride.

The figures are painted with the swift, seemingly effortless brushwork that has placed Tiepolo's sketches at the pinnacle of this genre. Here he modulates his technique from the lightly drawn gods, almost dissolved by Apollo's rays, to the more loaded brush and darker colors of the corner groups representing earthly bounty.

The Kimbell sketch differs significantly from the differently shaped ceiling that Tiepolo ultimately painted in 1740 in the Clerici palace, *The Course of the Chariot of the Sun*. To accommodate the proportions of the long gallery, Tiepolo was obliged to create a more complex program, with Apollo in his chariot at one end of the room, and Venus, Cupid, and Time at the other.

iovanni Battista Tiepolo's talent for devising pictorial programs that infused older traditions with an animated and luminous grandeur earned him international repute as the greatest decorator of the age. In the spring of 1754, shortly after returning to Venice from Würzburg, where he painted an inspired series of frescoes for the archbishop's palace, Tiepolo won the commission to fresco the ceiling of the newly constructed church of Santa Maria della Visitazione, known as the Pietà. The Kimbell oil sketch served as the model for executing the frescoes of the church. In this celestial vision, the Virgin, clothed in white to denote her purity and surmounting a blue globe, is escorted by a glory of angels as she rises toward the Trinity: Christ holding his cross, the dove of the Holy Spirit, and God the Father, who holds Mary's crown aloft as she is received into paradise, her eyes modestly cast earthward, mediating between heaven and earth. Along a curving balustrade marking the rim of the oval ceiling, angels lift their voices and play a panoply of instruments in jubilation.

During Tiepolo's day, actual music would have accompanied this celestial chorus. The adjacent Foundling Hospital of the Pietà, one of Venice's four charitable institutions that cared for orphan girls, was renowned for its school of music. Hidden behind several raised galleries, the choir and orchestra of young girls performed concerts written by eminent musicians including Antonio Vivaldi, who also taught violin at the Pietà earlier in the century.

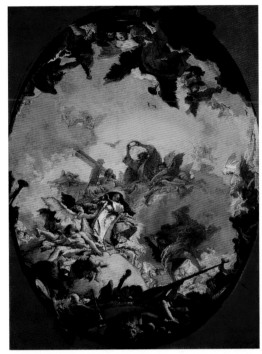

Oil on canvas; 40⅜ x 30⅜ in.
(102.6 x 77.3 cm)
Acquired in 1984

JOSHUA REYNOLDS
British, 1723–1792
Miss Warren (?), 1759

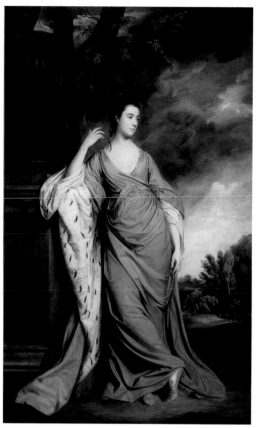

*Oil on canvas; 93¾ x 58¼ in.
(238.1 x 147.8 cm)
Acquired in 1961*

Having established a portrait practice in London, in 1749 Joshua Reynolds embarked on a journey to Italy, where during a two-year stay in Rome he studied the artistic canon of the antique, Michelangelo, Raphael, and the great Venetian masters. Upon his return he often cast his sitters in poses from these sources, creating a new historical or grand style based on "the simplicity of the antique air and attitude." Reynolds's position as the first president of the Royal Academy of Arts enabled him to fulfill his goal of elevating the status of the painter in his native Britain to that of a man of learning. Through the exposure of his works at the annual exhibitions at the Academy, and the *Discourses on Art* he delivered to its members and students, Reynolds became the preeminent arbiter of style in his day and exerted tremendous influence on the arts.

The sitter in the Kimbell portrait may be identifiable as the "Miss Warren" who appears in Reynolds's records as sitting for the artist between January 1758 and May 1759. Often incorrectly identified as Frances Warren, second wife of Sir George Warren, the wealthy member of parliament for Lancaster, she is, in fact, more likely to be Elizabeth Warren, his sister. This portrait is one of Reynolds's earliest essays in the grand manner, in which beauty and grandeur are achieved by avoiding the particularities of local fashions. Miss Warren's simple, wraparound morning gown displays the contours of her figure and lends the portrait a timeless, classical effect. Her idealized form has something of the quality and dignity of sculpture, with smooth, alabaster skin and graceful drapery folds. The proportions of the figure above the high waist are deliberately diminished, while her inflated hips and thighs swell like the oversized urn beside her, perhaps alluding to her female role as a fecund vessel.

Jean-Baptiste Greuze achieved fame for his morally uplifting narrative paintings influenced by the manner of seventeenth-century Dutch masters, but he was equally adept working in the pastoral, erotic mode brought to refinement by François Boucher. In 1756, while sojourning in Rome, Greuze received support from the Marquis de Marigny, who commissioned from him two oval paintings for the Versailles apartment of his sister Madame de Pompadour, mistress of King Louis XV, leaving the choice of subject to the artist. Greuze painted *Simplicity*, a girl pulling the petals off a daisy in a ritual of "he loves me, he loves me not." Despite the importance of the commission, Greuze did not hasten to finish the paintings. *Simplicity* took about three years to produce, and its pendant, *Young Shepherd Holding a Flower* (Petit Palais, Paris), showing a boy holding a dandelion and pensively making a wish for his love to be reciprocated, was not delivered until 1761.

The romantic sentiment and decorative style of *Simplicity* are typical of French court painting of the *ancien régime*. Skillfully capturing the nuances of emotion at the dawning prospect of love, Greuze works within the prescribed oval shape to lay stress upon the smooth curves of the girl's face, brows, and hair ribbons, her straw hat, and soft, cupped

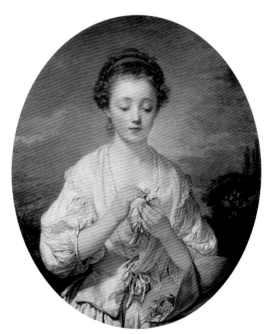

Oil on canvas; 28 x 23½ in. (oval) (71.1 x 59.7 cm)
Acquired in 1985

hands. A critic at the Salon of 1759, where *Simplicity* was exhibited along with other paintings by the artist, noted: "M. Greuze seems to prefer dressing his figures in white; it is one of the greatest difficulties in painting, worthy of the efforts of a distinguished artist." The refinement of tones is seen in the transparency of the girl's porcelain flesh, and the fluid brushwork of the creamy white costume, with its active play of delicate folds of fabric.

LUIS MELÉNDEZ
Spanish, 1716–1780
Still Life with Oranges, Jars, and Boxes of Sweets, c. 1760–65

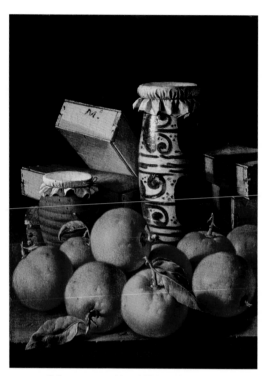

Oil on canvas; 19 x 13⅞ in. (48.3 x 35.2 cm)
Acquired in 1985

uis Meléndez, the greatest Spanish
still-life painter of his time, created a
remarkably bold coda to the genre
brought to prominence by masters of the
seventeenth century. As the most gifted
student admitted to the newly founded
Royal Academy of Fine Arts in Madrid in
1745, Meléndez could have anticipated a
prosperous career at the Spanish court.
Such expectations were dashed, however,
when he was expelled from the Academy
some years later because his father,
honorary professor of painting, had
denounced its directors over a dispute.
Trained in portraiture and employed for
some five years as a miniaturist upon his
return from a trip to Italy, Meléndez
eventually found his métier as a painter
of still life.

In this tightly compressed composition, Meléndez scrupulously renders the
textures and forms of the closely grouped
fruit and containers, highlighting the
glazed curve of a honey jar of Manises
pottery, one of his favorite motifs. The jar
is here rendered in white and green to
match the color of the leaves and
complement the oranges. A strong light
enhances the sharper geometry of the
sweet boxes, one bearing the artist's
monogram, and throws a shadow from
the honey jar across the receding boxes
at the right.

In 1772, claiming it was his intention
to depict "every variety of comestible
which the Spanish clime produces,"
Meléndez appealed to the scientific
interests of the prince and princess of
Asturias (the future King Charles IV and
his wife) and asked for their support for
the project. They agreed, but terminated
the commission in 1776 due to a dispute
over payment. By that time, Meléndez
had delivered forty-four pictures to the
royal couple, including some earlier
still-life paintings, and these later decorated the prince's country house at
El Escorial. Despite his exceptional
gifts, Meléndez died a pauper.

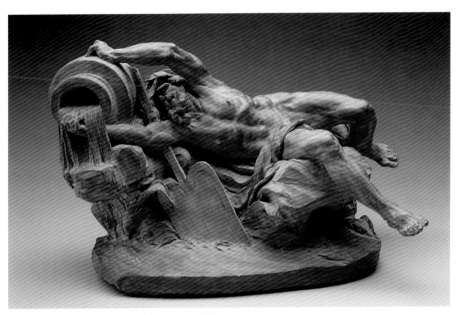

Terra-cotta; h. 11 in. (27.9 cm); l. 18 in. (45.7 cm)
Acquired in 1984

One of the outstanding sculptors of his age, Claude Michel, better known as Clodion, is today most admired for his small-scale terra-cottas. Though spirited and charming, Clodion's mythological scenes and putti are grounded in a solid academic training. He studied in the Parisian studio of his uncle Lambert-Sigisbert Adam, who created statuary for Versailles and other châteaux. In the autumn of 1762 Clodion departed for the French Academy in Rome, where he studied antique sculpture, Michelangelo, and especially Bernini.

Bernini's *Four Rivers Fountain* in the Piazza Navona in Rome, with its highly animated poses, forms the immediate backdrop to this terra-cotta, with its roiling, horizontally extended figure of the Rhine. The mighty river god's acrobatic feat is registered in the taut and rippled muscles of his arms, neck, torso, and thighs. His beard undulating like the water he personifies, he grips the mouth of the urn, causing the water to flow in two separate streams. The unusual subject derives from the Roman historian Tacitus's *Germania* (A.D. 98) and alludes to the Rhine dividing the territory of the Gauls on the west bank from that of the Germans to the east.

During his years in Rome, Clodion's small terra-cottas were already highly sought after by collectors and connoisseurs ranging from Catherine the Great of Russia to the artist François Boucher. The Kimbell terra-cotta, or one of the two similar versions now in the Victoria and Albert Museum, London, and the Fine Arts Museums of San Francisco, was exhibited at the Salon of 1773, two years after the artist's return to Paris.

GEORGE STUBBS
British, 1724–1806
Lord Grosvenor's Arabian with a Groom, c. 1765

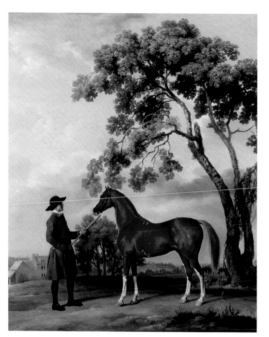

Oil on canvas; 39⅛ x 32⅞ in.
(99.3 x 83.5 cm)
Acquired in 1981

George Stubbs was the greatest painter of animals of his day. He was celebrated especially for his representation of horses, the forms and nature of which he captured with a remarkable understanding and sensitivity. As the son of a Liverpool currier and leather-maker, Stubbs's early exposure to animal carcasses no doubt inured him to the dissections he performed even as a boy. After a start as a portrait painter, in 1754 he traveled to Rome, where his study of antiquity

probably informed the classical design of many of his compositions, with their elegant curves, pleasing profiles, and allusions to relief sculpture. Upon his return from this brief sojourn, for nearly two years Stubbs single-mindedly pursued exhaustive anatomical studies at an isolated Lincolnshire farm. Unable to find a printmaker to render his subtle anatomical drawings, Stubbs taught himself engraving and produced *The Anatomy of the Horse*, published in 1766. He established his artistic reputation in London during the 1760s, offering a newfound naturalism and artistry in his animal paintings.

Stubbs's characteristically uncompromising spirit, and his quest for calibrated composition and balanced tones, are clearly evident in this portrait of Lord Grosvenor's young Arabian stallion. He employs a low horizon, with rolling hills and soft foliage, to effectively display the warm tones of the chestnut Arabian. (A reproductive print of the painting, published in 1771, shows that the landscape was originally a good deal more extensive to the left; the canvas seems to have been cut down on that side in the late eighteenth or early nineteenth century.) The sprightly mien of the colt, ears pricked and nostrils wide, is set in contrast with the reassuring demeanor of the groom. The artist meticulously portrays its genetic Sabino markings—the broad blaze, white stockings, and white spots on the belly and sides.

RICHARD WILSON
British, 1713/14–1782
Tivoli: The Temple of the Sybil and the Campagna, c. 1765

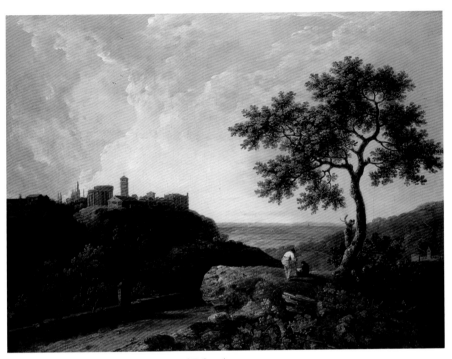

Oil on canvas; 29 x 38½ in. (73.6 x 97.8 cm)
Acquired in 1979

Tivoli, in the Sabine hills to the east of Rome, was from the seventeenth century a favorite destination for artists. The grandeur of its landscape, with its evocations of ancient glory, also made it a major destination for foreign visitors on the Grand Tour. Like the artist seen sketching in this picture, Richard Wilson, who was in Italy in the 1750s, must have passed many pleasurable hours drawing the dramatic site with its distinctive round Temple of Vesta, known as the Temple of the Sibyl. Tivoli and the Campagna (countryside) had also figured in the works of Claude Lorrain and Gaspard Dughet. Wilson's composition derives unmistakably from their classical land-scapes: a wedge of land framed by a tree, the hillside view of Tivoli, and the vista of the low plain as it extends toward Rome.

The Kimbell painting—a variant of a composition the artist first painted in 1752—was made after Wilson's return to Britain. By introducing the ideal landscape to the next generation, he played a major role in establishing the British school of landscape painters. Even John Constable, who professed no need to go to Italy, was influenced by Wilson and spoke of how his work "still swims in my brain like a delicious dream." The young J. M. W. Turner's debt was explicit: he copied the Kimbell painting, though omitting the large tree and figures (c. 1798, Tate, London), many years before he made his own trip to the Roman Campagna.

FRANÇOIS BOUCHER
French, 1703–1770
Juno Asking Aeolus to Release the Winds, 1769

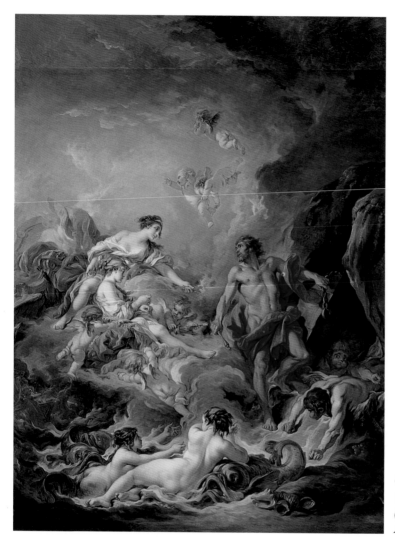

Oil on canvas;
109½ x 80 in.
(278.2 x 203.2 cm)
Acquired in 1972

Juno Asking Aeolus to Release the Winds is one of the six monumental mythologies that Boucher painted for a salon in the Parisian residence of a cultivated financier, Jean-François Bergeret de Frouville; four of these decorative paintings are at the Kimbell and two of a narrower format (*Venus on the Waves* and *Aurora and Cephalus*) are in the J. Paul Getty Museum, Los Angeles. The other Kimbell paintings represent *Mercury Confiding the Infant Bacchus to the Nymphs of Nysa, Boreas Abducting Oreithyia,* and *Venus at Vulcan's Forge.* The Kimbell's canvases were enlarged at top and bottom when they were acquired by Baron Edmond de Rothschild at the end of the nineteenth century for his hôtel in the Faubourg Saint-Honoré.

Bridging heaven and earth by means of diagonally disposed, nubile bodies and

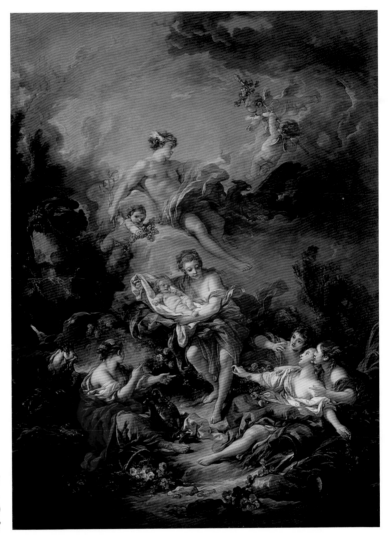

Oil on canvas;
107¼ x 79⅜ in.
(272.5 x 201.6 cm)
Acquired in 1972

pillowy putti in flight, Boucher's witty and dazzling compositions have come to typify the Rococo style at its most brilliant. He painted the present ensemble in the penultimate year of his life, but his virtuosity and energy remained undiminished. In it he depicts with great inventiveness how passion, enflamed by beauty and susceptible to jealousy, finds expression in those unbridled forces of nature, the Elements— turbulent winds, torrential waters, molten fires, and the bounties of the vine.

As related by the Roman author Virgil in the first book of *The Aeneid*, the goddess Juno, consumed by jealousy toward Venus, schemed to prevent the fleet of her rival's son, Aeneas, from reaching shore and founding a Trojan colony in Italy. To thwart the Trojans, Juno visited Aeolus, keeper of the winds,

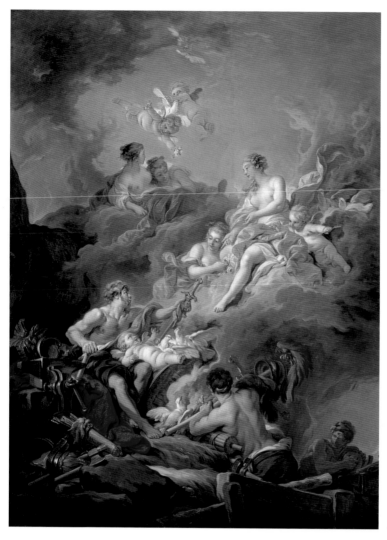

Oil on canvas;
107¼ x 80⅝ in.
(273.5 x 204.7 cm)
Acquired in 1972

and entreated him to provoke a violent storm that would destroy Aeneas's fleet. As enticement, Juno offered Aeolus her most beautiful nymph, Deiopea, in marriage. The presence of an alluring sea nymph reclining in the foreground reminds us that mighty Neptune, god of the sea, will prevail over the winds, and calm the insurgent waters.

At the center of *Mercury Confiding the Infant Bacchus to the Nymphs of Nysa* is the infant god Bacchus, born of Jupiter's illicit union with the princess Semele, who was transported by Mercury to Nysa for safe-keeping from Juno's jealous rage. The eagle bearing a lightning shaft, nestled in the clouds beside Mercury, alludes to Bacchus's fiery birth. As recounted in Ovid's *Meta-morphoses*, Zeus had fallen in love with Semele. To punish her wayward consort,

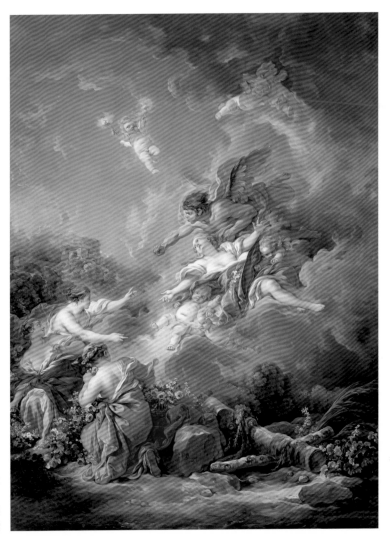

Oil on canvas;
107⅝ x 80⅝ in.
(273.3 x 205 cm)
Acquired in 1972

Juno tricked Semele into asking the god to appear to her in all his majesty. Powerless to deny her wish, Jupiter came to Semele, who was consumed by fire. However, the baby gestating in her womb was stitched into his father's thigh and spirited away to Nysa as soon as he was born.

Venus at Vulcan's Forge is drawn from the eighth book of *The Aeneid*. Succumbing to Venus's charms, Vulcan forges arms for her mortal son, Aeneas, champion of the Trojans against the Greeks.

Another scene from Ovid's *Metamorphoses*, *Boreas Abducting Oreithyia* illustrates the cold north-wind god seizing the lovely Greek princess, who had earlier spurned his advances. Overhead, a putto brandishes two torches, an allusion to the twin sons that Oreithyia later bore the wind god.

JEAN-ANTOINE HOUDON
French, 1741–1828
Aymard-Jean de Nicolay, Premier Président de la Chambre des Comptes, 1779

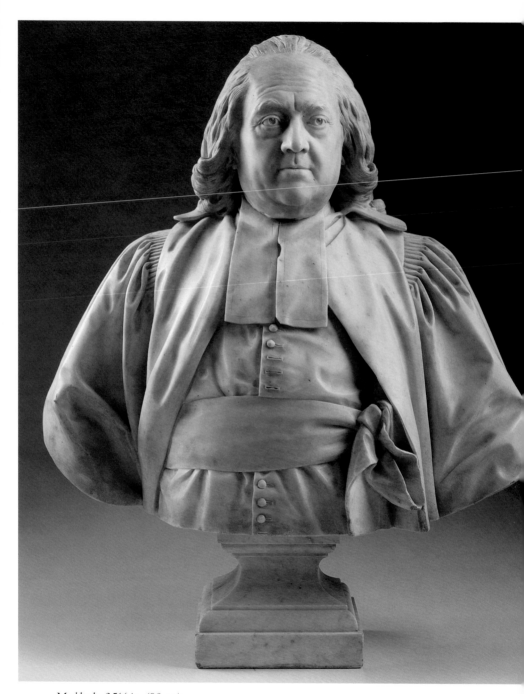

Marble; h. 35½ in. (90 cm)
Acquired in 1991

Houdon began sculpting at the age of nine and went on to receive an impeccable academic training in Paris and Rome. An associate member of the Academy in 1769, he exhibited regularly in the biennial Salon in Paris until the French Revolution. Between 1775 and 1789 the elite of French society sat for him, including members of the royal family, the aristocracy, and the financial and judicial nobility, as well as foreign princes and diplomats. In his portraits of the nobility and leading figures of the Enlightenment, Houdon achieved a new spontaneity and informality of expression without compromising his sitters' decorous and elevated presentation. His busts of Benjamin Franklin, Thomas Jefferson, and Jean-Jacques Rousseau, and his statues of George Washington and Voltaire, give convincing pictorial form both to the character and to the achievements of these great men, and have done much to convey their personalities to succeeding generations.

Houdon's portrait bust of Aymard-Jean de Nicolay, Marquis de Goussainville (1709–1785), was exhibited in the Salon of 1779, where it was described as "joining to the most perfect resemblance an elegance and nobility of form." Nicolay was a member of the *noblesse de robe*—nobility whose judicial and administrative functions dated back to the sixteenth century. As First President of the Chambre des Comptes, he was the senior official at the sovereign court responsible for the royal accounts and for the registration of all laws touching upon the Crown's domain, a position held by his family since 1506.

Although dressed in magistrate's robes, the sitter is portrayed without his wig, his long hair trailing behind his gowns as if in a private rather than public moment. Houdon's virtuoso handling is especially apparent in the carving of the delicate and energetic folds of drapery; the tension of Nicolay's sash pulling against his considerable girth only accentuates his commanding presence. Several buttons left undone on the robe add a note of studied informality. But it is in the modeling of the sitter's face and hair that Houdon's genius as a portraitist is most fully engaged, and the attention lavished on the modeling suggests the importance of this commission. The wrinkled forehead, fleshy chin, and sagging jowls, which convey Nicolay's acumen and experience, are testimony also to the sculptor's early and intense study of anatomy under the tutelage of a surgeon. The carving of the eyes is particularly masterful: Houdon first cuts out the entire iris, then bores a deeper hole for the pupil, taking care to leave a small fragment of marble to overhang the iris. The effect is a vivacity and mobility of expression that was praised even at the time, when Houdon was acclaimed as perhaps the first sculptor in the history of art to render eyes so convincingly.

ELISABETH LOUISE VIGÉE LE BRUN
French, 1755–1842
Self-Portrait, c. 1781

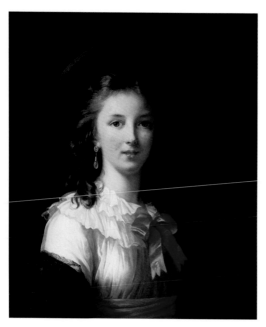

Oil on canvas, 25½ x 21¼ in.
(64.8 x 54 cm)
Acquired in 1949

This youthful self-portrait depicts Elisabeth Louise Vigée Le Brun at about age twenty-six, several years after she painted the first of her many portraits of Queen Marie-Antoinette, by which time she had already worked some ten years as a professional artist. Here she presents herself not as an artist, with palette and brushes, but as a charming and attractive lady of society—indistinguishable from her own patrons, including the queen and aristocratic ladies, whom she sometimes painted in similar informal attire. Largely self-taught, Vigée Le Brun copied old master and modern paintings, including works owned by the painter and art dealer who became her husband, Jean-Baptiste-Pierre Le Brun.

Recommended by the queen for membership in the Royal Academy in 1783, despite being disqualified by her husband's profession—academicians could not be connected to the trade in pictures—Vigée Le Brun soon acquired considerable fame and renown. Her paintings shown at the Salon were "the most highly praised . . . the topics of conversation at court and in Paris, in suppers, in literary circles."

This radiant self-portrait, which highlights Vigée Le Brun's healthy good looks and creamy complexion, also bears witness to her absorption of seventeenth-century Flemish art. Having visited Flanders and the Netherlands in the spring of 1781, Vigée Le Brun made good use of her study of Rubens in the delicate glazes used to render her translucent skin and the sparkling light catching her eyes and crystal earrings. Attentive to the latest fashions, Vigée Le Brun often showed her sitters in graceful poses, and outfitted in comfortable Grecian gowns and scarves. Here her simple muslin gown and elegant scheme of white, black, and cherry, along with her loose curls of hair, offer a refreshingly unfettered contrast to the towering, powdered coiffures and swathes of brocaded silk favored by more formal portraitists. Along with her costumes, Vigée Le Brun bestowed on her sitters something of her own appealingly glamorous persona. Her indomitable spirit sustained her after she fled Paris in 1789 at the onset of the Revolution. Welcomed throughout Europe and Russia, she reaped honors and great fortune as the favored portraitist of aristocratic society.

The Allen Brothers (James and John Lee Allen), early 1790s

Henry Raeburn was the leading portraitist in Edinburgh, Scotland, a center of the intellectual and artistic movement known as the Enlightenment, from about 1790 until his death in 1823. *The Allen Brothers* dates from early in his career, when his portraits show a remarkably experimental approach to composition, poses, and lighting effects, as well as the free, virtuoso brushwork for which he is best known.

Like many of Raeburn's patrons, the Allen brothers came from the Scottish landowning elite. John Lee Allen (born in 1781) and James Allen (born in 1783), the sons of John Allen of Inchmartine, were heirs to the considerable estates of Inchmartine and Errol on the north bank of the Tay estuary near Perth.

Despite their social status, the boys appear in an informal scenario, playing a game with a hat and a stick. The exact nature of the game is unclear, although it is presumably some form of mock fighting, perhaps a boyish version of jousting. Hats and caps raised on sticks were symbolic of Liberty, and, as such, common in the imagery of the French Revolution; this topical association may also have played into the way in which the portrait is staged. Whatever the case, the activity allows Raeburn to set off one against the other in a series of contrasts: the older boy standing and active, the younger seated (after a fashion) and passive; the older boy in profile and intent on his play, the younger in full face and apparently responding to the presence of the viewer.

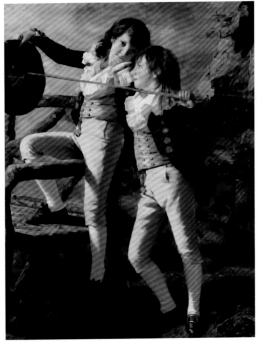

Oil on canvas; 59½ x 48⅞ in.
(151.1 x 124.1 cm)
Acquired in 2002

In his characterization of the boys, Raeburn hints at aspects of boyhood in general. The younger boy's expression and pose suggest a carefree innocence. Meanwhile his older brother jabs the stick into the lining of the hat, which is already ripped, with a look of determination, even destructive willfulness, that suggests innocence lost. Such a subtle and ambiguous vision was characteristic of the Romantic period, which gave birth to the idea of childhood as an interesting state in itself rather than a mere prelude to adulthood.

FRANCESCO GUARDI
Italian, 1712–1793
Venice Viewed from the Bacino, c. 1780

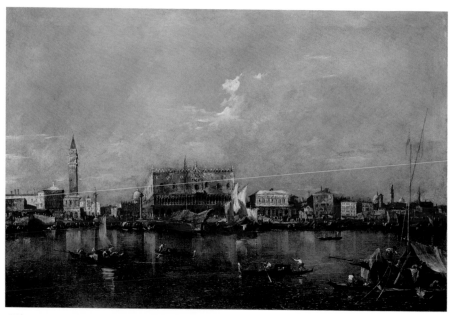

Oil on canvas; 24⅜ x 37½ in. (61.9 x 95.3 cm)
Acquired in 1970

Little is known about Francesco Guardi, whose family, originally from the Alpine region around Trent, was active as painters of devotional works. While he is remembered chiefly for his magical invocations of Venice, he initially worked with his older brother, Antonio, as a figure painter. Influenced as a view-painter by Canaletto, with whom he possibly trained for a time, Guardi also may have apprenticed in the studio of his brother-in-law, Giovanni Battista Tiepolo.

Compared to the neatly delineated pictures of his predecessor Canaletto, Guardi's views of Venice are painted with great brio and atmosphere. In this panoramic view from the *bacino*, or bay, Guardi presents an evocative image of the city's most famous facade. Rising at left is the campanile, or bell tower, next to the open space known as the Piazzetta, marked by the columns of Saint Theodore and the Lion of Saint Mark. At center is the imposing pink and white facade of the Doge's Palace, with the state galleon reserved for the doge moored at the quay, oars raised in waiting. The neighboring vessel with bright, unfurled sails docks adjacent to the dazzling white prisons. Gondolas and cargo boats ply water the color of slate, with reflections that enhance its glassy surface, in contrast to the light, fleecy sky above. Guardi's agile brush leaves traces of paint that glide on the surface of the canvas to create the miragelike image of the city on a lagoon, the forms quivering and dissolving in the sunlight.

Arriving in Paris in 1785, Louis-Léopold Boilly was witness to the collapse of the French monarchy, the struggle for modern republicanism, and the rise and fall of Napoleon's empire. Although he was denounced for the allegedly corrupt morality of his works in 1794, he survived the Revolution and went on to become the most gifted genre painter in France during the late eighteenth and early nineteenth centuries. He was also one of the period's most prolific portraitists.

This portrait was shown in 1812 and again in 1814 at the Paris Salon (the large, highly publicized, state-sponsored exhibition of contemporary art). It depicts a paymaster in the French administration, Monsieur Gaudry, instructing his daughter in geography. Boilly, as an intimate of the family, was said to have been present at this event many times. The little dog, whose face and paws are mimicked by the ornamentation of the chair, has been identified as "Brusquet," much admired in the family because his constant barking had once succeeded in scaring away a band of thieves who had broken into the finance ministry.

Historical geography was promoted as a field of study for both boys and girls in Napoleonic France, the maps of whose territories were subject to frequent revision with each new conquest. Here the sphinx and pyramid in the cartouche of

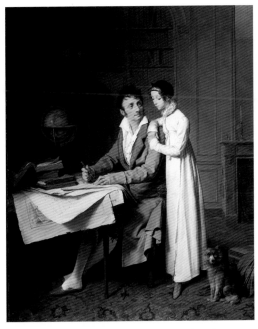

Oil on canvas; 29 x 23¼ in. (73.6 x 59 cm)
Acquired in 1990

the map no doubt refer to Napoleon's Egyptian expedition of 1798–1801; the globe shows Europe and Africa. The fine detail of *The Geography Lesson* is indebted to Dutch domestic genre paintings of the seventeenth century, many incorporating maps and books into middle-class homes. Indeed, Boilly himself had a notable collection of works by seventeenth-century genre masters such as Gerard Terborch and Gabriel Metsu.

FRANCISCO DE GOYA
Spanish, 1746–1828
The Matador Pedro Romero, c. 1795–98

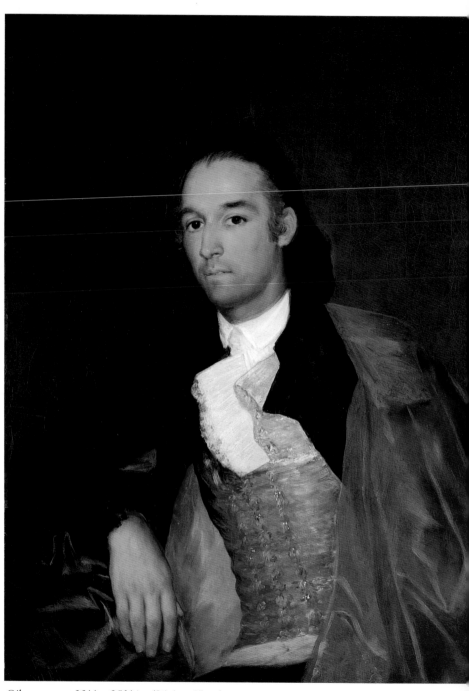

Oil on canvas; 33⅛ x 25⅝ in. (84.1 x 65 cm)
Acquired in 1966

Francisco de Goya, the most important Spanish painter after Velázquez, was, like his predecessor, a master portraitist. Unrivaled for his capacity to explore the depth and range of human passions, Goya created portraits that were boldly suggestive and pictorially striking. This portrait depicts Pedro Romero (1754–1839), one of the greatest toreadors of all time, idolized for his courage and control, as well as his handsome appearance. He was the foremost exponent of the classical school of bullfighting established by his family in Ronda, Andalusia. Romero was painted shortly before he retired from the bullring in 1799, at age forty-five, and several years after Goya had become completely deaf as a result of a serious illness.

The finery of Romero's costume does not upstage his charismatic good looks. Goya's study of Velázquez is apparent in the deft brushwork defining the rich fabric of his black jacket and the silver and pearl tones of his waistcoat, painted wet-in-wet, against the bright white of his shirt. The chromatic refinement extends to the mauve cape draped over his left shoulder and beneath his right arm, and the crimsons of his jacket lining and sash. The composure of the figure is in keeping with Romero's style of bullfighting; in contrast to the recklessness of his Sevillian rivals, Romero—who was said to have killed over 5,000 bulls without suffering injury to himself—relied on the skill and agility of his maneuvers. He was especially admired for his courage in confronting and subduing the bull with his elegant use of the cape, killing the animal with a single sword-thrust. Romero asserted that "the bullfighter should rely not on his feet but on his hands, and in the ring when confronting the bulls he must kill or be killed before running or showing fear." Here, Goya enlarged the initial expanse of the cape over Romero's black jacket, thereby balancing the prominent display of the matador's right hand, and magnifying the attributes of Romero's skill.

This portrait was greatly admired in Romero's day. A contemporary appreciated Goya's genius of characterization: "He breathes honor and sensitivity without showing any of the soulless ferocity of the gladiatorial customs." José de Vargas Ponce, who wrote a discourse in 1807 urging the abolition of bullfighting, called the portrait "the most finished and expressive from the estimable and agile brush of Goya." In his youth a professed aficionado, Goya exposed the cruelty of the bullfight when he returned to the theme in his brilliant print series of 1815–16, *La Tauromaquia*. His etching *Pedro Romero Killing the Bull*, however, underscores the matador's legendary skillful control.

ANTONIO CANOVA
Italian, 1757–1822
Head of a Woman, c. 1817

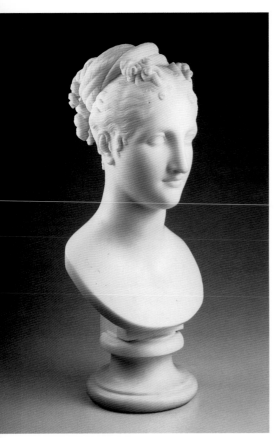

Marble; h. 22¼ in. (56.3 cm)
Acquired in 1981

The Venetian artist Antonio Canova was the leading sculptor of the Neoclassical movement. Traveling to Rome in late 1779, his virtuosity and stylistic innovation soon won him papal commissions and acclaim. Along with his French contemporary, the painter Jacques-Louis David, Canova set the standard for a new aesthetic based on the noble simplicity, grandeur, and ideal beauty of ancient art. With its elegant profile, smooth skin, and elaborate chignon, all familiar characteristics of such ancient prototypes as the Capitoline *Venus*, Canova's "ideal head" in pure white marble is a stunning example of his technical virtuosity as a carver.

Alongside his portrait sculptures, by 1811 Canova developed ideal heads as a sculptural type, some bearing the names of muses, such as Clio and Calliope. Around the same time he undertook his greatest masterpiece, *The Three Graces* (Hermitage, Saint Petersburg), as a commission from Empress Josephine. The exquisite heads of the three figures in this life-size ensemble are arguably the culmination of Canova's efforts to revitalize the ideals of classical female beauty. The Kimbell portrait relates to a statue of Polyhymnia, the muse of heroic hymns, made for Elisa Baciocchi Bonaparte (1812–17, Kunsthistoriches Museum, Vienna).

Despite the fact that members of Napoleon's family had been among Canova's most important clients, the sculptor was appointed by Pope Pius VII after the Battle of Waterloo to negotiate the restitution of famous paintings and antique statues that the emperor had looted from Italy. At the Allied Conference in Paris in 1815, Canova was aided by several British diplomats, including Charles Long, on whose advice the Prince Regent made a substantial contribution toward the cost of transporting these art treasures back to Rome. Canova presented this exquisite head to Long in gratitude. Similar heads were given to the Duke of Wellington (Wellington Museum, London), Lord Castlereagh (private collection), and William Richard Hamilton (Ashmolean Museum, Oxford).

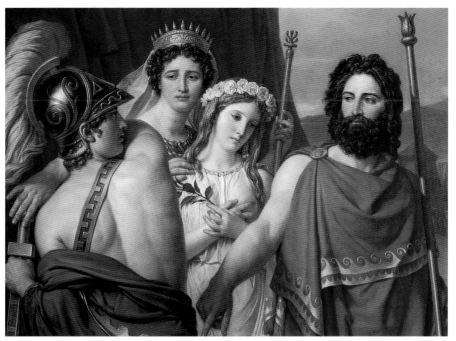

Oil on canvas; 41½ x 57⅛ in. (105.3 x 145 cm)
Acquired in 1980

The leading Neoclassical painter in Europe during the French Revolution and under Napoleon, David went into exile in Brussels after the Battle of Waterloo, in 1815. There he painted and exhibited *The Anger of Achilles*, which he prized as the culmination of his career-long effort to recapture the perfection of ancient Greek art.

The complex episode, which challenged David to render a spectrum of emotions from stoic courage and calm, heroic resolve, to grief and anger, is drawn from Euripides' *Iphigenia in Aulis* and Racine's seventeenth-century dramatic version of the same story. Agamemnon, king of the Greeks, has just revealed to the youthful Achilles that his daughter Iphigenia is not to be married to Achilles but sacrificed in order to appease the goddess Diana and so allow the Greek fleet to set sail for Troy. Observed from close up and cropped at waist level, David's seemingly speechless figures have scarcely enough room to act out the drama. Achilles angrily reaches for his sword, but Agamemnon's magnetic gaze and his authoritative gesture appear to freeze Achilles' outburst. Dressed as a bride, Iphigenia, who is portrayed like a Renaissance angel, clutches her heart, oblivious to this display of male confrontation. The reaction of her mother, Clytemnestra, mingling disappointment at Achilles' inability to act, with grief for her daughter, is apparently intended to mirror the mixed reactions that any spectator must feel as filial, spousal, and civic duties compete with one another.

JEAN-BAPTISTE-CAMILLE COROT
French, 1796–1875
View of Olevano, 1827

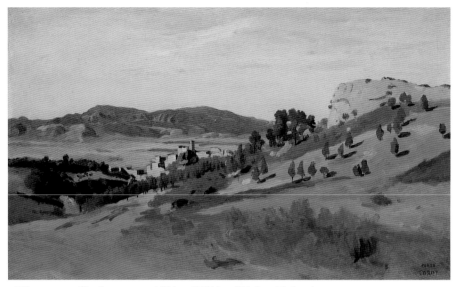

Oil on paper affixed to canvas; 10⅞ x 17⅞ in. (27.6 x 45.4 cm)
Acquired in 1980, with the assistance of a gift from Colonel C. Michael Paul

As the final stage in his artistic education, Corot went to Italy in the fall of 1825. During his nearly three-year-long stay, he toured the countryside so richly evocative of Latin literary classics, as well as the old master landscape paintings by Nicolas Poussin and Claude Lorrain that formed the fountainhead of the French tradition. Corot painted his Italian landscape studies as preliminaries for more traditional large landscapes with figures composed in the studio. But many modern viewers prefer Corot's oil sketches to the less spontaneous studio works developed from them. Figures, even secondary ones, are rare in these studies, with the implication that Corot recorded nature for its own sake rather than to provide background décor to some historical or literary narrative.

Working out-of-doors, Corot made around 150 oil studies in Italy. Taken as a group, these works constitute one of the earliest important manifestations of modern-art values, including a meteorological (rather than poetic) concern for light, a preference for unexpected points of view with a disregard for symmetry in composition, and a willingness to leave brushmarks visible for their own inherent beauty. Corot visited Olevano, about twenty-five miles east of Rome, toward the end of his Italian sojourn, in April and again during the summer of 1827.

Corot himself did not intend his Italian studies for public exhibition and left most of them unsigned. The red seal at the lower-right corner of the Kimbell painting, which reads *Vente Corot* (Corot Sale), was provided for the auction of the contents of the artist's studio after his death in 1875.

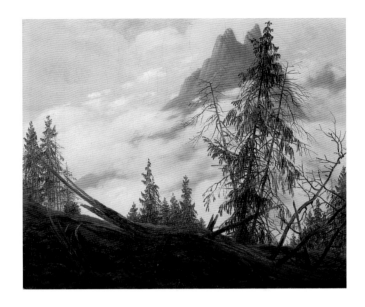

Oil on canvas;
9⅞ x 12¹⁄₁₆ in.
(25.1 x 30.6 cm)
Acquired in 1984

Friedrich is among the greatest of those Romantic artists in whose work spiritual yearning is the dominant theme. A close literary counterpart to his landscapes, in which sharply observed detail is laden with metaphorical or symbolic meaning, is the work of the English nature-poet William Wordsworth. Both epitomized an international trend in the years around 1800 to contemplate the state of nature, as opposed to the "civilized" states of humankind, for revelations about basic and eternal truths.

In this late painting, the artist observed a mountain wilderness with what appears to be photographic precision. Yet, like all Friedrich's works, this ostensibly ordinary scene is also open to interpretation as a spiritual text. While the rendition of the drifting clouds suggests a naturalist's awareness of meteorology, Friedrich almost certainly saw in them a symbolic meaning; veiling the distance and casting shadows across the landscape, they are an image of the shifting, imperfect conditions that nature provides for the illumination of the spirit. In the foreground a toppled tree is portrayed in matter-of-fact detail. It may symbolize mortality as a barrier to spiritual progress: according to some interpretations of Scripture, nature only became subject to death when the Fall of humankind corrupted the originally blissful landscape of Eden. Even the leafless evergreens in the middle distance (trees often understood as premonitions of eternity, given their relative immunity to seasonal change) bear witness to death. Finally, far off in the distance, as if in a separate realm all but inaccessible to human striving, Friedrich includes a fortresslike mountain peak—a revelation, perhaps, of the possibility of salvation.

When the Kimbell Art Museum acquired *A Mountain Peak with Drifting Clouds* in 1984, it became the first public collection outside of Europe to own a painting by Friedrich.

JOSEPH MALLORD WILLIAM TURNER
British, 1775–1851
Glaucus and Scylla, 1841

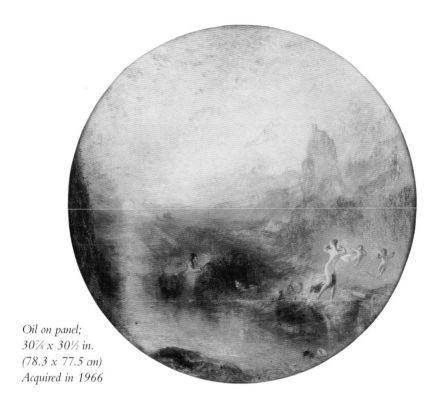

Oil on panel;
30⅞ x 30½ in.
(78.3 x 77.5 cm)
Acquired in 1966

J. M. W. Turner dominated British land-scape painting throughout the first half of the nineteenth century. Emulating the seventeenth-century French painter Claude Lorrain, Turner frequently included momentous events from the past within his landscapes as moral lessons. During Turner's lifetime and ever since, however, his paintings have been most admired for his virtuoso renditions of natural appearances, especially dramatic effects of light and weather.

The Kimbell painting includes a complicated mythological tale from the *Metamorphoses* of the Latin writer Ovid. We see the beautiful sea nymph Scylla fleeing from the outstretched arms of her would-be lover, the sea god Glaucus. The jealous and vengeful Circe, daughter of the Sun, who herself loved Glaucus, trans-formed him into a monster to frighten Scylla. Later, Circe changed Scylla into a rock. Turner possibly meant to indicate Scylla's fate with the two red outcrop-pings on the distant horizon. As for Circe, Turner apparently visualized her as the explosion of sunset light.

Various explanations, including a pref-erence for centralized compositions, have been forwarded for Turner's decision in the last decade of his life to paint circular-format works, almost always in pairs. *Glaucus and Scylla* was exhibited as a pair to *The Dawn of Christianity/Flight into Egypt* (Ulster Museum, Belfast) at the Royal Academy, London, in 1841.

Born at Ornans, near the Swiss border of France, Courbet came to Paris in 1840 to study law, but with characteristic assurance he quickly decided that his true calling was art. He at first specialized in swashbuckling self-portraits, reclining female nudes, and somber male portraits like the present work. Courbet's work was noticed by the Dutch contemporary art dealer H. J. van Wisselingh (1816–1884) at the Salon of 1846, and he invited the artist to visit Holland during the summer. As Courbet wrote to his family, "[Holland] is the only country where I can earn money right away. That is why I have to go and see what they like, study their old masters, see what their contemporary painters are doing, and get to know their art dealers. I already know one who will be most useful to me." While in Amsterdam he painted a portrait of van Wisselingh to present at a contemporary art exhibition in that city. "I had a unanimous ovation from the artists, all of whom by now I know," Courbet explained, "and many art lovers have come to see it and paid me the greatest compliments."

Rembrandt's art was a touchstone for Courbet, and the deep Rembrandtesque shadows in this portrait, while they obscure physical fact, suggest insights into the mood and character of the sitter and his world. Judging from Courbet's works of the late 1840s and 1850s, the Dutch seventeenth-century paintings that he saw in the Rijksmuseum in the summer of 1846 had made a lasting impression. The anticlassical and widely influential Realist art of the common people, advocated during those years by Courbet and his controversial friend, the poet Charles Baudelaire, which was based on the reality of modern life (its dark sides included), owed a considerable debt to the model of Rembrandt and his contemporaries.

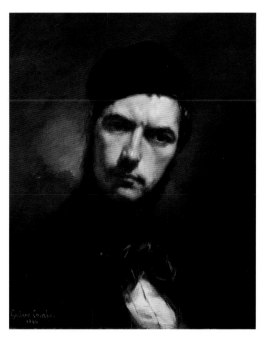

Oil on panel; 22½ x 18⅛ in. (57.2 x 46 cm)
Acquired in 1984

EUGÈNE DELACROIX
French, 1798–1863
Selim and Zuleika, 1857

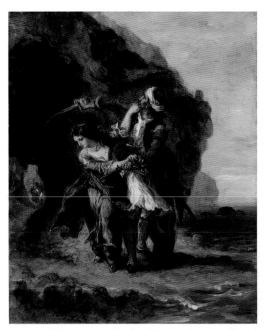

Oil on canvas; 18¾ x 15¾ in. (47.6 x 40 cm)
Acquired in 1986

Like many of his contemporaries, including Théodore Géricault, Delacroix proudly took inspiration from the best-selling Romantic poetry of Lord Byron. This painting is the last and most developed of the four canvases that the artist devoted to Byron's *The Bride of Abydos*, first published in 1813 and available in French translation by 1821.

Set in the Dardanelles of Turkey, Byron's poem relates the tragic fate of Zuleika, the daughter of the Pasha Giaffir, and her lover, the pirate Selim. In order to avoid a loveless marriage arranged by her father, Zuleika escapes at night from the harem tower in which she has been held. In Delacroix's painting the lovers await rescue in a grotto by the sea, pursued by Giaffir and his men, armed and bearing torches. When Selim fires his pistol to summon the aid of his comrades, who are waiting offshore, the shot signals their position to Giaffir. Sensing the approach of her pursuers, Zuleika tries to restrain Selim. In the tragic climax of the tale, Selim will be shot dead by Giaffir, and his body washed out to sea. Zuleika will die of grief.

Delacroix, a master of pose and gesture, portrays Zuleika and Selim in a dancelike embrace by the edge of the sea. The heart-pounding trauma of the incident is mirrored in the fluttering sweep of drapery, as Zuleika holds Selim back from the futility of confrontation and gently takes hold of him for a final embrace. The dawning light behind reveals the rocky silhouettes characteristic of the Normandy coast, where Delacroix often sketched during the late 1840s and 1850s. The colorful, freely brushed rendition of the rocks, water, and drifting clouds are precisely the qualities that made Delacroix's art so inspirational to the next generation of French artists, in particular the Impressionists.

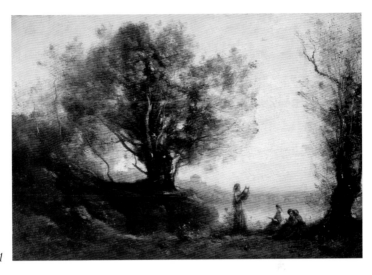

*Oil on canvas;
16½ x 24 in.
(41.9 x 61 cm)
Acquired in 1961*

The celebrated landscape painter Corot was among the leading members of the so-called Barbizon school, which placed a premium on working directly from nature, but he was simultaneously active as a painter of dreamlike fantasy landscapes. He undertook several works in response to the 1859 Berlioz production of Glück's celebrated opera *Orfeo*, about the musician of Greek mythology who enchanted all his listeners, even the animals. The largest of Corot's *Orpheus* paintings, exhibited at the Salon of 1861, is today in the Museum of Fine Arts, Houston. The considerably smaller Kimbell version depicts the beginning of the first act of this opera. Orpheus's beautiful bride has just died from the bite of a serpent. In mourning, Orpheus plays his lyre to three companions, who repeat a grouping of figures from Corot's *Homer and the Shepherds* of 1845 (Musée des Beaux-Arts, Saint-Lô). Orpheus, who appears somewhat femi-

nine in the Kimbell painting, is dressed in ancient fashion, whereas his seated female companions appear more contemporary, dressed in Italian folk costumes.

By the early 1860s, critics accused Corot of repeating more or less the same pastoral painting—a misty-morning landscape with a literary theme in the style of Claude Lorrain, the great seventeenth-century master. Yet Corot's ability to conjure long ago, faraway moods and his exquisite silvery tonal harmonies, no matter how formulaic, were greatly appreciated among his contemporaries, far more than his paintings done directly from nature in proto-Impressionist fashion. Among the hallmarks of Corot's theatrical landscapes are tiny flickers of white paint that suggest the sparkle of morning sunshine, a technique introduced by the great English painter John Constable. When first exhibited in Paris in the 1820s, Constable's matter-of-fact landscapes were an inspiration to the young Corot.

FREDERIC LEIGHTON
British, 1830–1896
Miss May Sartoris, c. 1860

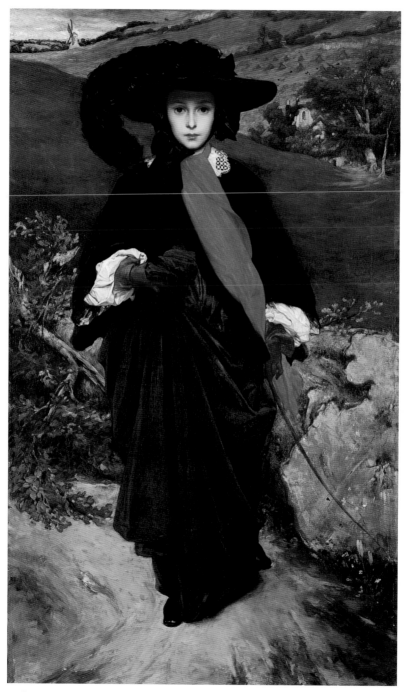

Oil on canvas; 59⅞ x 35½ in. (152.1 x 90.2 cm)
Acquired in 1964

This striking portrait was first exhibited only in 1897, when the Royal Academy presented a retrospective of the works of its recently deceased president, who had been both knighted and elevated to the peerage. The lender was Mary Theodosia (May) Sartoris, married since 1871 to a Mr. Henry Evans Gordon; she was painted about a decade earlier, at around age fifteen. The background landscape, presumably the Sartoris family properties in Hampshire, where Leighton visited in the early 1860s, includes a windmill, a field with rows of stacked wheat, and a country church. The dark tonality of the broad rolling lawn in the middle ground suggests an overcast day.

Carrying a riding crop and gathering up her dark blue riding habit to avoid dragging it in the dirt, the horseless equestrienne looks out of the painting with inscrutable wide eyes. As much as the sitter herself, however, the subject of the painting seems to be her extraordinary costume. Her hair is completely hidden under a broad-brimmed black hat tied at her chin in a bow and topped with a long black ostrich feather. Her black jacket with its white lace collar is boldly accented with a long scarlet scarf.

Leighton's close friendship with May's mother, the opera singer Adelaide Sartoris, began in Rome in 1853. Leighton had spent most of his childhood in Germany and Italy, where, as an art student, he became committed to the international revival of the Renaissance style. Indeed, Leighton made his reputation in 1855 when Queen Victoria purchased his monumental history painting depicting Cimabue, Giotto, and other Renaissance art pioneers (Royal Collection, on loan to the National Gallery, London).

Similarities to old master paintings aside, Leighton's slightly later portrait of May Sartoris has numerous counterparts among the full-length images of pensive females painted in the 1850s by leading English Pre-Raphaelite painters, including Arthur Hughes, John Everett Millais, and William Holman Hunt. The closest prototype for *Miss May Sartoris*, however, is the 1857 portrait of *Miss Daisy Grant* (private collection) by her father Francis Grant, who became president of the Royal Academy in 1866. In Grant's portrait the subject, dressed in black, appears, like May Sartoris, to stride out of an overcast landscape directly towards the viewer.

The inclusion of the cut-down tree just behind May is similar in spirit to the props in works by the American expatriate James Abbott McNeill Whistler, whom Leighton met in 1860. For example, in Whistler's *Symphony in White No. 1*, 1862 (National Gallery of Art, Washington), the model stands on a bearskin. The tree allows Leighton to indulge in varied painterly effects. Moreover, the invocation of autumn invites meditation on the seasons and the passage of time, accentuating the fragile beauty of the young girl.

CLAUDE MONET
French, 1840–1926
La Pointe de la Hève at Low Tide, 1865

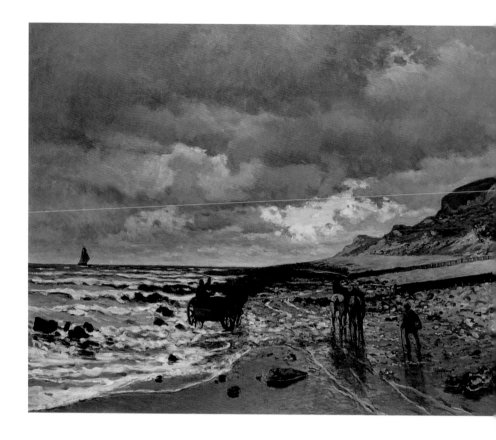

This magnificent beach scene near Le Havre, where the artist grew up, was one of two landscapes that launched Monet's career when exhibited in Paris at the 1865 Salon, the vast, well-attended survey of contemporary art sponsored by the French government. At the 1865 Salon, some viewers confused Monet's signature with that of the controversial Édouard Manet. When the older artist received compliments for a painting that he had not painted, he sought out Monet, thus initiating one of the richest dialogues ever between great painters.

Monet seemingly developed this large showpiece in direct response to similar compositions submitted to the Salon of 1864 by Charles-François Daubigny and his son Karl. (Around this time Monet owned a small landscape by Daubigny.) Daubigny had attempted to execute his Salon painting entirely on the spot, away from the shelter and convenience of a studio, in what would soon become

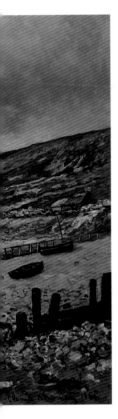

as far as the eye can see. The rocks at the right, described with brisk, creative brushwork, are especially indicative of Monet's unique talents, which were increasingly evident as he emerged as the leading Impressionist landscape artist.

The figures on the beach, all observed from the rear, appear in other works painted by Monet during the 1860s. Perhaps inspired by a work of 1862 by the Dutch Realist painter Jongkind, whom Monet met that year, the same horse-drawn cart appears in a snow scene painted in Normandy (Musée d'Orsay, Paris). A closely related snow scene (private collection) likewise includes the image of the man walking with a staff in *La Pointe de la Hève*. Finally, the pair of horses reappears in a farmyard scene that Monet painted at Chailly (private collection, Germany), where he worked in 1863 and 1865. Presumably Monet had drawings of such figural details that he would add as picturesque highlights. Such conventional means for finishing touches would become anathema to Monet in the later 1860s with the emergence of Impressionism and its challenge to make paintings on site, without after-the-fact studio alterations in detail or scale.

Monet insisted that an old black-and-white photograph of *La Pointe de la Hève* be included in a 1921 book about him, to record his beginnings. Perhaps as a result, this large work from his youth was traced, and in 1923 a dealer friend brought it to Giverny to keep the elderly artist company as he recovered from eye surgery.

Oil on canvas;
35½ x 59¼ in.
(90.2 x 150.5 cm)
Acquired in 1968

orthodox practice for so-called Impressionist landscapes. But in 1864 Monet still worked in more traditional fashion: he first painted *La Pointe de la Hève* at the site as a portable-scale work (private collection), which he then enlarged at his Paris studio during the first months of 1865 in preparation for the Salon. Most impressive in this large version, now in the Kimbell, is Monet's rendition of the muddy beach at low tide, the muted silvery tones of the foreground reflecting the low-hanging clouds stretching away

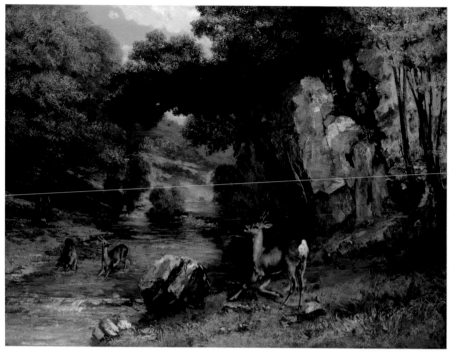

Oil on canvas; 38⅜ x 51⅛ in. (97.5 x 129.8 cm)
Acquired in 1968

Courbet was an avid hunter and painted such works as *Roe Deer at a Stream*, in which he seems to approach the deer—his quarry—unobserved, to appeal to patrons who shared his sporting interests. By depicting such swift and skittish creatures he also demonstrates his ability to make lightning-fast observations and renditions. In this respect, Courbet was challenging the efforts of his many talented young admirers—including Manet, Degas, Monet, and Renoir—who, in the 1860s, were already determined to depict the fast pace of modern life on Paris streets or at the racetrack.

Courbet boasted about painting directly from nature in proto-Impressionist fashion, but the fact that many of the animals in *Roe Deer at a Stream* are identical in pose to those in a closely related landscape of 1866 (Musée d'Orsay, Paris) reveals such claims to be exaggerated. In a letter written to his parents in 1866, Courbet explained that he had rented some deer from a Paris game butcher to serve as models. His tricks of the trade notwithstanding, Courbet's originality is evident in his economical and confident brushwork, which, in tandem with his use of a palette knife, suggests delicate textures like grass or leaves and rough ones like stone strata. With Courbet's "art for art's sake" emphasis on the physical qualities of paint, works like *Roe Deer at a Stream* inspired several generations of modern landscape artists, from Cézanne to Picasso and Matisse.

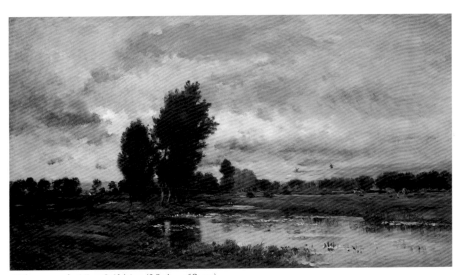

Oil on panel; 15 x 26¼ in. (38.1 x 68 cm)
Acquired in 1969

Daubigny was one of the foremost painters of the Barbizon school, a group of French artists active from the 1830s who celebrated the French landscape in their paintings during a period of unbridled industrialization and urbanization. He was a close colleague of other members of the famous group, in particular Corot, although in fact he seldom painted around Barbizon—which is a small village on the northern edge of the Fontainebleau forest.

Daubigny began to exhibit landscapes at the Paris Salons in 1838, but earned his living mostly as an etcher, often providing illustrations for books. His success as a painter began around 1850, when he won acclaim for his river views, despite his sketchy handling of paint. Already by the late 1850s, Daubigny's works were referred to as "impressions," because they lacked the sort of careful finish that was standard before the advent of Impressionism in the 1870s. In 1857 Daubigny

launched a studio boat as a way of easing the problems of transporting supplies, which, as an out-of-doors painter, he faced on his expeditions to work directly from nature. Monet, who would launch a studio boat of his own in 1873, kept a small landscape by Daubigny on his studio wall for inspiration when he began his career. It was Daubigny, moreover, who promoted Monet and Pissarro when all three artists sought asylum in London during the Franco-Prussian War.

The Kimbell landscape, painted in the summer of 1871, is an exquisite example of Daubigny's influential style. It shows a view along the Oise River, not far from the artist's home in Auvers. The windswept clouds in the sky, rendered with accents of impasto, animate the quiet, mirroring surface of the river, dotted with water lilies, with the sort of nature poetry that would become the essence of Impressionism.

CAMILLE PISSARRO
French, 1830–1903
Near Sydenham Hill, 1871

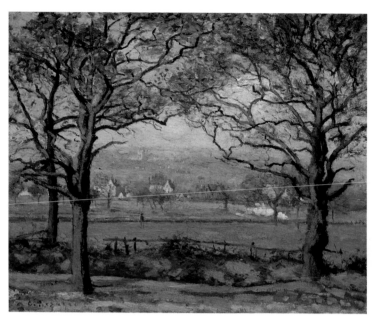

Oil on canvas;
17 x 21 in.
(43.5 x 53.5 cm)
Acquired in 1971

Camille Pissarro was one of the leading figures of the French Impressionist movement. He took part in the
first Impressionist show in 1874 and was
the only member to show his work in all
eight exhibitions organized by the group.
Pissarro was a modest and generous man
who exerted a strong influence on the
next generation of painters. He was, in
Cézanne's opinion, "a man to consult,
and something like the good Lord."

This crisply observed landscape, with
a commuter train puffing along in the
middle distance, depicts the suburban
neighborhood near Lower Norwood
(West Dulwich), south of London, where
the forty-year-old Pissarro, his companion
Julie Vellay, and their two children came
to live in December 1870. The vantage
point is just north of Sydenham Hill
Station, looking toward West Norwood

Cemetery. Pissarro's decision to relocate
from France was made in concert with
his mother and his brother, all realizing
the need to escape the chaos resulting
from the Prussian army's ongoing siege
of Paris. Their friends, the Monets, had
been in London since early October,
part of a colony of French exiles. In
London, Pissarro and Monet went to the
museums and studied works by Constable
and Turner, whose pioneering, freshly
observed landscape paintings had paved
the way for French Impressionism.

Judging from the absence of green
foliage, the Kimbell painting was executed
in early spring. An inscription on the
stretcher reads: "to my wife . . . C. Pissarro,"
suggesting that it was a wedding gift.
Pissarro and Julie Vellay married on
14 June 1871, just before returning
to France.

Jean-Baptiste Carpeaux was much sought after as a portraitist by prominent sitters, including members of the imperial household. Among his finest busts is this posthumous portrait of his older brother, Charles, a musician, who died in 1870 after long suffering. Carpeaux made an initial, rapid sketch in plaster (Musée du Petit Palais, Paris), which the sculptor's earliest biographers claimed was made entirely for himself as his brother lay ill. The Kimbell's terracotta cast, whose surface was remodeled with additional clay, preserves a sense of the artist's own physical involvement in the material through the sketchy handling, especially in the texture of the jacket and the hair. The back and side of the figure's coat show the traces of the artist's fingers in the process of forming, whereas the lines along the sleeves, apparently made with a stylus, are comparable to chisel marks still visible on a marble work in process. These textures, indications that the work is not "finished" by conventional standards, are richly suggestive, perhaps drawing upon the expressive power of the unfinished sculptures of Carpeaux's hero, Michelangelo. The hand and tool marks provide a sense of intimacy, suggesting that the viewer is watching over the shoulder of the sculptor at work in his studio. These same marks provide elegiac overtones to the bust: the rough, unfinished look seems in keeping with the subject's "unfinished" life. Whatever the case, by virtue of its exciting informal surfaces, this portrait is among Carpeaux's most modern works,

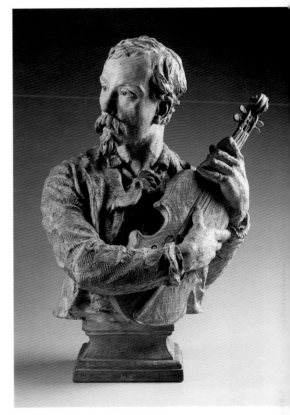

Terra-cotta; h. 27 in. (68.6 cm)
Acquired in 1984

anticipating the similarly modern-minded experimentation of Rodin.

Among the preeminent French sculptors of his day, Carpeaux remains best known for his influential sculpture of nude allegorical figures (*The Dance*, now Musée d'Orsay, Paris) commissioned for the facade of the new Paris Opera House, which was condemned as indecent and even vandalized shortly after completion in 1869.

GUSTAVE CAILLEBOTTE
French, 1848–1894
On the Pont de l'Europe, 1876–77

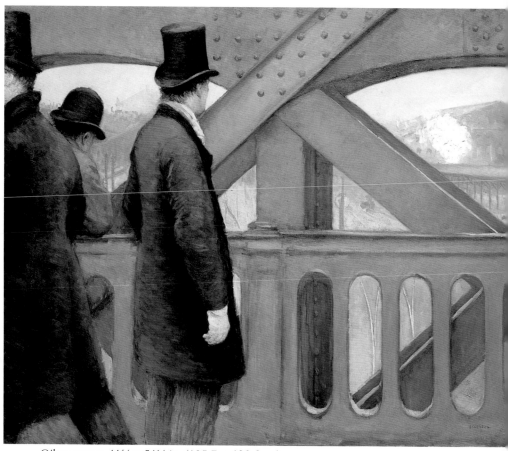

Oil on canvas; 41⅝ x 51½ in. (105.7 x 130.8 cm)
Acquired in 1982

Caillebotte was the most important
early patron of the so-called Impressionists: Cézanne, Degas, Monet, Pissarro,
Renoir, and Sisley. They invited him to be
in their second group exhibition in 1876,
and later that year Caillebotte wrote a
will promising his controversial collection
of works by the artists he championed to
the French state. In 1897 forty paintings
from Caillebotte's bequest went on view

at the Musée du Luxembourg, thus legiti-
mizing the status of Impressionism. Today
these works form the nucleus of the
collection at the Musée d'Orsay, Paris.

Although his closest artist friends were
Monet and Renoir, the key advocates for
loose brushwork and bright color, in his
own art Caillebotte preferred the sort
of conventional draftsmanship and unaf-
fected urban subjects dear to Degas. Like

Degas, Caillebotte limited himself as an artist to strictly subdued visual means. With its restricted, cool palette of blacks, blues, and grays, *On the Pont de l'Europe* looks something like a giant amateur snapshot, lacking such basic pictorial elements as facial expression, gesture, a ground plane, compositional balance, and an unobstructed background view.

In *The New Painting* (1876), Impressionist champion Edmond Duranty wrote: "A back should reveal temperament, age, and social position. . . ." Caillebotte includes three backs in *On the Pont de l'Europe*. Each figure has but one visible feature, an ear, and as a group the ears suggest the invisible mechanical din of the train station. Caillebotte's primary source for *On the Pont de l'Europe* was Manet's luminously painted *The Railroad*, 1872–73 (National Gallery of Art, Washington), showing a little girl from the rear as she looks through the bars of a fence at a smoke-filled railroad yard. Caillebotte's response to the Manet is quite different in effect. Like so many of his works, it is monochromatic, the persuasive blue tones corresponding in visual terms to the chilling cold in which the figures stand. The man on the left with his collar turned up and the principal figure, their backs turned toward each other as if mirror images, are dressed in identical fashion. The implication, perhaps, is that modern urban society appears no less regularized than modern engineering, with its mass-produced prefabricated parapets, girders, and rivets. For his composition, Caillebotte has adopted the geometric structure of the bridge, one pier of which bisects his picture vertically into two arched bays, these each subdivided by diagonal cross-bracing struts. The humanity of the figures resides in their freedom to escape the rigid symmetry. Since the figures and the activities in the train station are all obscured or fragmented, the abstract visual rhythms of the bridge's structure take priority in a very modern way.

The iron trellis of the *Pont de l'Europe* in fact overlooks the Saint-Lazare train station, which was famously portrayed by Monet in a dozen paintings made early in 1877 and included at the third Impressionist exhibition that year. It is at least possible that Caillebotte (who soon purchased three of Monet's variations on the station theme) refrained from showing his masterful *On the Pont de l'Europe* at the same exhibition in order not to compete.

ÉDOUARD MANET
French, 1832–1883
Georges Clemenceau, 1879–80

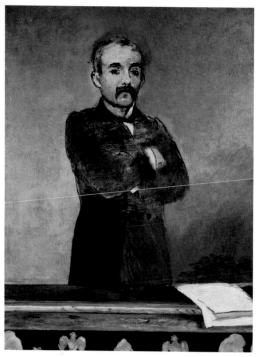

Oil on canvas; 45⅝ x 34¾ in.
(115.9 x 88.2 cm)
Acquired in 1981

Shortly after he became prime minis-
ter of France in 1906, Georges
Clemenceau (1841–1929) ordered
Manet's *Olympia* to be transferred from
the Musée du Luxembourg (where
contemporary art was relegated) to the
Louvre, thus granting old master status to
the controversial painter of modern life.
When the two first met is unknown, but
Clemenceau, just out of medical school,
left for America as a newspaper corre-
spondent in 1865, the year in which
Manet first exhibited *Olympia* in Paris.
Following his return in 1869, Clemenceau
entered the tumultuous French political
world of the 1870s as a radical leftist.

Manet, who often asked his friends to
model for him as themselves, seems to
have sought out political figures around
1879, when he initiated this painting of
Clemenceau. The rostrum at the bottom
of the Kimbell painting was probably
intended as an economical way to indicate
Clemenceau's incumbency at the time in
the Chamber of Deputies.

Manet typically exasperated models
with his insatiable need to revise, and
he never finished the portrait of
Clemenceau, begun on two different
canvases of identical size. Closely related
photographs of Clemenceau, found
among the papers of both artist and
sitter, suggest that the deputy was seldom
available to pose in person. The pose
with arms crossed may have been
suggested by a portrait of the baritone
Paul Barroilhet (1849, Fogg Art Museum,
Cambridge, Massachusetts) by Manet's
teacher and Clemenceau's friend, Thomas
Couture. Further, the painter and forceful
politician may have intended some allusion to earlier portraits of liberal reform-
ers in this stance, such as Paul Delaroche's
Comte Charles de Rémusat (1845, Musée
du Vieux Toulouse).

Manet's widow gave both incom-
pletely realized portraits to the politician
as keepsakes. Later, in 1905, Clemenceau
agreed to sell one of the versions to an
American collector; shortly afterwards
he sold the other (now the Kimbell
version) to a Parisian dealer. The American collector, Louisine Havemeyer, had
the unfinished lower portion of her
version removed and in 1927 donated
the work to the Louvre (today displayed
at the Musée d'Orsay).

By 1872 Degas had begun to specialize in genre scenes of women at
work, especially music hall performers
and ballet dancers. In his paintings of
these subjects he often included background figures pausing from tedious
labors to stretch or yawn, as if to underline his goal of capturing unedited
glimpses of daily life. It has been
suggested that the Kimbell drawing
might have originated as a study for a
never-realized detail in one of these
multifigured paintings.

Degas, who signed works only when
he sold or exhibited them (and rarely did
either), never signed this particular drawing. But the executors of his estate
stamped imitation signatures in red ink
on all the works left in his studio, and
Dancer Stretching was among them. The
status of its signature aside, this drawing
features many of the idiosyncratic hallmarks of Degas's influential style. As if by
oversight, Degas miscalculated the size of
the figure to that of the sheet of paper,
with the result that there is no room in
the composition for the figure's feet and
the fingers of her left hand. Nor did he
choose to erase the first lines with which
he searched to capture the figure's form,
even after he had finalized his observations. The visibility of the preliminary
drawings underneath the final one seems
intended to suggest how Degas needed to
rush in order to capture such a split-
second subject. The smudges and leftover
lines here also serve as "background" to
the final figure, who is therefore not situated in a recognizable space, like a ballet

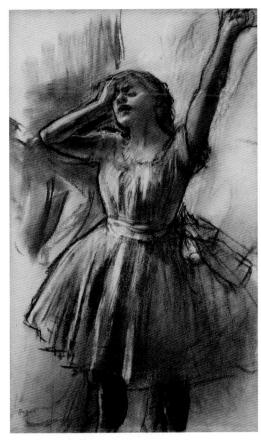

*Pastel on pale blue gray paper;
18⅜ x 11¾ in. (46.7 x 29.7 cm)
Acquired in 1968*

rehearsal room, but instead inhabits the
sheet of drawing paper, evolving from the
marks on it as the result of an artistic
process. Degas's decision to leave traces of
this process visible, and thus to "represent" not simply a dancer but the act of
drawing her, gives this work an expressly
modern character.

JAMES ENSOR
Belgian, 1860–1949
Skeletons Warming Themselves, 1889

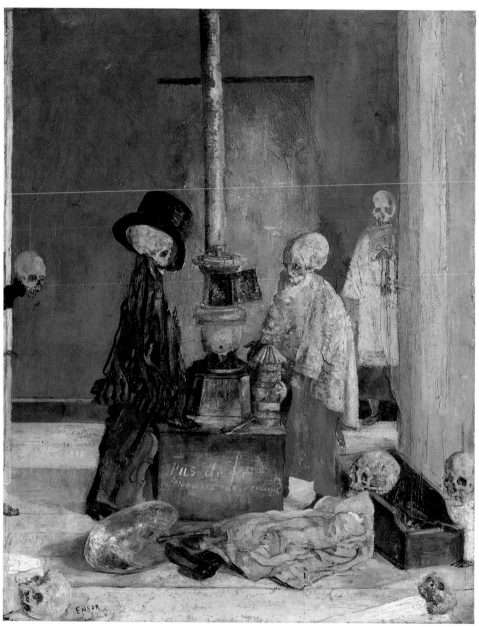

Oil on canvas; 29½ x 23⅜ in. (74.8 x 60 cm)
Acquired in 1981

James Ensor was one of the most original painters of the late nineteenth century. Populated with masks and skeletons, his macabre images are morbid commentaries on the human condition, his hometown of Ostend on the North Sea, Belgian history, and his own mortality. Human bones were regularly uncovered in Ostend well into the twentieth century, residue of the carnage there during early-seventeenth-century warfare, and Ensor retained childhood memories of their exhumation. In 1888 he made a little etching of himself as a reclining skeleton in slippers, entitled *My Portrait in 1960* (that is, at age one hundred).

Belonging to a group of closely related paintings from the late 1880s, the enigmatic work in the Kimbell's collection is among the artist's masterpieces. He has placed three dressed-up skeletons in the foreground around a stove on which is written *"Pas de feu"* and under it *"en trouverez vous demain?"*—"No fire. Will you find any tomorrow?" The skeletons are accompanied by a palette and brush, a violin, and a lamp. Presumably Ensor intended these items to symbolize art, music, and literature. If so, the probable implication here is that artistic inspiration, or patronage to support it, has expired in Ensor's world.

Understood as a scene in an artist's studio, *Skeletons Warming Themselves* resembles a vignette from the popular medieval and early Renaissance print cycles of the Dance of Death, each print portraying skeletons as an allegorical comment on the vanities of a particular profession or social type. In this tradition, Ensor may be satirizing the idea that painters can bring life to canvas. Rather than immortalizing his models, this painter has a studio littered with skulls from previous failed efforts. Curtains muffle the daylight coming through the window at right. While the models in absurd costumes warm themselves between posing sessions, a skeleton peers in from the left, possibly the artist, himself too dead to perceive anything wrong. The long vertical stripe of white paint at left, behind his neck— too tall for a door—is probably the edge of the ambitious canvas under way.

X-radiographs reveal another finished picture beneath this scene. It is a bust-length portrait of a young girl, probably painted before 1883. Ensor's reuse of an earlier canvas may reflect his own difficult economic condition in 1889. In 1895 Ensor made an etching of the same composition and entitled it *Squelettes voulant se chauffer (Skeletons Trying to Warm Themselves)*.

PAUL GAUGUIN
French, 1848–1903
Self-Portrait, 1885

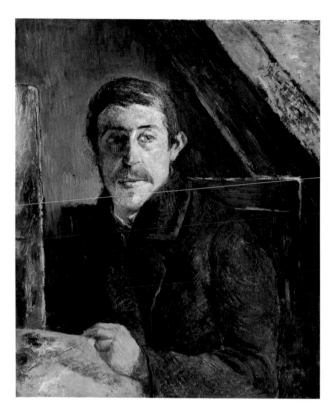

Oil on canvas;
25⅝ x 21⅜ in.
(65.2 x 54.3 cm)
Acquired in 1997

Gauguin assumed his role as renegade artist in 1885. Rather than remain jobless in Copenhagen with his Danish wife and their five children, the former stockbroker decided to return to Paris to follow his restless artistic conscience. Whether painted in Denmark or in France, this painting is the first of the many self-portraits in which Gauguin sought to explore his dark inner psyche.

Scientific examination of the painting has revealed that at first Gauguin portrayed himself in profile and included reproductions of his own paintings on the background studio wall. Turned to confront the viewer in the final work, he shows himself left-handed, like his image in a mirror, crowded in an attic space with a slanted beam, and cold, with the lapels of his heavy jacket wrapped together. Only his piercing eye escapes the bleak atmosphere.

Gauguin may indeed have intended to present himself as a prisoner. When he made a self-portrait for his new friend Vincent van Gogh in 1888, he explained: "It is the face of an outlaw, ill-clad and powerful like Jean Valjean [the criminal hero of Victor Hugo's *Les Miserables*]— with an inner nobility and gentleness. . . . As for this Jean Valjean, whom society has oppressed, cast out—for all his love and vigor—is he not equally a symbol of the contemporary Impressionist painter?"

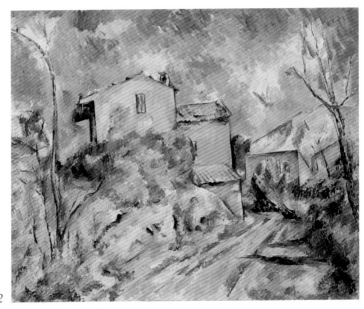

Oil on canvas;
25⅝ x 31⅞ in.
(65 x 81 cm)
Acquired in 1982

Provençal buildings with stucco walls and red-tiled roofs—often, as here, observed from a road turning into the picture—formed one of Cézanne's favorite subjects. Several seem to have appealed to him as portraits-by-proxy of their owners, but the identity of Maria, after whom the primary building in this work is named, remains a mystery. In terms of composition, the Kimbell painting is a reprise of *The House of the Hanged Man* (Musée d'Orsay, Paris), presented in 1874 at the first Impressionist exhibition and at the Paris World's Fair of 1889.

By the late 1870s, Cézanne had devised his hallmark manner of applying color in short parallel strokes, no differently for objects than for empty space. Here the distinctive way in which the trees are rendered with jagged broken lines, along with the density of the sky, relates stylistically to paintings that he made in 1895 at a quarry near Château Noir. It was at Château Noir, an unfinished and abandoned nineteenth-century building complex in the Gothic style, visible in the right background of the Kimbell painting, that Cézanne stored his art supplies beginning in 1887. Indeed, Cézanne's melancholy late paintings of Château Noir were painted from the path in front of the Maison Maria.

Landscapes such as this, in which Cézanne shows corners of rural France with simple domestic buildings, were a major source of inspiration for Braque and Picasso, and by extension for Cubism and early-twentieth-century art.

PAUL CÉZANNE
French, 1839–1906
Man in a Blue Smock, c. 1896–97

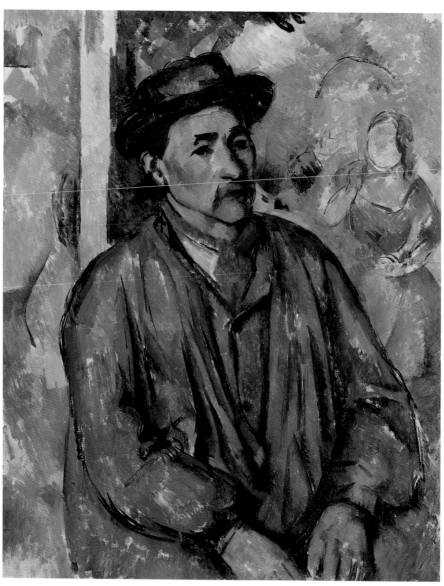

Oil on canvas; 32⅛ x 25½ in. (81.5 x 64.8 cm)
Acquired in 1980, in memory of Richard F. Brown, the Kimbell Art Museum's first director,
by the Kimbell Board of Trustees, assisted by the gifts of many friends

Starting around 1887, using his wife and son as models, Cézanne began to paint single figures with the same gravity he had developed in his landscapes and still lifes. Around 1890 he extended his options by enlisting workers from his family's estate in the south of France. The worker who posed for *Man in a Blue Smock* also posed for the famous *Cardplayers* compositions of the early 1890s. For the remainder of his career, Cézanne maintained his interest in making portraits of rural workers — if the term "portrait" can be applied to images of anonymous models posed as themselves in the studio.

In the background of *Man in a Blue Smock*, Cézanne represented the right-hand section of a folding screen that was his very first work of art (around 1859, Musée Granet, Aix-en-Provence); featuring elegant figures such as the woman with a parasol, this was a scene of leisure rendered in the pastoral spirit of an eighteenth-century tapestry. Juxtaposed in an ambiguous way next to the worker in the Kimbell portrait, this faceless woman perhaps suggests some mute dialogue between opposite sexes, differing social classes, or even between the artist's earliest and most fully evolved efforts as a painter.

Not counting his classical nudes in landscape settings, Cézanne had mostly abandoned figure painting after his portrait of the painter Achille Emperaire (Musée d'Orsay, Paris) was refused by the jury of the Salon of 1870. Left on deposit at the shop of the art-supply dealer Julien Tanguy — one of the only places works by Cézanne could be seen in Paris until the mid-1890s — the Emperaire portrait was a revelation around 1887 to young Post-Impressionist painters including Émile Bernard and Vincent van Gogh. Indeed, van Gogh's acclaimed portrait of Tanguy (Musée Rodin, Paris) seems to have been inspired by Cézanne's early portrait. In turn, the enthusiasm of these younger artists may have helped rekindle Cézanne's own lapsed interest in portraiture.

Another impetus for Cézanne's renewed interest in figure painting was the opportunity to reconsider Manet's work after the latter's death in 1883. When Cézanne had first come to Paris, in the 1860s, Manet's art had almost immediately become the most important touchstone for his development. On view in the Manet estate sale in 1884 were not only completed works, but also works in progress. Whether by design or coincidence, Cézanne's mature figure paintings, such as *Man in a Blue Smock*, bear a striking similarity to some of these never fully realized Manet paintings, with patches of bare canvas throughout. Although Cézanne sometimes suggested the flicker of light with small unpainted areas in his late landscapes, the blank patches in his figure paintings can be understood to express more abstract meanings. Among Cézanne's most important legacies was his pioneering demonstration, by leaving areas of canvas unpainted, that a painting could suggest not only what the artist saw, but also his pauses and hesitations during the exacting realization of his observations.

EDVARD MUNCH
Norwegian, 1863–1944
Girls on a Bridge, c. 1904

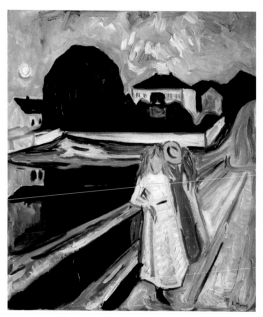

Oil on canvas; 31¾ x 27¼ in.
(80.5 x 69.3 cm)
Acquired in 1966

In 1889 Munch started spending peri-ods at the resort of Åsgårdstrand, popu-lar at that time with many artists and writers. While summering there in 1893, he developed the pictorial ideas that some years later would evolve into *Girls on a Bridge. The Storm* (Museum of Modern Art, New York) shows several of the town's houses as a backdrop for a group of women by the edge of the sea, and *The Scream* (National Gallery, Oslo) depicts the nearby pier as the background for an isolated figure whose face is a mask of anguish. In 1899 Munch used the same pier setting as the foreground for a paint-ing of a group of women with the houses of Åsgårdstrand in the background, and this was the first version of *Girls on a Bridge* (National Gallery, Oslo).

Following the lead of modern artists such as Monet and Renoir, who in the early 1890s began to play multiple varia-tions on a single compositional idea, Munch painted seven versions of *Girls on a Bridge* between 1899 and 1930, as well as half a dozen closely related works with groups of older female figures in the same setting. In all these, Munch depicted the pier with slanting lines receding dramatically into the background space. Among the *Girls on a Bridge* variations, the Kimbell's is one of the most freely painted.

Exaggerating line and color to create haunting, even ominous, moods, Munch portrays a world charged with emotions and anxieties. Here it is the setting, rather than the girls' poses and expressions, that suggests they may be brooding about their identities or desires. They appear absorbed, like the painter, in their obser-vations of the townscape under a full moon. The foremost girl turns away from her friends toward the viewer but her face is blank, an emotional riddle.

Bourdelle is generally acclaimed as the most important heir to Rodin, in whose studio he was an assistant from 1893 until 1908. Upon his separation from Rodin, however, Bourdelle sought direct inspiration in the work of the famous Neoclassical painter Ingres, a native of the sculptor's own hometown, Montauban. Bourdelle sculpted a portrait of Ingres in 1908 while developing *Penelope*, the pose for which, based on ancient Roman models, was among Ingres's favorites.

In Bourdelle's earliest versions, Penelope held a spindle to identify her as the steadfast wife of Odysseus, who, in Homer's epic account of the Trojan War, endures the long absence of her warrior husband by weaving a shroud. In the fully evolved, half-scale Kimbell version, the figure's identity as Penelope is manifest only from the ancient Greek costume and meditative pose. Both the elimination of the spindle prop, and the pose with arms brought close to the body, contribute to the sculpture's columnlike silhouette. Indeed, the heavy woolen pleats of Penelope's chiton are like the fluting on a Doric column. This architectural character is most evident in the final full-scale version of *Penelope*. Such monolithic simplicity was an ideal in early-twentieth-century sculpture, from Rodin to Maillol and Brancusi. Evoking the theories of Michelangelo, the sculptor Duchamp-Villon told his students that an ideal sculptural form could be rolled down a hill without any breakage. Bourdelle's *Penelope* is a particularly successful example of this sort of modern monumentality.

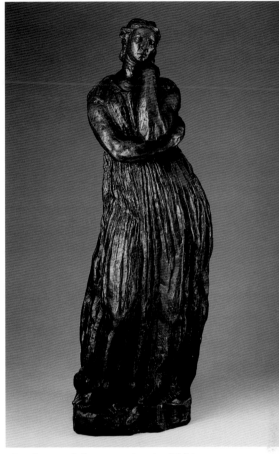

Cast bronze, dark green patina; h. 47⅛ in.
(119.7 cm)
Acquired in 1969

In its lack of specific attribute, and massive arms and legs, the *Penelope* resembles the big-bodied female allegorical figures in Renoir's works of the early twentieth century. Indeed, the nude subjects of both Bourdelle and Renoir herald the new classicism (the so-called "return to order") so evident in the works of Picasso, Matisse, and Derain from the World War I years onward.

PABLO PICASSO
Spanish, 1881–1973
Nude Combing Her Hair, 1906

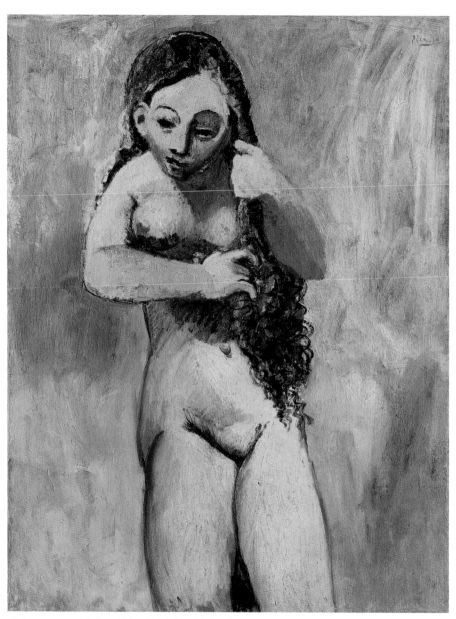

Oil on canvas; 41½ x 32 in. (105.4 x 81.3 cm)
Acquired in 1982

Based on the classical *Venus Anady-omene* type of figure—in which the goddess, rising from the sea, wrings out her hair—*Nude Combing Her Hair* attests to the engagement with classicism that preoccupied Picasso throughout his career. It was, however, always a process of selective and critical adaptation: the woman's masklike features exemplify his habit of stylizing the classical prototype, and the deliberately crude brushwork (especially evident in the shadow around the figure's arm, her hair, and the sketchy, neutral background) marks a deliberate gesture against the idealism of classical art.

The professional model for *Nude Combing Her Hair* was Fernande Olivier (born Amélie Lang), who entered Picasso's life in 1904. Her presence helped motivate him to abandon his somber Blue Period subjects in favor of the female nude themes so successful at the turn of the century with Degas, Renoir, and other avant-garde artists. Matisse also, to whom Picasso was introduced in 1906, had just begun to stress female nude themes in both paintings and sculpture, and works like *Nude Combing Her Hair* may be understood as Picasso's response to this powerful artistic rival.

Picasso created numerous works with similar subjects in 1905–6, for the most part fragmentary or sketchy in appearance. Whatever the cause for his obsession with this particular figure type, the raw power of the masklike face in works like the Kimbell painting may reflect his exposure to a medieval statue of the Virgin in Gósol, Spain, where he spent the summer of 1906. Judging from x-radiographs of the Kimbell painting, Picasso first showed the figure in a crouching pose, afterwards repainting the lower part of the figure as a standing, adolescent nude. Like so many of Picasso's dramatically reworked canvases of this time, with boldly modern disjunctions between adjacent parts, *Nude Combing Her Hair* represents both its obvious subject and the artistic act in the process of realization.

GEORGES BRAQUE
French, 1882–1963
Girl with a Cross, 1911

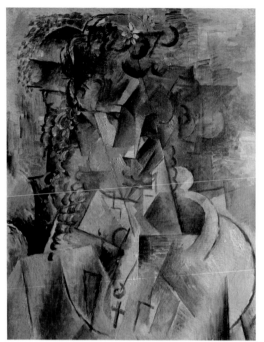

Oil on canvas; 21¼ x 17 in. (55 x 43 cm)
Acquired in 1989

Beginning in late 1907, Braque and
his new acquaintance Pablo Picasso
began to paint objects as highly simplified
geometric forms, expressing solidarity
with the most idiosyncratic tendencies in
the art of Cézanne—especially that of
juxtaposing unaligned observations of
adjacent parts of a single entity, like a
house, bottle, or face. Matisse, whose own
works at this time emphasized rich color,
is generally credited with coining the
term "Cubism"—and he used it to
describe Braque's overcast landscapes and
shadowy still lifes. By late 1909, however,
Braque and Picasso had extended the
Cubist premise to such a degree of analy-
sis by fragmentation that their somber
gray and ocher paintings appeared mostly
abstract, except for scattered, geometric-
shaped vestiges of recognizable imagery,
such as an eye, the bridge of a nose, a
cascade of hair in curls, or a necklace
with a cross. The implication was that
solid matter and the space surrounding it
had interpenetrated one another, resulting
in a new visual order.

In *Girl with a Cross*, the head (or rather
its disembodied details) emerges like an
apparition amid a rich interplay of highlighted and shaded facets, thinly scumbled
and atmospheric in mood. What appears
to be a round white ceramic pot at the
right, more solidly painted than the
woman, mysteriously occupies the space
where her shoulder should be. Orchestrating details in this way, Braque creates
an unprecedented visual impression of
presence, absence, and movement, all
dissolved together into a single space-time
diagram.

In early July 1911, Picasso left Paris for Céret, a small town near Arles in south-western France. Braque joined him there in August and the two painted their ultimate "Analytical Cubist" works in intense dialogue. Analytical Cubist painting is characterized by complex linear scaffolds—in this case long vertical lines at roughly equal intervals and sets of isosceles triangles—and by scores of small brush marks, interlocking and overlapping like pieces of a jigsaw puzzle in progress. While most of the marks in *Man with a Pipe* are baffling in terms of representation and serve primarily to establish visual rhythms, a few fragments of graphic information are legible. Easily spotted just above the middle of the painting, the white clay pipe helps locate the man's head, with its half-lightened, half-darkened mustache, suggesting how one side of his face is turned toward some source of light. The eye and nose can be discerned by extrapolating from the placement of the mustache. A white rectangular shape at the bottom, a piece of paper, indicates where to look for the man's hands. *Man with a Pipe* presumably represents the interior of a dimly lit, smoke-filled café (hence the letters *est* detached from the word *restaurant* and the letters *AL*, seemingly printed to the right of a mostly white rectangle, to suggest *journal*, meaning "newspaper" in French). A man with a similar mustache, smoking a similar pipe, appears in another Céret painting by Picasso, *The Poet* (Peggy Guggenheim Collection, Venice).

Around 1910 both Picasso and Braque had begun to work with particularly dark palettes. Possibly the nocturnal moods

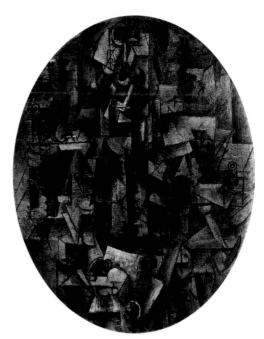

Oil on canvas; 35¾ x 27⅞ in. (oval) (90.7 x 71 cm)
Acquired in 1966

evoked were intended as a challenge to seeing in conventional terms, as if the painters wanted to invite viewers to strain their eyes to experience a difficult new way of looking. A similarly melancholy mood had been a hallmark of Picasso's 1901–4 blue-period paintings, which often portrayed figures in cabaret settings. The oval format of the dark Analytical Cubist works, which had often been employed by Rembrandt (who also used a dark palette) and other portrait painters, offered a formal resolution to the centralized composition of the portrait. Following Braque's introduction of the oval for Analytical Cubist works in the spring of 1910, Picasso painted nearly three dozen compositions in this format by the end of 1913.

PIET MONDRIAN
Dutch, 1872–1944
Composition VII in Color, 1914

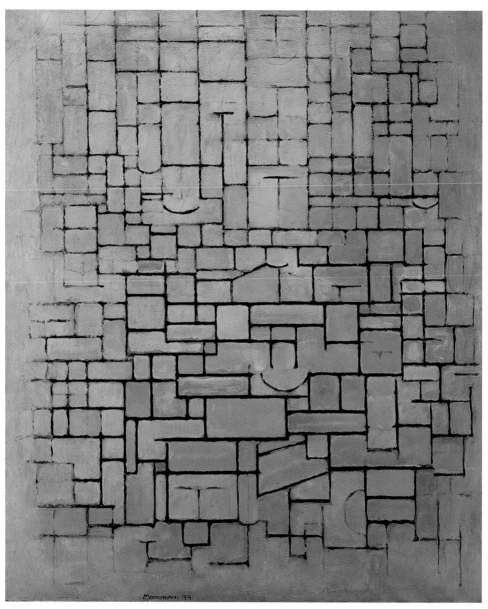

Oil on canvas; 47½ x 39⅞ in. (120.6 x 101.3 cm)
Acquired in 1983, Gift of The Burnett Foundation of Fort Worth in memory
of Anne Burnett Tandy, 1983

From the age of fourteen, when Mondrian decided to become a painter, he specialized in calm landscapes, often with isolated buildings and shadowy twilight effects of dull gold and silver. Starting around 1908, he was deeply influenced by the bright colors of Fauvism, applied in rows of rectangular brushstrokes to indicate such textures as stonework. But his exposure to the Cubism of Braque and Picasso in 1911 quickly converted him to ever deeper abstraction, and brought him back to the coloration of the poetic works of his early career. The scumbled atmospheric tones of ocher, blue gray, and pink in *Composition VII in Color* are typical of this development.

Mondrian moved to Paris in 1912 and developed his own luminous style of Cubism with paintings of trees and clusters of buildings. He based a series of compositions, including the Kimbell painting, on the complicated geometry of the streetscape near his studio in Montparnasse. He may have been inspired in part by Monet's close-up images of Rouen Cathedral from the early 1890s, each recording delicate golden, pink, and blue tones of reflected daylight. In these Cubist-inspired works, Mondrian "drew" his subject with a scaffold of black lines within, across, and

around which he delicately added color as if orchestrating atmospheric effects.

"The masses generally find my work rather vague," he wrote in January 1914, around the time he painted *Composition VII in Color*. "I construct lines and color combinations on a flat surface, in order to express *general beauty* with the utmost awareness. Nature (or that which I see) inspires me . . . but I want to come as close as possible to the truth. . . . I believe it is possible that, through horizontal and vertical lines constructed with *awareness*, but not with *calculation*, led by high intuition, and brought to harmony and rhythm, these basic forms of beauty, supplemented if necessary by other direct lines or curves, can become a work of art, as strong as it is true."

Mondrian first exhibited the Kimbell painting and its horizontal-format counterpart (Museum of Modern Art, New York) at the 1914 Salon des Indépendants in Paris, each listed in the catalogue simply as *Tableau* ("Picture"). Later that same year he revised them prior to an exhibition in The Hague, for which he entitled the Kimbell painting *Composition I*. The next year he exhibited the painting twice more, each time with a different title: *Composition H* and then *Composition VII in Color*.

JOAN MIRÓ
Spanish, 1893–1983
Heriberto Casany, 1918

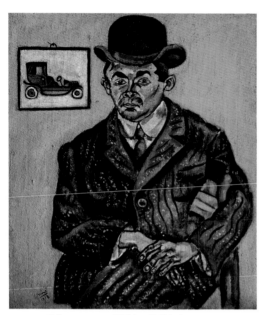

*Oil on canvas; 27⅞ x 24⁹⁄₁₆ in.
(70.2 x 62 cm)
Acquired in 1984*

"Here in Barcelona, we lack courage,"
Miró wrote in late 1917 to his
studio-mate Enric Ricart. "We, the
younger generation, could get together
and exhibit every year, all together under
the name of the 'Chrome Yellow Salon,'
for example, and pronounce virile mani-
festos. . . . We have to be men of action."
During the next few months Miró,
Ricart, and several associates banded
together, not as the Chrome Yellow group,
but as the "Courbets," in honor of the
nineteenth-century French Realist famous
for inciting controversy at official exhibitions. Their devotion to modern French

painting notwithstanding, the Courbets
were committed both to Catalan tradition
and to radical pictorial innovation. Among
the three works that Miró presented when
the Courbets first showed together in
1918, this portrait of his art-school friend
Heriberto Casany, with his spindly fingers
and the undulating folds in his tweed suit
jacket, resembles saints depicted in
medieval Catalan frescoes with gold backgrounds. Casany's attribute is quintessentially modern: a framed cartoonlike image
of an automobile, which apparently refers
to his father's cab-rental business. The lilac
tones in the background of the automobile image are intentionally discordant
with the intense orange yellow background, which is roughly and unevenly
brushed.

Treated in Fauvist fashion, with
disconcerting green, yellow, and violet
shadows, Casany's schematized features
appear animated with a life force. As Miró
explained later, ". . . even in my portraits,
where I tried to capture the immobility
of presence, . . . I tried to get the vibra-
tion of the creative spirit into my work."
Miró's treatment of his friend's fine
haberdashery, his rendering of the stripes
and texture with undulating lines and
white specks, makes the inanimate tweed
as vividly "alive" as the sitter. Just such
attention to minute details would become
the basis for the highly poetic, pulsating
pictorial language Miró developed in
the following decades to evoke tilled
fields, starry nights, and nature in all
its abundance.

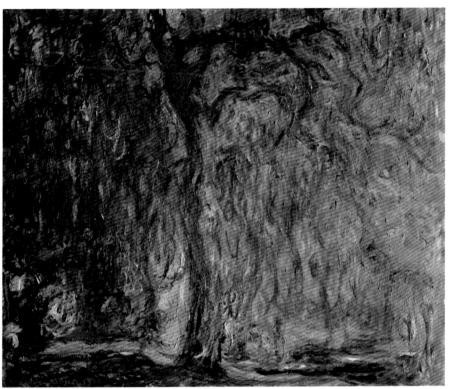

Oil on canvas; 39¼ x 47¼ in. (99.7 x 120 cm)
Acquired in 1996

Monet had painted ten *Weeping Willow* paintings by 1919, apparently in mournful response to the mass tragedy of World War I. Due to the war, Monet's luxurious compound at Giverny was for the most part emptied of his children's families and his household staff, who were either called into service or moved away from the advancing German army. His only surviving son was in constant danger at the front. At times Monet could hear artillery fire, but he refused to leave, preferring to share the fate of his gardens.

As a group, the *Weeping Willow* paintings are characterized by shadowy colors and writhing forms, as if Monet intended to express the grieving mood not simply with the subject, but also through an expressionist style of painting. They were among the very few easel-scale paintings that Monet made after 1914, when he claimed his failing eyesight was best suited for working in larger formats. The particular tree portrayed in *Weeping Willow* had pride of place on the bank of Monet's water garden, with its exotic water lilies. The tree's trunk, its cascading branches, and its reflection are all incorporated into his greatest artistic legacy, the mural-scale *Nymphéas* canvases, which were his preoccupation from 1914 until his death.

FERNAND LÉGER
French, 1881–1955
Composition, c. 1920

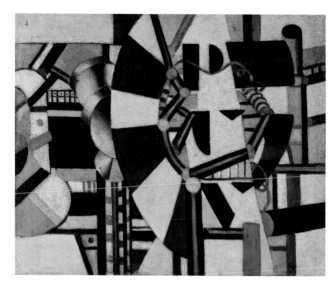

*Oil on canvas;
23¼ x 28⅞ in.
(60.3 x 73.4 cm)
Acquired in 1985*

Léger usually painted several different variations of each of his pictorial ideas, and many of the same elements in the Kimbell painting, arranged in similar interrelationships, appear in four other paintings, all dated 1920. Aside from what appear to be rods, wires, and the stenciled letters *P*, *U*, and *V* (presumably taken from some poster or sign observed on the street), it is impossible to identify specific objects in this almost totally abstract composition. But judging from Léger's other more explicitly representational works of the immediate post–World War I era, the colorful fragmented and segmented forms, all geometrical in outline, are most likely related to elements of modern machinery and architecture. Already before World War I, in a lecture presented in Paris, Léger stressed that condensation, variety, and fragmentation were the essential visual qualities of motorized, commercialized, twentieth-century experience and hence of modern painting.

Léger gave the Kimbell painting to his lifelong friend, the poet and art critic Blaise Cendrars (1887–1961), who favored the rhythms of just such fractured and fragmentary observations in his influential writings. After the war, in which they both saw combat, Léger provided illustrations for Cendrars's book *I Have Killed* (1918). Their close relationship is apparent in a poem entitled *Construction*, which Cendrars wrote in 1919: "Color, color, and more colors . . . / Here's Léger who grows like the sun in the tertiary epoch. . . . Painting becomes this great thing that moves / The wheel / Life / The machine / The human soul / A 75 mm breech / My portrait."

The work remained in Cendrars's collection until acquired by the Kimbell in 1985. As a result, its condition remains pristine; never varnished nor relined, it provides a benchmark for understanding the delicate textures and matte surfaces essential to Léger's aesthetic.

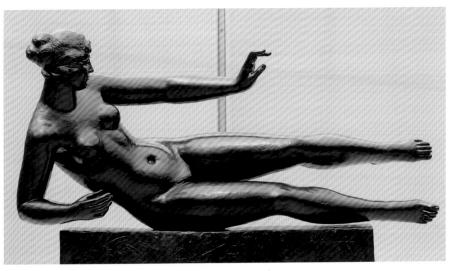

Bronze; 50¾ x 92¾ x 38 in. (129 x 235.5 x 96.5 cm)
Acquired in 1967

This is one of eight bronze and lead sculptures corresponding to the stone figure for a monument commissioned from Maillol by the city of Toulouse, France. It honors the crew of the hydroplane Croix du Sud, which left on 7 December 1936 for the twenty-fourth transatlantic crossing of a newly established mail service between France and South America, and disappeared after take-off. In Toulouse, the figure, balanced on its right hip, is positioned on an undulating drapery, perhaps to suggest wind or waves.

According to the art historian John Rewald, who visited Maillol at his winter studio in Banyuls while work on the sculpture was under way, Maillol based his idea upon a small terra-cotta he had made around 1900 showing a woman reclining on billowing drapery, as if to represent a Greek goddess at court in the clouds or on the sea. Since classical antiquity, the image of the healthy nude woman has symbolized beauty, truth, and innocence, among other abstract ideals. Maillol's own interest in the general pose first appears in his paintings of bathers around 1895, derived from works on this theme by Gauguin and Renoir.

Maillol's first work in the form of a recumbent female nude evolved from his commission to create a monument to Cézanne (finished 1925, Musée d'Orsay, Paris), whose own paintings of bathers were made in dialogue with works by Renoir. According to Rewald's account, Maillol developed the pose for *L'Air* by cutting up a version of the figure he had already developed for the Cézanne monument and subtly rearranging the parts. "Nevertheless," Rewald concluded, "the artist thus created an altogether original work which appears still more beautiful than the initial statue."

PIET MONDRIAN
Dutch, 1872–1944
Composition No. 8, 1939–42

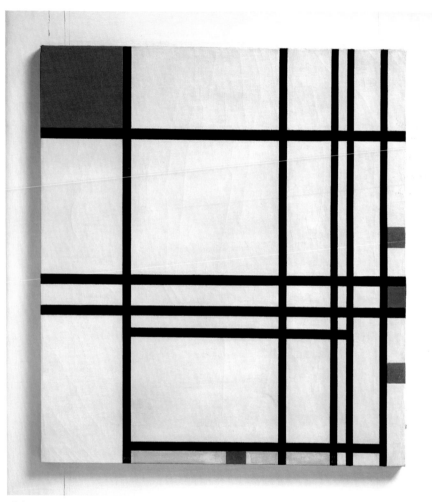

Oil on canvas; 29½ x 26¾ in. (74.9 x 67.9 cm)
Acquired in 1994

The austerely abstract style of Mondrian's grid paintings restricts itself to straight horizontal and vertical lines, and the rectangular shapes resulting from their crossing; their palette is simply black, white, and the primaries: red, yellow, and blue. The artist's intuitive arrangement of these elementary pictorial means in balance and harmony expressed his concept of "dynamic equilibrium." As he wrote: "Observing sea, sky, and stars, I sought to indicate their plastic function through a multiplicity of crossing verticals and horizontals. . . . The clarification of equilibrium through plastic art is of great importance for humanity. It reveals that although human life in time is doomed to disequilibrium, notwithstanding this, it is based on equilibrium. It demonstrates that equilibrium can become more and more living in us."

Begun in 1939 in London, where Mondrian had fled from Paris the year before, *Composition No. 8* was completed in New York, where he arrived in 1940 to escape the quickly spreading dangers of World War II. The Axis attack on Pearl Harbor in December 1941 took place just as he put the finishing touches to the work for a January 1942 exhibition. In most respects *Composition No. 8* is one of the culminating paintings in a stark, hallmark mode that Mondrian had developed by 1921 in dialogue with his fellow Dutch artists of the De Stijl movement. But a new sense of adventure, characteristic of Mondrian's final New York works, is expressed in such details as the absence of black bordering lines for the red rectangles located along the right and bottom edges.

Composition No. 8 retains its vibrant, unvarnished surface and also its original frame. Mondrian himself claimed, as far as he knew, to be the first artist to bring the painting forward from the frame rather than setting it within; in so doing, he eliminated the tendency of the traditional frame to lend an illusionistic depth to the painting. The wide, recessed borders enhance the ease and safety of handling his works and also harmonize with their spare aesthetic.

JOAN MIRÓ
Spanish, 1893–1983
Constellation: Awakening in the Early Morning, 1941

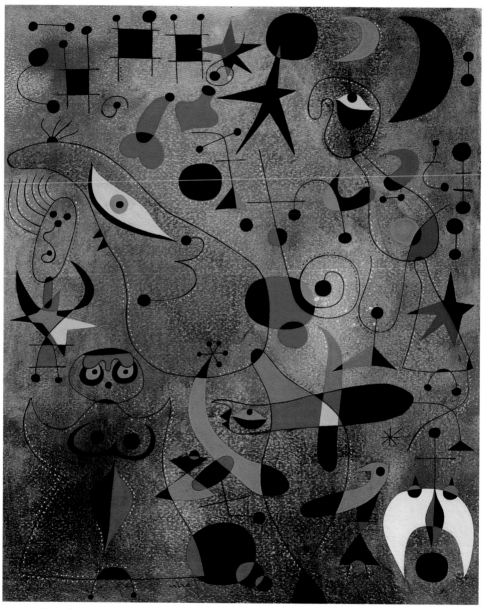

Gouache and oil wash on paper; 18⅛ x 15 in. (46 x 38 cm)
Acquired in 1993, with the generous assistance of a grant from Mr. and Mrs. Perry R. Bass

Awakening in the Early Morning is the fifteenth in a series of twenty-three small gouache and oil wash paintings on paper known as *Constellations*. For these small works, Miró extended the playfully fantastical style that he had invented in the 1920s, partly in response to the art of children and the madcap mosaics of Antoni Gaudí (1852–1926), whose park designs and buildings had transformed Miró's native Barcelona into one of the epicenters of modern design.

Teeming with weird, doodled creatures afloat in fluid fields of color, the small *Constellations* evolved, surprisingly enough, from Miró's aspirations in the late 1930s to work on a mural scale. In 1937 he moved into a building in Paris where his neighbor was the American architect Paul Nelson, who had a summer home at Varengeville on the Normandy coast. As if in response to the painter's brief article of May 1938 entitled "I Dream of a Large Studio," Nelson invited Miró to spend the summer as his guest in 1938 and paint a mural in his home. Miró returned to Varengeville the following summer and chose to remain there after France declared war on Germany in September 1939. In January 1940 he wrote to his dealer, Pierre Matisse, son of the famous artist, that the *Constellations* were under way, describing them as "very elaborate paintings . . . [with] a high degree of poetry." A month later he had already begun fifteen to twenty *Constellations*: "I feel that it is one of the most important things I have done, and even though the formats are small, they give the impression of large frescoes." He could not send any to his dealer, he explained, "[because] I must have them all in front of me the whole time—to maintain the momentum and mental state I need in order to do the entire group."

In May 1940 the Nazi offensive into Normandy forced the Miró family to flee south. They reached Majorca in July, and it was there that the Kimbell *Constellation* was finished. At this time, Miró later explained, "The night, music, and stars began to play a major role in suggesting my paintings. Music had always appealed to me . . . especially Bach and Mozart, when I went back to Majorca upon the fall of France." The series was smuggled to New York, where part of it was exhibited at the Pierre Matisse Gallery in January 1945. Symbolic of the survival of great art in the face of the ongoing war, these small works had important implications for American painters such as Jackson Pollock as they created abstract compositions permeated with free-floating lines and forms.

HENRI MATISSE
French, 1869–1954
L'Asie (Asia), 1946

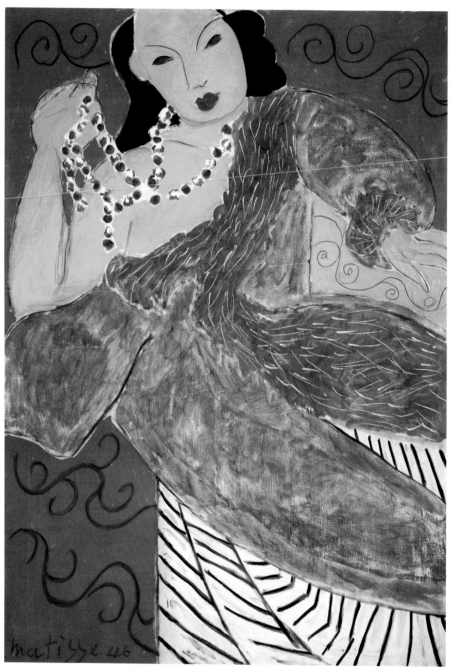

Oil on canvas; 45¾ x 32 in. (116.2 x 81.3 cm)
Acquired in 1993

Coming nearly at the end of Matisse's long career, *L'Asie* culminates his obsession with the representation of the isolated female figure in rich, exotic costumes and settings. In the work's title he was perhaps alluding to a well-established tradition in European art in which female figures were used to symbolize each of the continents. Or it may have been suggested by one of his favorite costumes, a Chinese coat lined with white fur from a Siberian tiger, here rendered in violet and blue and worn over a haute-couture striped gown. While the golden ocher skin tones of the model are characteristic of Asian peoples, the model apparently came from the Congo. Moreover, her eyes are blue and green, as if reflecting the colored beads of her necklace.

Matisse worked on *L'Asie* between his return to the hill town of Vence, in the south of France, in late November 1945, and his departure for Paris in June 1946. It was painted in his studio at the Villa Le Rêve, to which he had withdrawn in June 1943 to escape the Allied bombardment of Nice. Shortly after its completion Matisse lent *L'Asie* to his friend Pierre Bonnard, who wrote of the picture: "The red there is wonderful late in the afternoon. . . . What an intense life the colors have, and how they vary with the light! I make discoveries every day, and I have you to thank for this pleasure and instruction."

The thinly painted surface of *L'Asie*, with its fluid and seemingly rapid, spontaneous drawing, possesses an appearance of effortlessness that masks the painstaking efforts Matisse put into creating this late masterpiece, with its startling intensity of color, animated drawing, and lightness of handling. Infrared reflectography has uncovered traces of an earlier state of the composition with a black quadrant in the lower left, enlivened by arabesque lines, and a signature and date of 1946 scratched into the paint, revealing the white ground beneath; these appear in a photograph of the work published in 1951. In *L'Asie*'s finished state, Matisse converted the black quadrant to a flaming red, unifying the background as a decorative space, and redrew the arabesque lines, as well as his signature and the date, with black crayon. The earlier state of *L'Asie* documented in the photograph may have been only one of several revisions before Matisse brought the painting to its brilliant conclusion. He wrote in 1948: "I have always tried to hide my own efforts and wanted my work to have the lightness and joyousness of a springtime which never lets anyone suspect the labors it has cost."

JOAN MIRÓ
Spanish, 1893–1983
Woman Addressing the Public: Project for a Monument, 1980–81

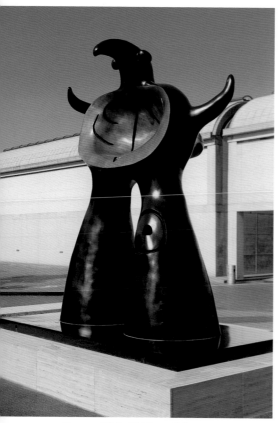

Bronze; 12 ft. 2½ in. x 8 ft.
(372.1 x 243.8 cm)
Acquired in 1996

With its peculiar proportions and anatomy, Miró's huge fantasy monument *Woman Addressing the Public* is indebted to the artist's lifelong study of the imaginative and expressive powers of the art of children. He first realized its design in 1971 as a twenty-inch plaster maquette painted white, with color accents for the eyes, arms, and sexual organs. He then made a collage with a photograph of the maquette pasted onto a photograph of the entrance to the Los Angeles County Museum of Art, intending the work as a monument of welcome and maternity. Unable to realize the project in Los Angeles, Miró submitted it as a proposal for Central Park, dedicated to the children of New York City, which did not materialize. In 1978, the Hirshhorn Museum and Sculpture Garden, in Washington, expressed interest in commissioning the still unrealized *Woman Addressing the Public*, but the project was once again abandoned. It would be nearly a quarter of a century before his playful "monster" would finally have a place of honor outside an important museum, the Kimbell. The final work, cast in an edition of four when the artist was eighty-seven, weighs roughly three tons.

The art of children was indeed a major source of inspiration for Miró, and whimsical creatures related in appearance to *Woman Addressing the Public* began to appear in his paintings and drawings in the 1920s. It was only after World War II, however, that he began to fashion little statuettes of similar figures, perhaps inspired by the surreal sculptures of his fellow countryman Picasso. Miró began to develop his ideas as sculpture at full scale in the 1950s and 1960s, in effect embarking on a second career as a sculptor expressly interested in art for public spaces. The female creature with arms outspread was his favorite sculptural subject, and *Woman Addressing the Public* is his grandest and ultimate statement of the theme.

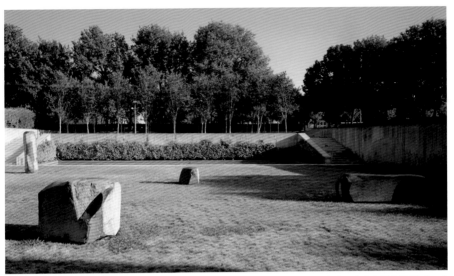

Basalt; left to right: h. 84 in. (213.4 cm); h. 40 in. (101.6 cm); h. 24 in. (61 cm); l. 96½ (245.1 cm)
Acquired in 1983, gift of the Isamu Noguchi Foundation in honor of Louis I. Kahn and the
Kimbell Art Museum. With thanks and goodbye to Shaindy Fenton

Around 1980, the great twentieth-century stage designer, furniture maker, and sculptor Isamu Noguchi was inspired to create a sculptural ensemble for the grass courtyard on the south side of the Kimbell in honor of the architect Louis Kahn. The two men had been friends—they worked together in the early 1960s on a never-realized playground for Manhattan's Riverside Park—and in 1961 Noguchi had created an outdoor sculpture plaza in downtown Fort Worth for the former First National City Bank building. Arranged on the Kimbell site in August 1983, *Constellation* makes a most successful addition to the spirit of the building through allusion to one of Louis Kahn's favorite topics, the prehistory of architecture. In particular, it recalls the mysterious menhirs that are among the earliest structures made by humankind.

Drawing upon his American-Japanese heritage, Noguchi deserves much of the credit for introducing into Western sculpture the spirit of Japanese garden design, with carefully chosen rocks placed to create a setting of intuitive harmony. His first major project of this kind was the garden for the UNESCO headquarters in Paris, finished in 1958.

Given his longstanding interest in lunar themes, it was perhaps the basaltlike moon rocks brought back to earth in 1969 that encouraged Noguchi to use basalt monoliths as a primary material in the 1970s. He much admired the quality of these obdurate stones, which were carved in his studio on the island of Shikoku, Japan. The igneous rock, rich in iron and black augite, weathers brown; by leaving it untouched on some sides while chiseling and polishing it on others, Noguchi made his material yield a palette of different colors.

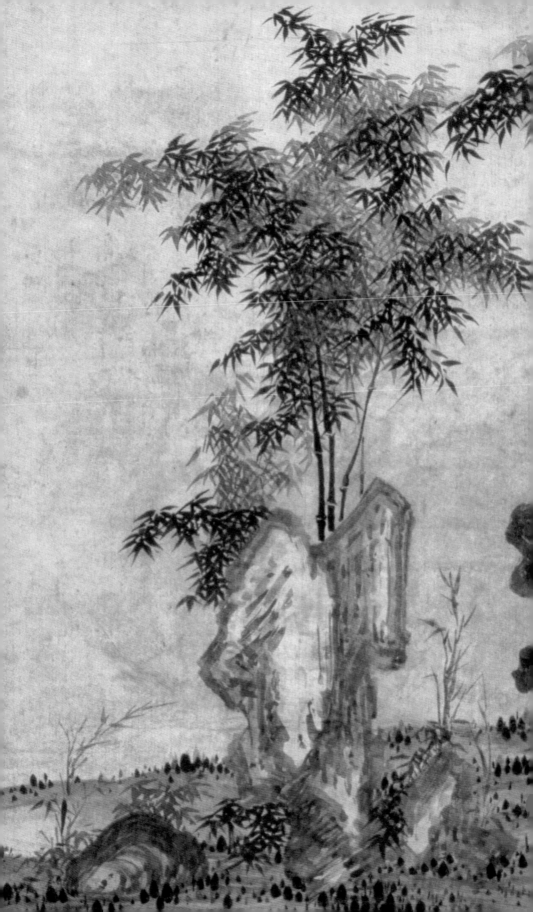

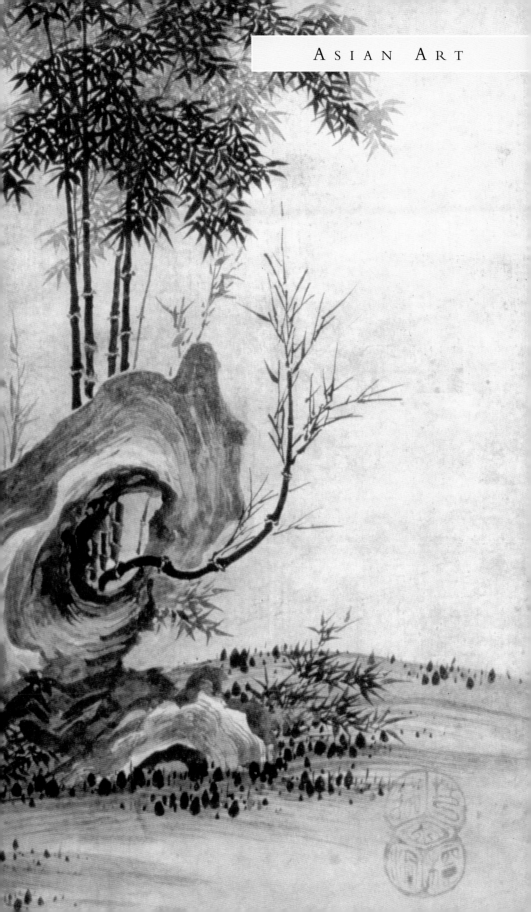

Seated Buddha with Two Attendants
Mathura, Uttar Pradesh, India; Kushan period, A.D. 82

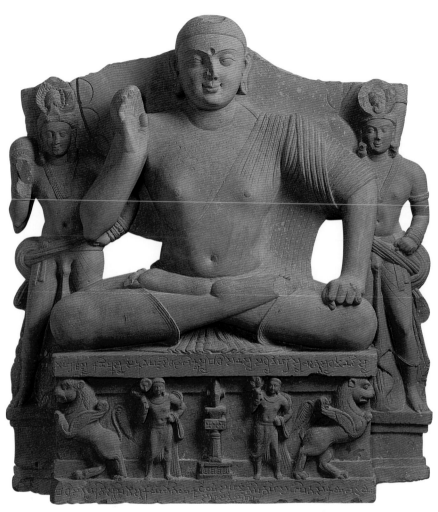

Red sandstone; h. 36⅛ in. (93 cm)
Acquired in 1986

The earliest images of the Buddha and bodhisattvas appear in the first century A.D., during the Kushan period. The Kushans ruled from the first to third century in much of northwestern India and the ancient region of Gandhara (parts of present-day Pakistan and Afghanistan). The artistic conception of the Buddha in human form grew out of theological changes that resulted ultimately in the formation of the Mahayana (Great Vehicle) sect, and which created the need for devotional images as spiritual aids. Two distinct styles of sculpture emerged during the Kushan period, one associated with the region of Gandhara and one with the city of Mathura in present-day Uttar Pradesh. Mathura was the second capital of the Kushans and a major center of art production, which developed there out of the indigenous Indian traditions, and made much use of the local mottled red sandstone.

This *Seated Buddha with Two Attendants* conforms to a standard early Mathura type. In his personification as Shakyamuni, the teacher, the Buddha is portrayed as a traditional yogi, seated on a throne, and dressed in the guise of a monk. A diaphanous robe is worn over the left shoulder leaving the right shoulder bare. The sensitive modeling of the soft, plump flesh gives little hint of the musculature underneath but still endows the body with a sense of solidity and mass. The hair is smooth like a cap, and the cranial bump *(ushnisha)*, now missing, would have appeared as a twisted bun or coil of hair *(kapardin)*. The right hand is raised in the gesture of reassurance *(abhayamudra)*. As prescribed by the scriptures, the palms of the hands and soles of the Buddha's feet are marked with the lotus and the wheel, symbols of his divinity and teaching. Carved in high relief with generously modeled and sensuous torsos, the royal attendants flanking the Buddha have similar stylized facial features and archaic smiles as their lord. The sculpture is carved in the form of a stela and includes other symbols and figures referring to the Buddha's life and exalted status as a universal monarch. The large halo behind his head represents the sun and proclaims his divinity. The pillar, topped by a wheel centered in the relief panel of the throne, is symbolic of preaching and refers to the Buddha's first sermon at Sarnath. The two figures holding flywhisks, flanking the pillar, and the rampant lions signify the Buddha's royal heritage.

The sculpture is inscribed with a date (year 4 of Maharaja Kanishka) and states that it was installed by Dharmanandi, a companion of the Buddhist monk Bodhisena, in his own worship hall with his parents and paternal aunt Bhadra.

Standing Bodhisattva
Pakistan (ancient region of Gandhara); Kushan period, 2nd–3rd century A.D.

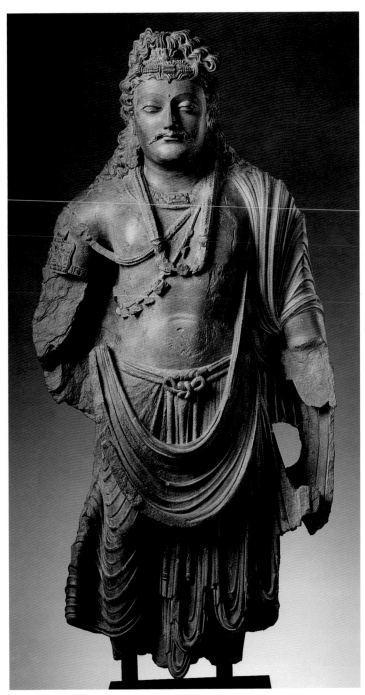

Gray schist; h. 59⅛ in. (150.2 cm)
Acquired in 1997

Representations of bodhisattvas emerge at the same time as images of the Buddha in both Gandharan and Mathuran art, in the first century A.D. Enlightened beings who voluntarily postpone their own achievement of *nirvana* in order to assist mankind on the path to salvation, bodhisattvas are sometimes shown in Gandharan art as attendants to the Buddha and sometimes stand alone. They possess some of the same superhuman traits as the Buddha, having elongated earlobes and the tuft of hair between the eyebrows *(urna)*, and display similar gestures *(mudras)*, but bodhisattvas lack the cranial protuberance *(ushnisha)*. At first their images were distinguished from those of the Buddha primarily by their secular attire, such as a turban and earrings, a sophisticated coiffure and mustache, and noble robes and jewelry, all alluding to the Buddha's life as a prince before attaining enlightenment. Eventually, individual bodhisattvas were also identified by the attributes they held in their hands or symbols worn in their hair.

This majestic figure of a *Standing Bodhisattva* is lavishly attired in the rich dress and jewelry of a Kushana prince or nobleman from the ancient region of Gandhara (parts of present-day Pakistan and Afghanistan). The powerful, fleshy torso, the rounded musculature of the chest and abdomen, and the long, flowing hair further emphasize the figure's regal bearing. The strong, round chin, straight nose, and smooth oval face adorned by an elegantly twirling mustache reflect the mixture of races and cosmopolitan nature of first millennium Gandharan art and culture. Although strongly Hellenizing in profile, the figure is dressed as a thoroughly Indian ruler, wearing the *dhoti*, bare-chested, with a sash casually slung over the shoulder and draped in an elegant curve over the forearm. The juxtaposition of distinctly Western classical features, particularly the realistically rendered drapery and musculature, with the indigenous elements of dress and attributes, typifies Gandharan Buddhist sculpture.

Although both arms are missing, the position of the left arm indicates that it held a water pot *(kundika)* containing *amrita* (the elixir of life) and a symbolic promise of salvation in the future, the spiritual role of the bodhisattva Maitreya, the Buddha of the Future. In this case, the right arm would have been raised in the *abhayamudra*, the gesture of reassurance.

Standing Buddha
Pakistan (ancient region of Gandhara); Kushan period, c. 2nd–3rd century A.D.

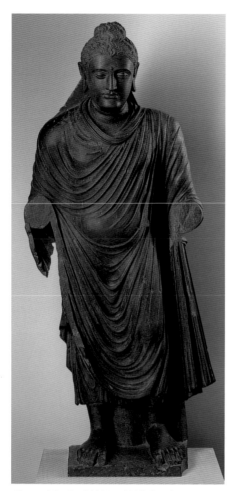

Gray schist; h. 51½ in. (130.8 cm)
Acquired in 1967

It was during the Kushan period (first to third century A.D.) in India that the image of the Buddha was first realized in human form and the basic repertoire of Buddhist iconography was established. Among the elements specified in the early literature are the *lakshana*, auspicious physical attributes or marks on the Buddha's body indicating his status as a supernatural being. The most important *lakshana* were:

the *ushnisha*, the cranial bump on top of the Buddha's head, and the *urna*, the tuft of hair between the eyebrows, both signs of the Buddha's superior wisdom; webbed fingers and toes on the hands and feet; and wheel markings on the palms of the hands and soles of the feet.

One of the two distinct styles of sculpture that emerged during the Kushan period was produced in Gandhara (parts of present-day Pakistan and Afghanistan) between the first and sixth centuries. Typically carved from gray schist, Gandharan sculptures were iconographically similar but stylistically distinct from their Mathuran counterparts in northern India. Gandharan art was heavily influenced by contact with the Greek and Roman traditions of the Mediterranean world. From the fourth century B.C., when Alexander the Great conquered as far east as the border of India, until the fifth century A.D., these regions maintained frequent trade and other contacts with the Mediterranean.

This Gandharan *Standing Buddha* image would have been carved into a rock-temple niche. Monastic robes cover the figure's shoulders in heavy folds of naturalistic drapery deriving from classical models. The serene, idealized face, here blending classical and Indian types, is smooth and oval-shaped with a straight nose and well-defined eyes, shown half-closed as if in a state of meditation. The hair is rendered in wavy lines, culminating in the *ushnisha*, here depicted as a wavy topknot. The *urna* is conceived as a raised circle between the brows. The arms would have been raised in one of the five standard gestures *(mudras)* that the Buddha makes.

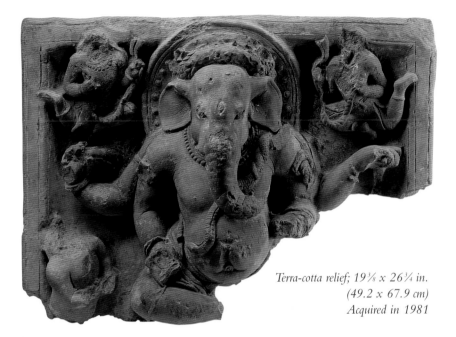

Terra-cotta relief; 19⅜ x 26¾ in.
(49.2 x 67.9 cm)
Acquired in 1981

It was not until the Gupta period (A.D. 320–600) that the forms of many Hindu deities became standardized, and the art of this period is therefore considered India's classical age. Sensuously modeled figures with softly rounded contours and a lively, elegant silhouette characterize the highly sophisticated style of sculpture that was produced during this period.

Ganesha is the elephant-headed son of Shiva, one of the three most important deities of the Hindu pantheon, and his consort, the goddess Parvati. He is widely worshiped as the remover of obstacles and the bestower of good fortune, prosperity, and health. The origin of his hybrid body—consisting of an elephant's head with one tusk and an infant's torso with distended belly—is related in Hindu legends. Parvati is said to have created Ganesha in human form to act as her door guardian. When he refused to admit Shiva to Parvati's chamber, the god cut off the child's head. In order to placate the distressed Parvati, Shiva replaced the head with that of the first living thing he could find—an elephant. Hindu deities are often depicted with multiple heads and arms, a physical expression of the multiplicity of their superhuman powers. Due to the damaged condition of this superb terra-cotta relief, it is no longer possible to identify the deity's usual attributes—an axe, a rosary, and a bowl of sweetmeats—which would have been held in his hands. The serpent hanging across his torso signifies his relationship to Shiva, who also bears this attribute.

Many Hindu brick temples were decorated with terra-cotta plaques such as this one. The plaques are distinguished by their naturalistic modeling, well illustrated in the sensuous and powerful sculpting of this image, which is unusually expressive, and notable also for its large size and early date.

Standing Female Deity
Rajasthan, India; Medieval period, 10th or 11th century

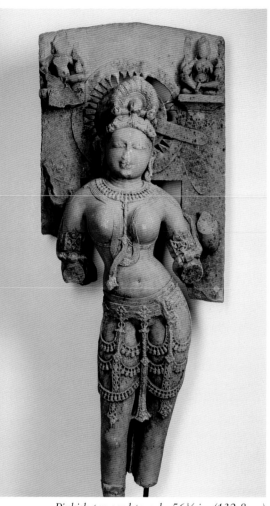

Pinkish tan sandstone; h. 56¼ in. (132.8 cm)
Acquired in 1968

The Medieval period (c. A.D. 600–1200) in India witnessed an unprecedented growth in temple building. Throughout India, both the external walls and interior spaces of temples were copiously decorated with exquisitely carved stone sculptures. Most of the temples are Hindu or Jain, for in both of these religions the building of temples and consecration of images is the surest means of gaining liberation *(moksha)* from the endless cycle of rebirth. The interior shrines of the temples are generally reserved for images of the primary deities to which the temples are dedicated, while the sculptural programs include a vast array of gods, goddesses, dancers, and musicians, as well as mythological and other narrative scenes.

Fertility goddesses of different types were an important component of early Indian nature cults and were eventually assimilated into the symbolic repertoire of later Indian religious art. These youthful, sensuous figures personify fertility, maternity, and Indian ideals of feminine beauty, various guises expressing different aspects of the female character—triumphant and fierce, as well as passive and dependent.

This delicately carved figure of a goddess, with its softly rounded forms and crisply delineated ornamentation, is typical of temple sculpture from the western Indian state of Rajasthan. The large size of the figure and attendants attest to her importance, and the halo and sword projecting from behind her head signify her power. However, since two of the original four arms, and all the attributes they held, are missing, her identity cannot be firmly established. It has been suggested that she may represent one of the sixteen Jain Vidyadevis (goddesses of learning); Mahamanasi, the sixteenth Vidyadevi, bears a sword as one of her attributes. If this is the case, then the small seated figures in the corners are probably a *yaksha/yahski* couple (male and female nature deities), often found with Jain figures.

The last significant phase of Buddhism as a dominant religion in India occurred under the Pala and Sena dynasties (c. A.D. 730–c. 1197), which ruled eastern India (the present-day states of West Bengal, Bihar, and Bangladesh) from the late eighth to the early thirteenth century. As the Buddhist holy land was located in and around south Bihar, monks from all over Asia made pilgrimages to eastern India to study and visit its famous sites. A prodigious amount of art was produced during the Pala period, but, with the destruction of many Buddhist monuments and sculpture during the Muslim invasions of the twelfth century and the subsequent rise of Hinduism as an organized religion, little of its architectural context survives.

The increasing complexity of imagery and iconographic detail in late Pala art paralleled the growing popularity of Esoteric Buddhism in eastern India. Khasarpana Lokeshvara, the Esoteric form of the immensely popular bodhisattva of compassion, Avalokiteshvara, was created by the absorption of Hindu elements into Buddhism and appears frequently in Pala art. In this stela, the youthful, bejeweled figure is seated on a double-lotus throne, surrounded by lotus blossoms and the deity's four standard attendants: the goddesses Tara and Bhrikuti to the left and right of the bodhisattva's knees; and, on the base, the needle-nosed Sucimukha, who imbibes the nectar of grace, at the left rear, and the plump, fearsome Hayagriva at the right front. In addition, the princely Sudhanakumara, who carries a book under his left arm, is shown at the front left of the base, while two tiny

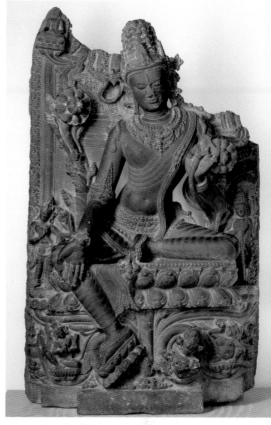

Gray schist; h. 49¼ in. (124.9 cm)
Acquired in 1970

figures of the donor couple are shown kneeling behind Hayagriva. Due to damage to the upper part of the stela, only one remains from the figures of the five jina Buddhas, the rulers of the Buddhist universe. The elegant proportions, attenuated waistline, richly carved surface decoration, complex iconography, and almost feminine poise of the bodhisattva are hallmarks of the mature Pala style.

Standing Buddha Shakyamuni
Nepal; Lichchhavi dynasty, 7th century A.D.

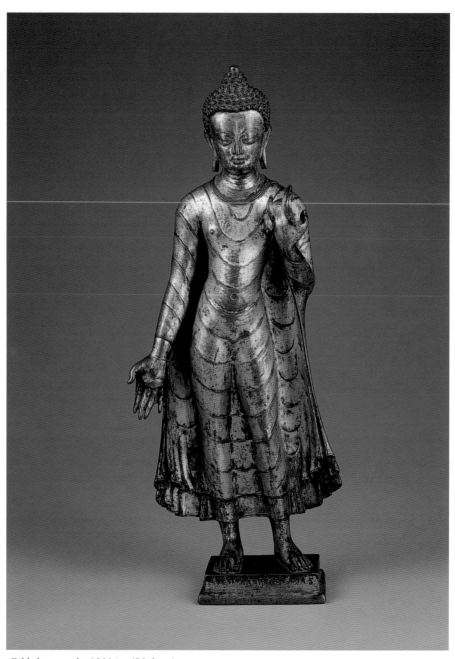

Gilded copper; h. 19¾ in. (50.2 cm)
Acquired in 1979

Nepal derived much of the inspiration for its art and culture from its southern neighbor India. Both Hinduism and Buddhism were introduced from India at an early date, with Buddhism enjoying its greatest success between the eighth and the thirteenth centuries. The early Buddhist sculpture of Nepal is nearly indistinguishable in style from Indian work of the Gupta period (A.D. 320–600), combining as it does the Sarnath and Mathura idioms of north India. Much of Nepalese art was created by a minority community known as the Newars, highly skilled and creative metalsmiths who were concentrated in the Kathmandu Valley. This image is a rare, early example of bronze sculpture, a tradition that was to flourish in Nepal in the following centuries.

The slim, richly gilded figure represents the historical Buddha, Shakyamuni, Sage of the Shakya clan. He displays a number of the physical signs that had come to represent the Buddha's divinity—the cranial protuberance (ushnisha), elongated earlobes, three parallel folds in the neck, webbed fingers and toes, and palms marked by a wheel. He stands in a graceful pose with the weight on the right leg and the hip thrust gently out.

The smooth, fleshy contours of the body are revealed by a thin, clinging garment with cascading pleats delineated into a threadlike surface design. The upper end of the robe is gathered in the left hand, the right bestowing the gesture of charity (varadamudra). While the clearly delineated striations of the garment completely covering the body show the influence of Mathura Buddhas, the transparency and wide flaring hem of the robe are more typical of images from Sarnath. The "snail-shell" pattern of curled hair, half-closed eyes, and lack of an urna between the eyebrows are typical Gupta features. The Nepalese origin of the sculpture is most evident in the expression of the face.

The important inscription on the base is in a script derived from Gupta India that was in use in Nepal during the Lichchhavi period (c. A.D. 300–879). The Lichchhavis, from Bihar in north India, entered the Kathmandu Valley in the third century A.D. and gave rise to an artistic tradition that originally borrowed from Tibet and India but increasingly evolved into a distinctly Nepalese style. Although the inscription is undated, features of the script allow it to be assigned to the seventh century, which is consistent with the style of the image.

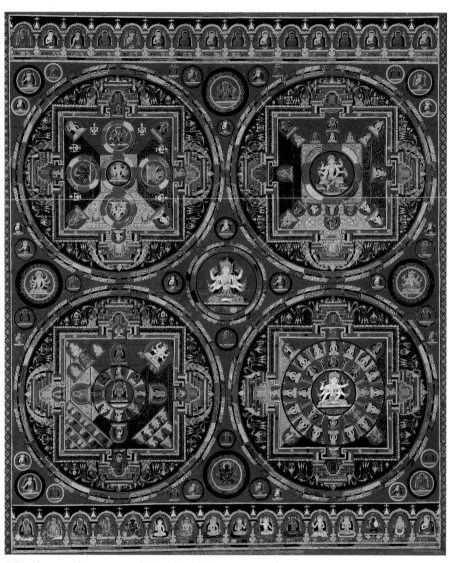

Thangka, gouache on cotton; 35 x 29 in. (88.9 x 73.7 cm)
Acquired in 2000

Most Tibetan art was created in connection with the complex rituals and meditational practices of Vajrayana Buddhism (the Diamond Path), in which mandalas (cosmic diagrams) are employed as visual representations of the sacred realms inhabited by a host of deities. Used as aids in the process of spiritual enlightenment, *thangkas* are painted portable scrolls that depict sacred icons or mandalas. Forming a focus of visualization and meditation, the *thangka* is also believed to house a deity, acting as an intermediary between the practitioner and the divinity.

This extraordinary *thangka* is from a series of paintings that illustrate mandalas from the *Vajravali* (Diamond Garland) text. They were commissioned by the monk Ngorchen Kunga Sangpo (1382–1456), founder of the Ngor monastery, in honor of his late teacher Lama Sasang Pakpa (died c. 1380) sometime between 1429, the year he founded the monastery, and his death in 1456. An inscription at the top of the painting identifies this *thangka* as the "fourteenth painting of the *Vajravali*." Along the bottom border are three sets of inscriptions. The central inscription reads: "May the heart's intent of the holy glorious Lama Sasang Pakpa be fulfilled." The right inscription reads: "Bless the monk Kunga Sangpo." Two mantras are inscribed at the left.

In this highly complex and elaborate work, four individual mandalas have been incorporated into an all-encompassing mandala of the Five Pancharaksha Goddesses. In the upper left is a mandala of these goddesses, popular deities for protection against sickness, misfortune, and calamity, at the center of which is the twelve-armed golden goddess Mahapratisara, surrounded in the four directions by the other four Pancharaksha goddesses, and eight other goddesses. The upper-right mandala depicts the six-armed golden goddess of wealth, Vasudhara, accompanied by eighteen deities, all associated with wealth and

prosperity. The lower-right mandala portrays the three-faced, eight-armed, white Ushnishavijaya, goddess of long life, surrounded by eight Ushnisha deities. The mandala at the lower left is that of Bhagvati Mahavidya, who is white and six-armed and sits in the upper-right corner of the mandala. In the center are nine planetary deities. The subsidiary imagery in this mandala is associated with protecting the initiate from negative planetary influences.

Interwoven around the four mandalas in the main field is another, floating mandala scheme consisting of the Five Pancharaksha Goddesses, who appear at the four cardinal directions and in the center, surrounded by thirty-five small Buddhas of Confession. Along the top border are sixteen seated Buddhas in niches. At the bottom, the row of sixteen seated figures consists of fifteen Buddhist forms of the World Gods, and the donor lama, Kunga Sangpo, the last figure on the right.

A classic mandala from one of the most famous sets of its type, this exquisitely painted and exceptionally well-preserved work is accorded added importance by the rarity of dated material from this period of Tibetan art.

Harihara
Style of Prasat Andet, Kompong Thom, Cambodia; Pre-Angkor period, c. A.D. 675–700

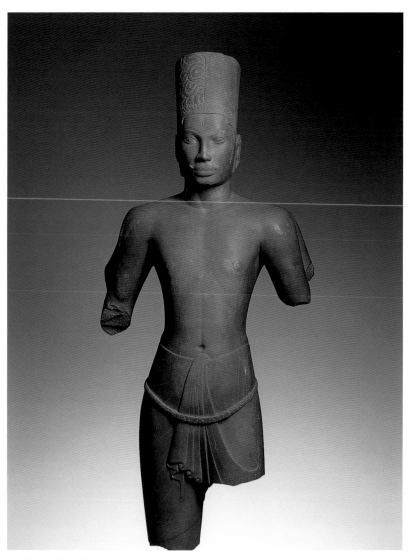

Sandstone, h. 45½ in. (115.6 cm)
Acquired in 1988

Before the emergence in the early ninth century of the powerful Angkor kingdom, which dominated Cambodia as well as large areas of Vietnam, Thailand, and Laos, this region was divided into a number of early Khmer cultures. Contact with India had already seen the introduction of Buddhism and Brahmanism, along with associated sculptural and architectural styles. While this Indian heritage is still evident, by the sixth century Khmer sculpture clearly demonstrates the naturalism and mastery of sculpture in the round that was to distinguish future Cambodian art. This pre-Angkor sculpture (sixth to eighth century) is unsurpassed in its grace and spirituality, its remarkable naturalism of anatomy and stance, and its restraint in decoration. This image of the Hindu deity Harihara, with its delicately modeled musculature, supple articulation of limbs, and slender torso draped in a simple *sampot*, is characteristic of the finest pre-Angkor style.

The cult of Harihara was of great importance in early Cambodia, combining the potency of two of the most powerful Hindu gods, Shiva and Vishnu. Shiva (Hara), embodiment of the forces of destruction and fertility, is indicated on the sculpture's proper right by the matted and twisted locks forming his characteristic headdress *(jakamukata)* and by half of his potent third eye. Vishnu (Hari), preserver of the world who will give rise to Brahma, the creator, after a cosmic sleep following the end of the current cycle of existence, is implied in the tall miter on the left. Harihara embodies the equilibrium between these two irreconcilable forces that is necessary for cosmic balance.

Some Harihara images are distinguished by garments and attributes from head to feet, but this one is identifiable only from its head details. The almond-shaped eyes, delicately traced brows, and subtly molded lips and nose have the particularity of portraiture, an individualized treatment that may represent the royal patron who commissioned the sculpture. It strongly resembles the National Museum of Cambodia's Harihara statue from the seventh-century monument of Prasat Andet. In Angkor times, Khmer monarchs chose posthumous names incorporating the name of the deity with whom they wished to be identified, but in the absence of any inscription we can only surmise that intention here.

The Bodhisattva Maitreya
Prakhon Chai, Buriram province, Thailand; Pre-Angkor period, late 8th century A.D.

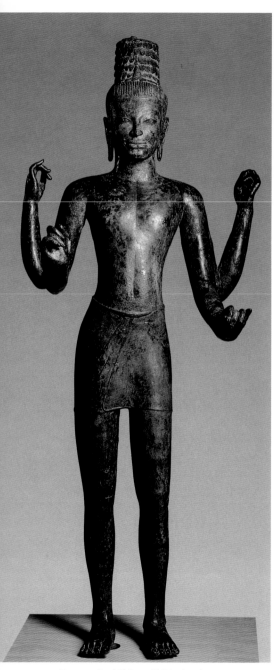

Bronze; h. 48¼ in. (122.5 cm)
Acquired in 1965

Buddhism and Brahmanism probably spread from India to Southeast Asia early in the first millennium, when traders established inland and maritime routes connecting the Mediterranean with China and the states between, including India. The religions coexisted harmoniously for centuries, often modified by local beliefs. While a number of pre-thirteenth-century rulers espoused Brahmanism, there were also many important Buddhist establishments in the region. Even in kingdoms with Hindu monarchs, Buddhist monks played a role.

The earliest Buddhist images in Southeast Asia were probably brought from India. Mostly bronze, they provided the techniques and the stylistic vocabulary that emerged in later Southeast Asian productions. By A.D. 600, regional characteristics had developed that clearly distinguish the sculptures of Champa, Thailand, Myanmar, Cambodia, Java, and Sumatra from their Indian models and also from each other.

Among the most distinguished pre-Angkor bronzes are those unearthed in 1964 in Prakhon Chai, in northeastern Thailand. This region was under the sway of Cambodia from the sixth century, when chieftains of the mountains separating Thailand and Cambodia pushed Khmer hegemony further west, influencing architecture and sculpture in the region until the fourteenth century. The Kimbell's Maitreya, one of the largest and most

Nao Bell
Possibly Hunan province, China; Western Zhou dynasty,
c. 10th century B.C.

This impressive, heavily cast *nao* bell is ornamented on each side with eighteen conical studs arranged in three rows, separated by bands of scrolling thunder pattern *(leiwen)* decoration, and surrounded by borders of fine thread-relief. The flat underside is embellished with deeply cast scrolling volutes. The tubular shank bears a raised collar decorated with two highly stylized animal masks *(taotie)*, constituted by large, rounded "eyes" amid a scroll pattern.

During their brief period of manufacture in the second and first millennium B.C., ritual chime bells bore a political and intellectual significance hardly suggested by their function as musical instruments, and embodied some of the highest technical skills of Chinese civilization. Originating along the middle reaches of the Yellow River in the north of China during the Anyang period of the Shang dynasty (c. 1350–1045 B.C.), the *nao* represents the earliest form of chime bell from any culture in the ancient world. It has no clapper and would produce sound by being mounted on a wooden stand with its mouth pointing upwards, and then being struck on the outside with a T-shaped wooden mallet. Each bell had two points of contact that would produce different tones.

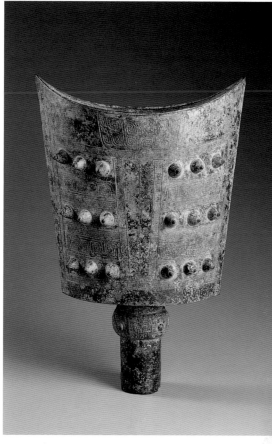

Bronze; h. 19 in. (48.3 cm)
Acquired in 1995

This *nao* bell is an exceptionally fine example of the southern type produced in the region of the Yangzi River, in Hunan province, in the early Western Zhou dynasty (c. 1100–771 B.C.). While northern *nao* bells were produced in sets of three and formed part of a ritual orchestra, *nao* bells of the southern type are all single specimens and never form part of a chimed set. Although similar in shape to northern *nao*, southern *nao* are much larger, heavier, more elaborately decorated, and may have served a very different ritual function. Rather than musical instruments in a ritual orchestra, the southern *nao* may have functioned more like Buddhist temple bells or later European church bells.

Jar with Stamped Decoration

Probably Jiangxi province, China; Eastern Zhou dynasty, 7th–4th century B.C.

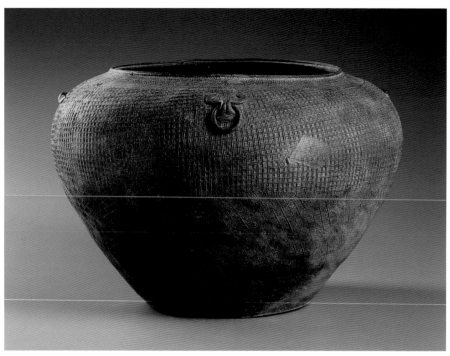

High-fired earthenware; h. 10⅜ in. (26.4 cm)
Acquired in 1996

The ceramics of the early first millennium B.C. from Jiangxi province in central China are characterized by stamped or impressed geometric designs on high-fired earthenwares, predominantly on vessels of simple forms with high shoulders, short necks, and broad mouths. The *Jar with Stamped Decoration* has an unusually wide, buoyant form and is decorated with three bands of delicately stamped geometric designs: a wave pattern of fine, closely spaced lines around the mouth; a "waffle" pattern where double parallel lines crisscross to form multiple squares on the shoulder; and hatched squares aligned diagonally on the body. On opposite sides of the shoulders

are two pairs of applied handles: one set of rings (one lost) attached by lugs, and one pair of horizontal twisted cords.

Despite the freedom with which the pot was thrown and decorated, there is considerable refinement in its simplicity of shape and crispness of design. During the Eastern Zhou dynasty (770–221 B.C.), one extreme within the ceramic tradition was distinguished by its magnificent imitations of the ornate bronzes of the period. This jar represents the other extreme—simple, elegant, "true" ceramic forms decorated with integrated surface designs based largely on contemporary fabric and textile patterns. Its comparatively large size and varied decorative

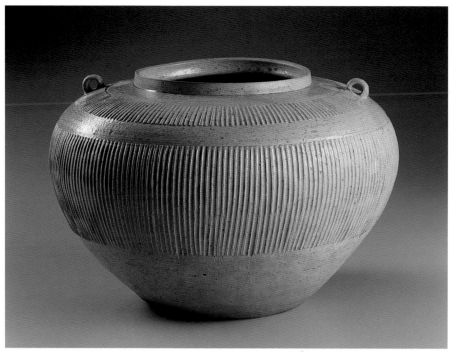

Stoneware with yellowish green glaze; h. 9⅝ in. (24.5 cm)
Acquired in 1995

patterns indicate that it may have been used for ritual as well as utilitarian purposes.

From the end of the Warring States period (475–221 B.C.) through the Han dynasty (206 B.C.–A.D. 220), glazed stoneware vessels were routinely produced in northern Zhejiang and southern Jiangsu provinces to serve as funerary storage jars. These vessels, many of which derive their shapes from bronze *guan* (ritual jar) or *hu* (ritual wine vessel) prototypes, are typically decorated in an overall stamped pattern, or with a combination of incised lines and raised bands or ribs. Their glaze, restricted to the upper surfaces, was probably produced by sifting

dry wood-ash, or a mixture of dry clay and ash, over the damp pots before firing. These proto-porcelaneous wares are the predecessors of the finer kaolin-clay, high-fire wares developed toward the end of the Tang dynasty (A.D. 618–907).

The shape of the *Jar with Ribbed Decoration*, as well as its lug handles, imitates bronze *jian* vessels (ritual water vessels), but in the process of simulation, the potter has adapted the form and decoration to this older and more venerable art form. The smooth, regular profile is evidence of being worked on a potter's wheel. It was probably placed in a tomb burial, and would have contained foodstuffs for the deceased.

Horse and Rider
Probably Shaanxi province, China; Western Han dynasty, 2nd–1st century B.C

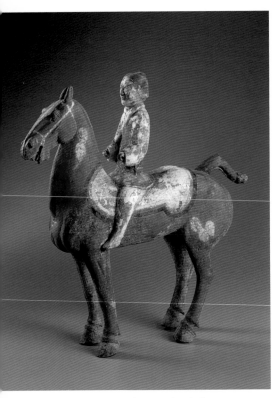

*Earthenware with painted polychrome
decoration; h. 22⅜ in. (57.5 cm)
Acquired in 1994*

Tombs of the Han dynasty (206 B.C.–
A.D. 220) were typically furnished
with model figures and other objects
believed to be necessary for a safe journey
to the afterlife. Historical records indicate
that when important military officials
died, the imperial Han court would

give them elaborate funerals, including
a full military cortege. It is likely that this
figure of a horse and rider was originally
part of a model funerary retinue
comprised of soldiers and cavalrymen
that would have been placed in such a
tomb. It is closely related stylistically to a
group of military figures excavated in a
Western Han (206 B.C.–A.D. 9) tomb in
Yangjiawan village, Shaanxi province.

To meet the increased demand for
burial goods during the Han dynasty,
these figures were produced in great
numbers. Despite their standardized
types, and simple sculptural techniques,
however, the Kimbell group displays great
vitality of form and considerable descriptive and expressive power.

As with much Western Han sculpture,
the artist has here focused attention on
the figures' heads. That of the horse is
boldly sculpted and precisely rendered,
suggesting the physical attributes of the
Samanthian breed from Xinjiang province
in Central Asia, prized by the Chinese
for its superior strength and speed. The
rider's face is characteristic of the period,
with simple and abbreviated, yet naturally
modeled, features. In both figures, the
strong contours help to define a sense of
volume and mass, enhanced by the addition of colorful pigments, which delineate
the rider's costume and the horse's saddle
and harness. Despite their relatively
modest size, the pair possess a monumental quality normally associated with
more massive Han stone sculptures.

Cocoon-Shaped Jar with Cloud-Scroll Design
Possibly Luoyang, Henan province, China; Western Han dynasty,
late 2nd or early 1st century B.C.

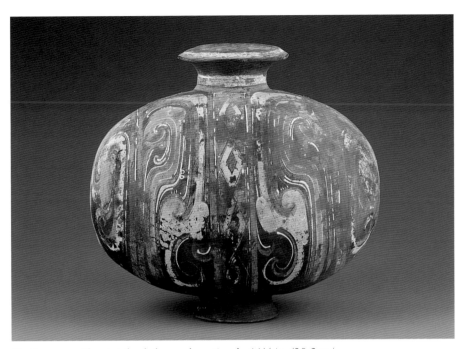

Earthenware with painted polychrome decoration; h. 11½ in. (29.2 cm)
Acquired in 1995

This handsome jar, dating from the Western Han dynasty, would have served as a mortuary object *(mingqi)*, placed in a tomb as a substitute for the more valuable bronze and lacquer vessels used in daily life. Along with a variety of other funerary earthenware objects, attendant figures, and animals, richly decorated vessels of this kind were intended to serve the spirit of the deceased in the afterlife.

The silk industry, dating back to the third millennium B.C., was a principal source of wealth for the Chinese economy during the Han dynasty. The distinctive, plump ovoid form of this jar imitates the silkworm's cocoon, a shape that appears to have been produced only from the end of the Zhou dynasty (c. 1100–221 B.C.) through the Western Han period.

In these later examples, the surface of the jar was either burnished before firing to a glossy black or painted after firing with designs in white, green, red, and lavender. These designs are similar to those seen on lacquer objects of the period. On this painted example, the drifting cloud-scroll *(yunwen)* motif, which flanks a central vertical panel of diamond-shaped lozenges, is evocative of the celestial realms of a Taoist immortal paradise. During the reign of the Han emperor Wudi (140–87 B.C.), fascination with the idea of the celestial journey and the Taoist search for immortality reached a climax, and gave tangible definition to the ethereal decoration of painted earthenware vessels such as this.

Standing Dog
China; Eastern Han dynasty, c. 1st century A.D.

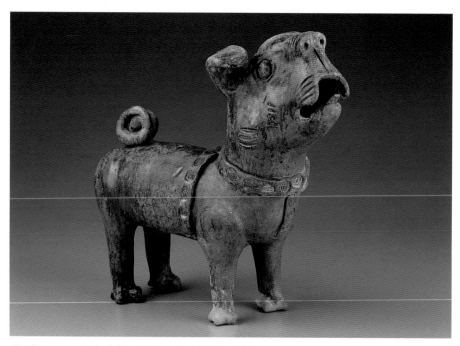

Earthenware with lead-fluxed glaze; h. 12¼ in. (31.1 cm)
Acquired in 1995

During the Eastern Han dynasty (A.D. 25–220), sculptors produced images of various dog types—among them mastiffs and chows—that were then included with the human and other animal figures placed in tombs. Dogs were generally fashioned standing on all fours or in recumbent attitudes. Chow dogs are usually shown in harness, reflecting their use for pulling small sleighs. Some are shown with a bell hanging from the collar. This animated figure of a chow dog from the Eastern Han dynasty was made from red earthenware covered in a dark green glaze. The dog's sturdy, compact body stands firmly planted, his head slightly raised in an alert expression with snarling mouth, cocked ears, and tightly curled tail—a fine illustration of

the Han artist's ability to embody the spirit of the animal in sculpted form.

The technique of glazing pottery was brought to new levels of sophistication during the Western Han dynasty. The earthenware surface was covered with a lead-fluxed glaze, containing copper or iron as a colorant, and fired to earthenware temperatures (600–800 degrees Celsius) in an oxidizing kiln. Copper green and iron yellow/brown make up the normal palette of Han glazed pottery, which provided the foundation for the development of the three-color *(sancai)* glazes of the Tang dynasty (A.D. 618–907). Most Han dogs are covered with a green glaze; however, there are also reddish brown examples, the result of a high content of iron in the lead.

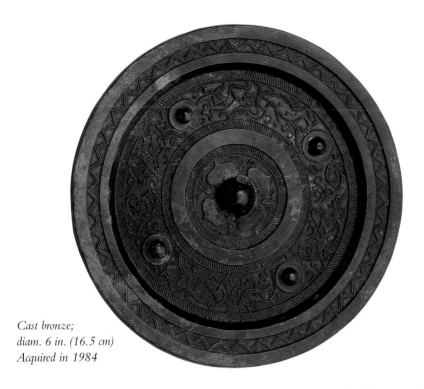

Cast bronze;
diam. 6 in. (16.5 cm)
Acquired in 1984

In ancient China, mirrors served both as functional articles of daily life and as sacred objects possessing powers of their own. Produced from at least the Shang (c. 1600–1100 B.C.) through the Tang dynasty (A.D. 618–907), from around the fourth century B.C. the custom had developed of placing mirrors in tombs. The Chinese believed that mirrors had the ability not only to reflect the truth, and thus ward off evil demons who could not bear to look upon themselves, but also to radiate light and thus illuminate the tomb for eternity. Often more than one mirror was placed in the tomb, not with the other funerary objects, but close to the body of the deceased.

In characteristic Chinese fashion, both the geometric motifs and naturalistic forms used to decorate this mirror have symbolic meaning. The four prominent, raised bosses that divide the field into four parts refer to the four cardinal directions and quadrants of the universe. Seven real and fantastic animals follow each other around the band. As is typical in such contexts, the group includes three of the traditional "spirit animals" of the four directions: the Green Dragon of the East; the White Tiger of the West; and the Red Bird of the South. The Black Tortoise of the North is here replaced by a pair of rodentlike quadrupeds. The two remaining animals cannot be identified. The eighth figure is a creeping human with fringes on his arms and legs, possibly one of the Taoist immortal "feathered men." Tiny bosses scattered seemingly at random over the surface represent stars grouped as constellations.

Jar in the Shape of a Stupa
Shaanxi, Shandong, or Henan province, China;
Northern Qi period or Sui dynasty, late 6th or early 7th century A.D.

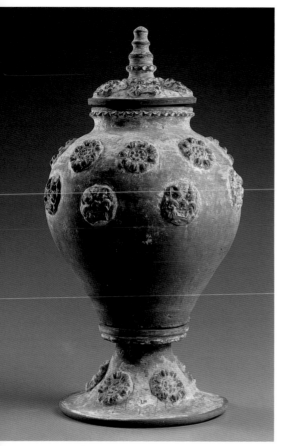

Earthenware with traces of painted polychrome
pigment; h. 19⅛ in. (45.6 cm)
Acquired in 1994

This unusual pottery jar illustrates the early assimilation of Buddhist motifs to the decoration of Chinese mortuary objects. Exceptionally for such objects, all three of its separate components have been preserved in an excellent state. The swelling, ovoid body resembles the shape of a stupa (in China, a pagoda), a traditional Indian structure that houses relics of the Buddha and marks the site of a sanctuary. The shoulder of the vase is decorated with bands of lotus roundels above monster masks, both in relief. The cover, which imitates the top of the stupa, consists of a series of simplified "umbrellas" crowned by a jewel and a band of relief monster masks. The body is supported by a separate flared stand that echoes the design of lotus roundels. Traces of the original white, red, and black pigment decoration are evident on the surface of all three components.

With the introduction of Buddhism into China in the third century A.D., the lotus became a pervasive motif in secular as well as religious art, symbolizing both the Buddha himself and Buddhist purity. The lotus petal roundels on this piece are based on lotus pedestals found in early Chinese Buddhist sculpture. The fantastic monster masks have their origin far to the west, where they may have been borrowed from the Gorgon mask of Greek mythology. In Chinese Buddhist iconography these masks assume the role of guardians of the Buddhist law. Here they may have served to expel evil influences from the grave, as this jar would have been among the diverse assemblage of objects included in a Chinese tomb of the late sixth or early seventh century. In this capacity, it may also have functioned as a container for some relic or sacred token belonging to the deceased.

The masks on this jar are similar to mask reliefs on a four-gate limestone pagoda that dates from the Northern Qi period (A.D. 550–77) to the Sui dynasty (A.D. 581–618), now in the collection of the Metropolitan Museum of Art, New York.

The first high-fired stonewares with a white body and a transparent glaze were made in Hebei province at the end of the sixth century. Around the same time there appear the first three-color *(sancai)* glazes, which reach their height of technical and artistic development in the Tang dynasty (A.D. 618–907). The three colors that made up the *sancai* palette were amber, green, and cream, the latter composed of a transparent glaze over a white slip. Throughout the Tang dynasty these colors were used both individually and in various combinations.

At this time, foreign goods and ideas were making their way along the silk route to the capital at Chang'an (modern-day Xi'an), impacting cosmopolitan Tang society and art. The influence of Central Asian, Hellenistic, and Persian models can be seen in the shapes and designs of many Tang vessels. This amphora-shaped vase, a typical shape of the Tang period, was modeled after Hellenistic Greek prototypes. It has been translated into a Chinese idiom through the substitution of double-stranded loop handles, ending in dragon's heads biting the rim, for the ordinary loop variety, and by the use of a single-color glaze. The finely crackled, barely tinted glaze falls in a graceful swag that separates the glossy upper body from the unglazed portion below.

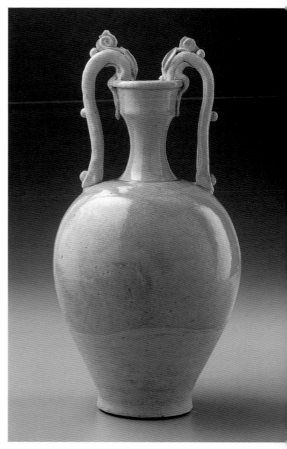

White stoneware with transparent glaze;
14⅞ in. (37.8 cm)
Acquired in 1969

Court Lady

Probably Shaanxi province, China; Tang dynasty,
first half of 8th century A.D.

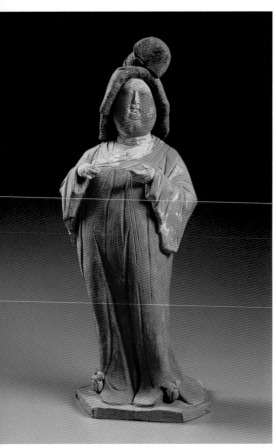

*Gray earthenware with painted polychrome
decoration; h. 16⁷⁄₁₆ in. (41.8 cm)
Acquired in 2001*

The Tang dynasty (618–907 A.D.) was a period of great prosperity and productivity, and the practice of sumptuous burials has left a rich legacy of Tang funerary sculpture. One of the most engaging and distinctive groups of such figures are those representing ladies of the court. This animated and charming example stands in a gracefully swayed pose, her petite hands held in a conversa-tional gesture in front of her swelling form. She wears a white long-sleeved jacket tucked into a full-length red robe, which is belted above her bosom, with a long scarf draped over her shoulder. The thick robe falls in looping folds to her feet, leaving her upturned, *ruyi*-shaped, triple-cloud shoes visible. Her hairstyle, known as a *gaoji* (upswept topknot), is stiffly lacquered and folded, with a clump of hair separated and bound into a fan shape in the front, all held in place by two crescent-shaped combs. Her plump, heavily made-up cheeks are offset by exquisitely delicate eyes, nose, and slightly parted lips, reflecting the contemporary ideal of voluptuous beauty.

The Tang sculptors' careful attention to details of fashion and physiognomy allows us to trace in their works the changing fashions of ladies at court during this period. The slender, elongated bodies with tight-fitting garments charac-teristic of such figures throughout the seventh century give way in the early eighth century to a new aesthetic that favored a fuller and more rotund physique and loose, billowing robes. This new fashion for ladies of ample form was probably set by Yang Guifei, the imperial consort of the emperor Xuan-zong (reigned A.D. 712–56). Dressed in elegant clothes with their hair arranged in elaborate coiffures and their faces beautified with cosmetics, these figures of aristocratic Tang women possess a singular grace and charm.

While most Tang figures were mold-made, this example clearly has been extensively modeled by hand.

Earth Spirit
Probably Shaanxi province, China; Tang dynasty,
first half of 8th century A.D.

The inclusion of fantastic animal guardians among the retinue of Chinese tomb figures began in the Northern Wei dynasty (A.D. 386–534) and continued into the Tang dynasty (A.D. 618–907). Also called earth spirits, or *zhenmushou* (grave-quelling beasts), these guardians took the form of fantastic hybrid creatures composed of various animal and sometimes human elements, and were placed in tombs in pairs to ward off malevolent beings who might threaten to intrude.

Brilliantly painted with pink, red, orange, and black pigments, and highlighted with gilding, the Kimbell's fierce figure of an *Earth Spirit* stands in a rampant posture of conquest as it subdues a snarling beast upon a rockwork base, its left arm entwined with a serpent. The spirit's triple horns, bulging eyes, and bare-teethed grimace add to its ferocious appearance. Black stripes on the forearms and forelegs terminate in sharply clawed hands and feet, and undulating flames emerge from its head, shoulders, and right leg. A gilded tondo, finely painted with a group of figures (possibly musicians, who may also be foreigners), set against a luxuriant floral panel, embellishes the figure's chest.

The composite elements of the *Earth Spirit*, such as the large horns, claws, fangs, and tiger stripes, presumably conferred upon it the fearsome qualities of these animals. The evil that the *Earth Spirit* is quelling is in the form of the

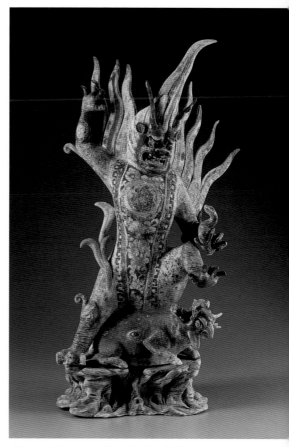

Gray earthenware with painted polychrome decoration; h. 26⁵⁄₁₆ in. (68.4 cm); with rockwork base, 30½ in. (82.6 cm)
Acquired in 2001

horned, hoofed beast that he tramples underfoot. The eye on the side of the beast's belly may represent the "third eye," an indication of the influence of Esoteric Buddhism prevalent during the early Tang period.

Bodhisattva Torso
Probably Shanxi province, China; Tang dynasty, c. A.D. 775–800

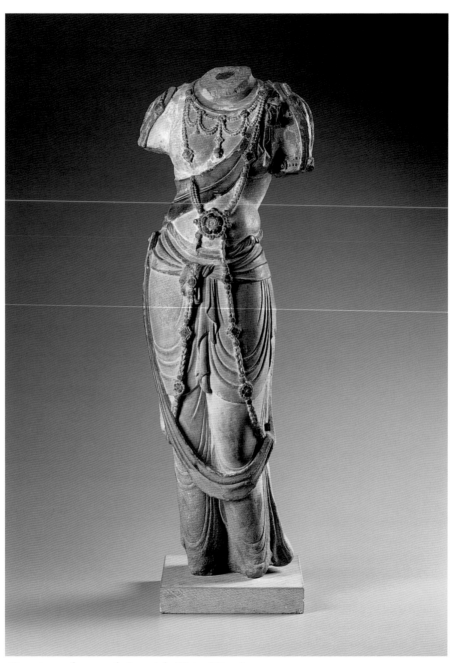

Stone, traces of gesso and pigment; h. 39 in. (99 cm)
Acquired in 1987

Buddhism was introduced into China from India during the Eastern Han dynasty (A.D. 25–220) and for the next six centuries underwent a gradual process of assimilation into Chinese art and culture. The evolution of Chinese Buddhist sculpture from archaic and columnar to fleshy and sensuous reached its culmination in the Tang dynasty (A.D. 618–907), by which time Chinese Buddhist sculpture in the round shows a masterful adaptation of foreign Indian style to indigenous traditions. The finest Tang sculptures, like the Kimbell figure, are voluptuous and tactile, their sumptuous garments carved to accentuate the contours of the body, with flowing scarves and clinging ropes of beads to emphasize its curves. Bodhisattvas and attendant figures stand or sit in a relaxed *tribhanga* stance, the weight shifted to one leg and hip. This Tang International style became the model for the transmission of Buddhist sculpture to the rest of East Asia.

This torso, adorned in a simple skirt with a scarf across the chest and a long, elaborate necklace, represents a bodhisattva attendant to the Buddha, one of a class of divine beings who put off their own final nirvana to help humankind on the path to enlightenment. The complex decorative treatment of the garments combines with a sense of confident repose to make this one of the most successful creations of Tang sculpture. The pronounced *tribhanga* pose, with the left knee slightly bent; the fleshy, volumetric treatment of the body; and the thin drapery reflect continuing Indian influence, here of the Gupta period (A.D. 320–600). The skirt, or *dhoti*, gathered and loosely tied at the waist, is sculpted into graceful folds and naturalistic curves that reinforce the sense of movement in the body. The necklace, crossed in front and looped around the sides to the back, is crisply carved with individual beads and studded with medallions. The torso is distinguished by its remarkably thick, full body when viewed from the side and by the sharp, precise quality of the carving.

Judging from the type of gray limestone used, the sculpture probably comes from Shanxi province in north China, where it would originally have been sculpted within a rock-cut cave temple.

Manjushri on a Lion
China; Southern Song or Jin dynasty, c. 1150–1300

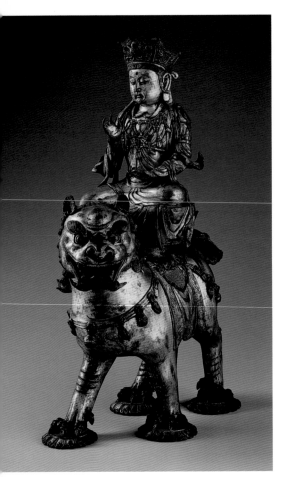

Gilt bronze; h. 21¹³⁄₁₆ in. (55.4 cm)
Acquired in 1987

Of the many deities that played a role in Chinese Buddhism, Manjushri (in Chinese, Wenshu), the bodhisattva of wisdom, is among the most appealing. One of the three most important bodhisattvas in East Asia, Manjushri is said to have originated in China from the mountains associated with Mount Wutai, a famous Buddhist monastic center. He was worshiped in China as the embodiment of knowledge and the guardian of sacred doctrines. Usually presented as a youthful, bejeweled prince, he is often shown seated on the back of a lion, and carries a book of truth and a sword that cuts through the darkness of ignorance. Depictions of Manjushri mounted on a lion were popular from the Tang dynasty (A.D. 618–907) onward, and in this form he was most frequently paired with the bodhisattva Samanta-bhadhra, these two figures flanking the historical Buddha Shakyamuni in a triad.

Among the Buddhist sculptures of China, bronze images occupy a very prominent place. Some of the finest religious works, especially during the Song dynasty (960–1279), were executed in this medium. Although paintings of Manjushri dating from the thirteenth to the fifteenth century are still extant, sculptures—particularly gilt-bronzes of this size—are extremely rare. This beautifully proportioned and superbly detailed example is a very rare, complete image of the divinity, preserved in excellent condition. Its precise dating remains problematic due to the paucity of related material. Stylistically, the bodhisattva and lion are consistent with Southern Song (1127–1279) or Jin dynasty (1115–1234) works. The facial features of the deity and details such as the three-pointed crown, sleeved garment, and necklace, find parallels on a monumental stone sculpture in the Dazu cave in Sichuan province, dated 1154.

Meiping Vase
Jiangxi province, China; Yuan dynasty,
first half of 14th century

*Bowl Carved with Design
of Boys among Peonies*
Jiangxi province, China;
Southern Song dynasty, 12th century

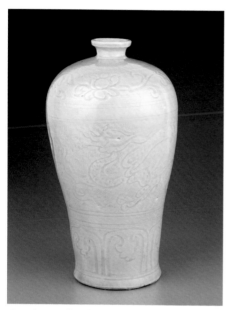

*Porcelain with pale greenish blue glaze
(qingbai ware); h. 12½ in. (31.8 cm)
Acquired in 1968*

Among the finest porcelain wares ever produced, *qingbai* (bluish white) constitutes one of the main groups of porcelain manufactured during the Song dynasty (960–1279). It is characterized by a fine, white, pure clay body of sugary structure, surprisingly thin and highly translucent potting, and a glaze that varies from strong bluish green to pale blue or almost white. Designs were incised, carved, and molded; incised wares were often worked with a thin, pointed tool and a comblike instrument.

The extremely fine *Bowl Carved with Design of Boys among Peonies*, dating from the Southern Song dynasty (1127–1279), bears an almost transparent icy blue glaze. The swirling decoration of two bald-headed boys and peony scrolls is incised in fluid forms of great vigor and move-

ment. Designs showing two or three small boys climbing among flowers are very common in *qingbai* wares. The peony symbolizes spring and is an omen of good fortune. The cherubic boys crawling on all fours probably allude to the wish for male progeny. An unusual feature is the Chinese character *zhang* carved in the center of the bowl, which probably denotes the surname of the family work-shop that produced the piece.

Qingbai wares of the Yuan dynasty (1279–1368) continue the tradition of Song *qingbai* wares, although the porcelain body is generally heavier. The term *meiping* (plum blossom vase) describes a tall vase with a wide shoulder and small mouth. The decoration on this *Meiping Vase* is arranged in three registers: carved floral scrolls on the shoulder, a carved dragon twisting through combed pattern clouds in the center register, and an upright band of incised, stylized petal motifs on the bottom register.

*Porcelain with pale blue glaze (qingbai ware);
diam. 7¾ in. (19.7 cm)
Acquired in 1995*

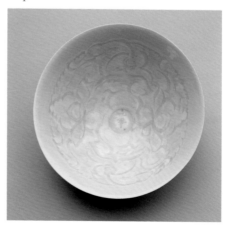

Vase with Fish and Foliate Scroll Design
China; Yuan dynasty, 14th century

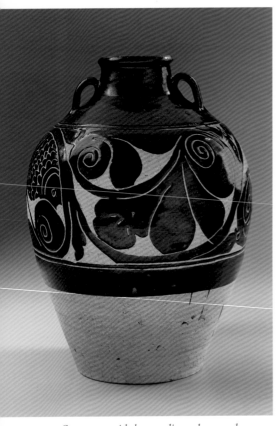

Stoneware with brown slip and green glaze (Cizhou ware); h. 15¾ in. (40 cm)
Acquired in 1970

Cizhou is the designation for a large and varied group of cream-colored stonewares decorated with painted designs under a transparent glaze, or by incising, stamping, or carving into a colored slip. First developed in the Song period (960–1279) and named for the kilns in the Cizhou area of Hebei province, they were made throughout north China from the tenth to the fifteenth century. While there is a considerable variety of slips, glazes, and vessel shapes, all Cizhou wares share a distinctive decoration in which large-scale motifs play on the contrast of light and dark tones. Cizhou wares are somewhat unrefined and were generally made for everyday utilitarian use in the homes of the middle class.

This vase's bold design of large foliate scrolls and fish was achieved by incising and removing areas of a dark brown slip that had been applied to the whole vase. Initially, the slip was cut away from the lower third of the jar to reveal the cream-colored body of the stoneware. The deeply incised outlines of the floral design and some details, most notably the eyes and the scale pattern of the fish, were then cut through the remaining slip. Finally, the background area of the floral design was scraped away. The result is a striking design that exploits the juxtaposed contrast of light and dark tones, and the differing textures of the glossy slip and matte stoneware.

Arhats (in Chinese, *lohans*) were the
original disciples of the Buddha, to
whom he first preached his doctrine at the
Deer Park in Sarnath. An arhat (which
means "worthy one" or "perfected saint")
is an enlightened being of exceptional
wisdom and is endowed with supernatural
powers. One of an arhat's primary roles is
to serve as guardian and advocate of the
Buddhist Law *(dharma)*. In China, certain
arhats or groups of arhats became the focus
of religious devotion. Worship of a group
of sixteen arhats was set forth in an Indian
sutra, *A Record of the Abiding of the Dharma
Spoken by the Great Arhat Nandimitra,*
which was translated into Chinese in the
mid-seventh century. By the end of the
tenth century, two additional arhats were
added, one paired with a tiger and the
other one with a dragon. The dragon,
regarded as a divine animal in China long
before the advent of Buddhism, personified
potentially fearsome natural phenomena
associated with water, thunder, and rain.

In this dramatic composition, a seated
arhat—accompanied by a guardian king,
a monk, and a child—confronts a dragon
as its emerges from a body of water. The
figures are rendered in a fine, linear ink
technique familiar in Southern Song
(1127–1279) painting, the thin ink
outlines being almost obscured by the
colors applied to the garments; the
landscape setting is painted with bolder,
more expressive brushwork. The turbulent
water, fluttering robes, and wide-eyed
expressions of the figures imbue the scene
with considerable movement and tension.
The arhat, depicted with an intense and
slightly malevolent expression, appears to
be subduing the force of the dragon with

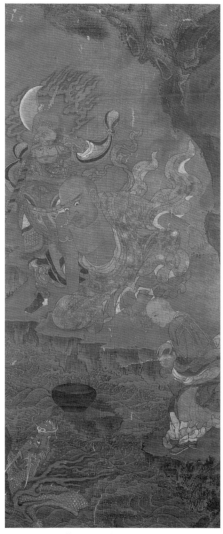

*Hanging scroll; ink and mineral pigments on
silk; 48¼ x 20¾ in. (122.5 x 52.7 cm)
Acquired in 1987*

his gaze, drawing the beast into his magic
alms bowl, which sits on a rock between
them. The dragon's act of submission to
the arhat glorifies the supernatural power
of the Buddhist saint.

Seated Arhat
Shanxi province, China; late Yuan to early Ming dynasty, c. 1300–1450

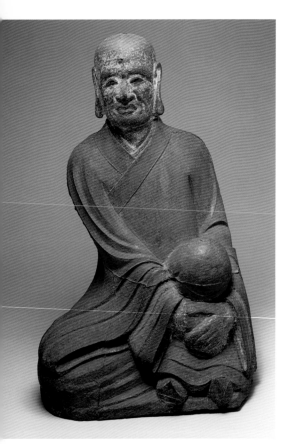

Cast iron, traces of pigment; h. 30¹¹/₁₆ in. (78 cm)
Acquired in 1984

This engaging portrait represents an arhat (in Chinese, *lohan*), one of a group of "perfected beings" who, in the Buddhist faith, were the original disciples of Shakyamuni Buddha. Like bodhisattvas, arhats have attained perfection but have delayed entering nirvana and becoming buddhas so that they may aid others in seeking enlightenment. Arhats were regarded as having achieved extraordinary spiritual levels that endowed them with superhuman capabilities. Usually appearing in groups of four, sixteen, eighteen, or even as many as a thousand, the arhats were depicted as monks and ascetics, sometimes with exaggerated features such as long eyebrows or domed heads, and some were associated with particular attributes. Although lists identifying each arhat exist, the descriptions are generally vague, and the precise identification of individual figures remains difficult.

The realism and humanity of the Kimbell arhat's face contrast with the simplified but rhythmical form of the body to produce a portrait of great character and presence. An inscription on the back of the statue names a large group of donors who commissioned and paid for the work, and gives the name of the temple, Yuhua, in Shanxi province, to which it was donated and where it may have been installed as part of a larger group of arhat portraits. Although it is similar to a group of arhats dated to the fifteenth century, this statue possesses a finer definition of drapery and facial detail, which suggests a somewhat earlier date.

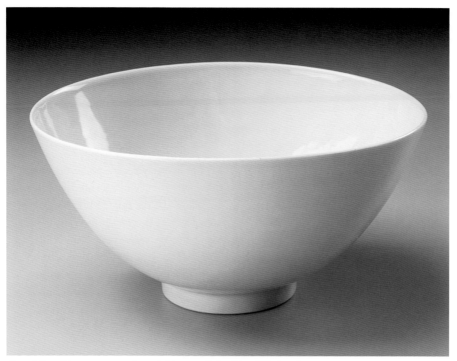

Porcelain with transparent glaze (white ware); h. 4 in. (10.1 cm)
Acquired in 1971

During the Ming dynasty (1368–1644), an inward-looking period in Chinese history, the standards and styles in much artistic production were set by the emperors. In the early Ming, the establishment of kilns that produced porcelains exclusively for the use of the imperial court made the city of Jingdezhen, in Jiangxi province, the most important ceramic center in China, and it was during this period that the manufacture of porcelain reached its peak. One of the great achievements of the Jingdezhen kilns was a glaze referred to as "sweet white" *(tianbai)*, which was favored by the Yongle emperor (reigned 1403–24) for ceremonial use at court. The best of these white wares have a thin, fine-grained, pure white body and a glaze that is transparent and glossy, without any tinge of color. The walls of these wares were so thin that they were often called "bodiless."

Many monochrome white porcelains of the early fifteenth century repeat the shapes of contemporary blue-and-white vessels and copy the blue designs in incision or low relief. A particularly popular device was to execute the ornament as *anhua* (secret decoration), which was so delicately incised that it is scarcely visible unless held up to the light. This lotus-shaped bowl is incised with such decoration in an interior pattern of radiating petals and wave border in molded slip, and an incised scrolling floral vine and key fret border on the exterior.

Flat-Sided Flask
China; Ming dynasty, early 15th century

Dish with Melon Design
China; Ming dynasty, early 15th century

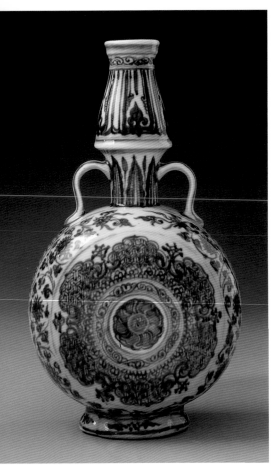

*Porcelain with cobalt oxide pigment under transparent glaze; h. 13⅛ in. (33.3 cm)
Acquired in 1968*

in the Yuan dynasty (1279–1368), using cobalt imported from the Middle East. Extant Yuan examples, however, are scarce, and the large-scale production of blue-and-white wares began with the establishment of the imperial kilns at Jingdezhen, in Jiangxi province, during the Yongle era (1403–24) of the early Ming dynasty.

These three elegant porcelain vessels exemplify the technical and decorative excellence of the finest Ming blue-and-white wares. The *Flat-Sided Flask* is known in bronze vessels dating to the sixth century B.C. in China, but the particular form of this vessel, with its angled, tubular neck and loop handles,

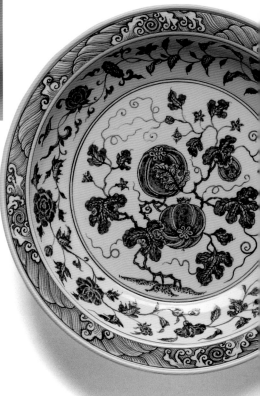

Blue-and-white wares produced during the Ming dynasty (1368–1644) begin a new chapter in the history of Chinese ceramic art. Although cobalt was used as a blue coloring agent earlier in China, the application of cobalt oxide pigment to plain porcelain wares before glazing is thought to have begun

is thought to have been based on Islamic
metal prototypes. The flask was
constructed from several pieces of molded
clay that were joined before firing. Its
decoration features a medallion of
radiating cloud-collar points that are
filled with an abstract woven pattern; at
its center is a flower blossom in a depres-
sion. Geometric and floral scrolls, set in
concentric bands around the sides of the
vessel, further emphasize the round shape.
The density of the design is characteristic
of early-fifteenth-century products of
the Yongle and Xuande (1426–35) eras
of the early Ming dynasty.

The precise, fluid decoration of the
large *Dish with Melon Design* is orderly
and spacious, in contrast to more
crowded designs on fourteenth-century
wares. The flat rim is decorated with a
pattern of rolling and cresting waves; the
cavetto is filled with an open scrolling
floral vine; and the center medallion
contains an unusual and exceptionally
well-painted design of melons, leaves, and

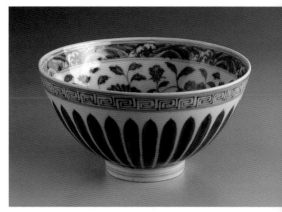

*Porcelain with cobalt oxide pigment under
transparent glaze; h. 4¼ in. (10.6 cm)
Acquired in 1970*

twisting tendrils. The mastery of the artist
is particularly evident in the modeling of
the fruit and leaves, in which unpainted
areas of white are skillfully transformed
into highlights.

The *Lotus Bowl* represents a popular
type of the Yongle and Xuande periods,
which seems to imitate the shape of the
lotus flower's seedpod. Most of these are
unmarked, but the Kimbell's bowl bears a
six-character Xuande reign mark on the
bottom in underglaze blue reading, *Da
Ming Xuande Nian Zhi* ("Made in the
period of the Xuande reign of the Ming
dynasty"). While the choice of borders
and flowers can vary, in general the decoration of these bowls is remarkably consistent, suggesting that they were mass
produced. The interior of this bowl is
decorated with a combination of scrolling
flowers and a wave border; and on the
exterior, stylized lotus petals and a key fret
border. The color and intensity of the
blue are typical of the period.

*Porcelain with cobalt oxide pigment under
transparent glaze; diam. 17⅛ in. (43.4 cm)
Acquired in 1970*

Round Dish with Pommel Scrolls
China; Ming dynasty, 15th–16th century

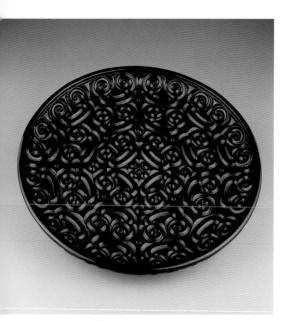

*Carved black lacquer with red layers (tixi);
diam. 13⅞ in. (35.2 cm)
Acquired in 1993*

Since at least the Shang dynasty (c. 1600–1100 B.C.), the Chinese have employed lacquer in an industrial as well as an artistic capacity. Being impervious to liquids, acid, and to a certain extent heat, lacquer made an excellent protective coating for materials such as wood, leather, and textiles. The artistic properties of lacquer were also exploited in a number of ways: combined with pigments it was used as a painting medium; it could be inlaid with precious materials such as mother-of-pearl or engraved with gold; and built up to a certain thickness it could be carved in a variety of techniques. Considered a luxury item, lacquerware with elaborate decoration was reserved for use by the elite classes and the court.

Carved, "marbled" lacquer *(tixi)*, a variety unique to China, was made from at least the Song dynasty (960–1279) onwards. In this labor-intensive technique, several layers of thin lacquer in varying colors are applied to a wood substratum, each layer being left to harden before the next is added. Once this coating has built up to a considerable thickness, grooves may be cut into the lacquer, revealing a series of colored bands. This large, deeply carved dish has seven alternating bands of lacquer, four black ones sandwiching three thin red ones. The interior of the dish is carved with a design of three concentric rows of pommel scrolls *(jianhuan)* encircling a quatrefoil floret, a decorative scheme commonly employed on *tixi* lacquers. The pommel-scroll motif, a trefoil pattern, takes its name from the shape of the ring-pommel of early Chinese swords. The exterior is carved with a classic or "fragrant grass" scroll *(xiangcao)*, and the dish stands on a sturdy foot-ring. The black lacquer surface layer has been highly polished to a lustrous shine, enhancing the overall decorative effect. The wide grooves with U-shaped troughs are indicative of *tixi* lacquers dating to the mid-Ming dynasty.

Colorful flower-and-bird paintings were created by court painters during the Ming dynasty (1368–1644) to decorate the grand halls of imperial palaces, where they could also serve as metaphors for the emperor and his court. This superb early Ming example draws on a tradition of flower-and-bird painting that can be traced back to the early Song dynasty (960–1279).

Yin Hong was the third generation of a family of professional painters who served the imperial court from the early to mid-Ming era. Although Yin Hong served in the academy during a period when the careers of many court painters suffered from diminished imperial patronage, he was nonetheless recognized by his contemporaries for his skill at depicting "feathers and fur."

This handsome painting evokes the passage from winter to spring with a combination of camellias and blossoming plum. It was probably painted as part of a monumental suite of seasonal paintings. It is one of only four of Yin Hong's works to have survived and bears his signature and seal. Unlike more naturalistic flower-and-bird compositions of Song date, the rocks, water, trees, blossoms, and birds are treated here as stylized formal elements in a grand design. Dark washes of ink and vigorous strokes form interlocking planes of strong, flat forms. The jutting boulders and the twisted bough of plum retain subtle gradations of tone that give volume to these shapes. Rich green leaves and red-and-white blossoms animate the diagonals with touches of brilliant color. The birds—little bulbuls and the red-breasted minivet (on the prunus branch),

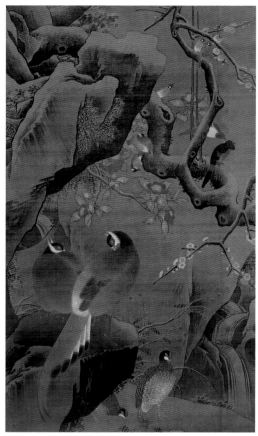

Hanging scroll; ink and mineral pigments on silk; 66½ x 40½ in. (168.7 x 102.7 cm)
Acquired in 1982

partridges (lower-right foreground), and brown-eared pheasants (on the rock cliff) — contribute to the patterned effect and tactile richness of the surface. Beyond its highly decorative qualities, the subject of the painting is also an allusion to imperial allegiance; the pheasants are symbolic of bravery and steadfastness, while the partridges represent the faithful followers of the emperor.

WANG ZHAO
Chinese, active 1500–1525
The Three Stars of Happiness, Wealth, and Longevity, c. 1500

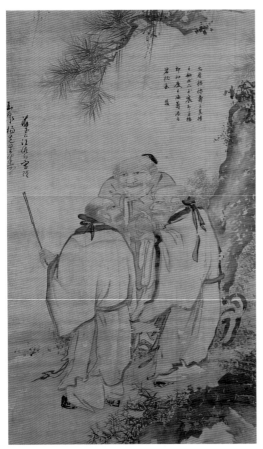

Hanging scroll; ink and light colors on silk;
62½ x 37½ in. (158.7 x 95.2 cm)
Acquired in 1985

Wang Zhao, an artist from Anhui province, is recorded only briefly in the biographies of his day. He is described as an eccentric person whose skill was repeatedly recognized and praised. He was not a literati, but followed the styles of the artists associated with the Zhe school and the Ming academy.

This bold and lively painting of three figures beneath a pine tree depicts a trio of Taoist deities known as the Three Stars of Happiness, Wealth, and Longevity, who are charged with caring for the well being of individuals. In popular legend each god is derived from a historical person, and although grouped as a trio here, each is worshiped separately. The vigorous brushwork, notable in the strong outlines of the figures and in the trunk of the tree, is typical of the expressionistic style favored by Chan (Zen) priest-painters, which was particularly suited to Taoist divinities and themes. Wang's inscription at the left states that it was painted for Master Yuan Yuquan in celebration of his birthday.

The Star of Happiness (Fuxing) is generally associated with a sixth-century civil official who persuaded his emperor to release the dwarfs taken forcibly from his hometown to serve as entertainers at court. Fuxing is the figure at the center rear who wears the robes of a civil bureaucrat. The Star of Wealth (Luxing), pictured on the left, is personified by Shi Fen, a Chinese peasant who became a general and allied himself with the founder of the Han dynasty (206 B.C.–A.D. 220). As a reward for his conquests he received both honors and great wealth. The Star of Longevity (Shouxing) is a deity who fixes the time of death for each individual. His presence as a star was a sign of peace; his disappearance, a sign of war. Shouxing stands on the right and holds the peach of immortality in his hands.

This painting of wild narcissi and short sprigs of young bamboo growing at the base of a rock is a masterwork of the artist Chen Jiayen, a relatively obscure painter from Jiangsu province. The expressionistic style of Chen's work follows a long tradition of literati painting produced in and around the city of Suzhou. Forcefully executed with quick, bold brushstrokes in soft gradated tones of ink wash, the primary forms of the Kimbell painting have a remarkable solidity. Darker ink is used to define the short, spiky leaves of bamboo, while the gently curving leaves of the narcissi are left white within a lighter ink outline.

What appears to be an unassuming painting of rocks and flora is, in fact, a thinly veiled expression of the artist's innermost thoughts and emotions. The scroll is an important work in Chen's oeuvre, the earliest of his paintings to include a poem and the combination of bamboo, rocks, and narcissus. The mood of the poem, written on New Year's Day, 1652, is one of despair and desolation, a reflection of contemporary events. At the end of the Ming dynasty (1368–1644), China fell to foreign Manchu invaders who established the Qing dynasty (1644–1911); Chen's painting dates to this turbulent period in the early years of the Qing. The poem also alludes to other events in Chinese history: the Tang-dynasty An Lushan rebellion (755–63), which similarly left the country destroyed, and to the Han dynasty (206 B.C.–A.D. 220) poetess Ban Jieyu, who laments her feelings of grief and abandonment. Like most Chinese paintings of plants and flowers, especially those

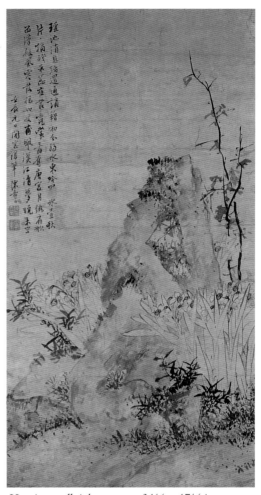

*Hanging scroll; ink on paper; 31½ x 17⅛ in.
(80 x 43.5 cm)
Acquired in 1984*

executed in monochromatic ink, this work has a moral significance. Despite the bleak overtones of the poem, Chen has painted bamboo, which bends in the wind but will not break, and narcissi, harbingers of spring, to symbolize the strength and self-regeneration needed to give hope to a fallen nation.

Pedestaled Ceremonial Bowl
Korea; Old Silla period, 5th–6th century A.D.

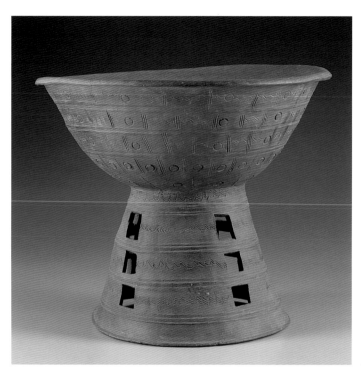

Gray stoneware;
h. 13 in. (33 cm)
Acquired in 1996

This large pedestaled bowl probably served as a ceremonial vessel or as a support for a large round-bottomed jar. Made for use by the living, it was no doubt later included in a tomb as part of a funerary offering. Its aesthetic appeal derives from its imposing proportions, its strong, solid form, and its harmoniously integrated decoration of square apertures and combed patterns.

By the fifth century A.D., Korean potters were producing high-fired gray stonewares. Characterized by their robust forms and unglazed surfaces, most Old Silla period (57 B.C.–A.D. 668) pots exhibit little surface ornamentation other than an occasional combed wave pattern or incised configuration of circles and chevrons. The decorative use of

geometric perforations is restricted largely to pedestaled bowls.

The Kimbell bowl is comprised of two parts. The high, hollow pedestal is punctuated by four stacks of three square perforations cut into horizontal bands of wavy, combed decoration. The large bowl above bears more combed wavy bands, here divided by vertical incisions into panels, some bearing incised circles. It was originally thought that the bases of Korean pots were perforated so that chips of wood could be burned within to warm the vessel's contents, but the lack of soot on the undersides contradicts this hypothesis. It is now believed that the cutouts were most likely added for decorative effect.

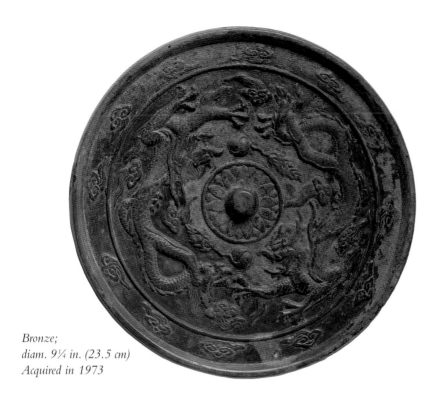

Bronze;
diam. 9¼ in. (23.5 cm)
Acquired in 1973

Bronze mirrors were essential items in the toilet sets of aristocratic ladies. A significant number of them survive through the East Asian custom of placing such luxury objects in tombs, to be used by the dead in the spirit world. The ability of mirrors to reflect images and light led to the belief that they had the power to radiate light for eternity, thus magically illuminating the interior of the tomb. This custom, which originated in China as early as the fourth century B.C., appeared in the tenth century in Korea. Although Korean mirrors made in the Koryo period (936–1392) follow contemporary Chinese prototypes in form and design, they generally have a softer definition of sculptural detail because of the lower tin content of the bronze.

On this mirror, two lively dragons chasing pearls or flaming jewels decorate the primary field around a central lotus-petal medallion. In the East, dragons are connected with water, rain, and thunder, and thus symbolize the spring season and fertility. The significance of the pearl or jewel is not known. The reverse side would have been highly polished, forming an excellent reflecting surface. The boss in the center has a transverse opening for the loop of a braided silk tassel that would have served as the mirror's handle, while the mirror was supported by a lacquered wood stand.

Bowl
Korea; Koryo period,
12th or 13th century

Cosmetic Box
Korea; Koryo period,
12th or 13th century

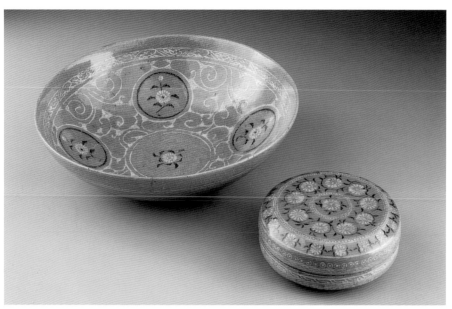

*Stoneware with dark green and white inlay
and celadon glaze; diam. 7¼ in. (18.4 cm)
Acquired in 1970*

*Stoneware with black-and-white inlay and
celadon glaze; diam. 3⅝ in. (9 cm)
Acquired in 1972*

One of the most significant contributions of the Korean potter to ceramic art was the technique of slip-inlay *(sanggam)* on celadon wares of the Koryo period (936–1392). Developed around the mid-twelfth century, the technique quickly became a national specialty. The inlay was produced by first incising or stamping designs into the clay, and then filling the depressions with white or black slip before glazing and firing. Slip-inlay decoration was quite sparing at first; later, the designs occupied more and more of the vessel surface.

This shallow bowl demonstrates the variety of decorative effects that can be achieved with slip-inlay technique. The chrysanthemum blossoms on the exterior and in the center of the interior medallions were stamped and then filled with white slip. The greenish black leaves and surrounding design were freely carved with a V-shaped knife. In a technique known as reverse inlay *(yoksanggam)*, the background of the curling, gray green foliage, rather than the leaves themselves, was carved out and filled with white slip.

Cosmetic boxes and small squat oil bottles were among the wide variety of forms made in this technique for the court and aristocrats of the Koryo dynasty. The boxes all have flat lids with rounded shoulders, a shape that had its origins in the metalwork of the time. The decoration on the lids generally consists of geometric or floral designs and is closely linked with lacquerwork of the period. This cosmetic box is inlaid with yet another variation on the familiar motif of chrysanthemum flowers and leaves.

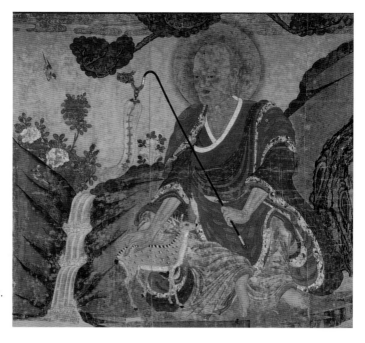

*Ink, mineral
pigments, and gold
on silk; 31 x 35 in.
(78.7 x 88.9 cm)
Acquired in 1995*

Although Confucianism was the official state religion of the Choson period (1392–1910), Buddhism survived in Korea as a kind of folk religion with a large admixture of indigenous Shamanist and Chinese Taoist elements. The precincts of large Buddhist temples often included three small side shrines *(sam song kak)* dedicated to Shamanist deities who had been adopted by Korean Buddhism: San Shin (the Mountain Spirit), Tok Song (the Lonely Saint), and Ch'il Song (the Seven Star Spirits).

The resulting blending of the iconographies of Korean Shamanism and traditional Buddhism can be seen in this painting of an arhat and deer. The sparsely bearded figure of an old man holding a walking staff resembles conventional depictions of San Shin, the most popular deity in the Shamanist pantheon.

However, his bald head surrounded by a halo and monk's robes suggests a Buddhist holy man, or arhat (in Korean, *nahan*). Replacing the tiger normally associated with San Shin is a deer, a traditional Buddhist symbol of longevity; the pink polocho, the small flower to the immediate left of the arhat's shoulder, is likewise a symbol of long life. The nearby peonies symbolize prosperity and progeny and may therefore allude to San Shin's capacity to bestow children. The pine tree and waterfall are conventional elements of Mountain Spirit paintings, with the pine also symbolizing venerable old age and endurance.

The skillful conception and execution of this very fine work suggest the hand of a master monk-painter, and it is most likely to have hung in a Buddhist temple or shrine.

Jar with Sculptural Rim
Japan; Jomon period, c. 2500–1000 B.C.

Female Figurine
Japan; Jomon period, c. 1000–200 B.C.

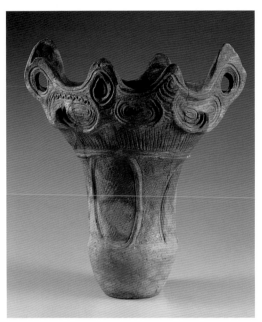

Low-fired clay; h. 16½ in. (42 cm)
Acquired in 1974

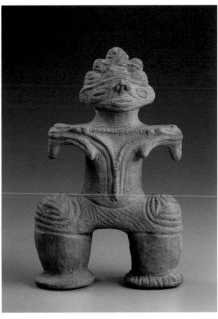

Low-fired clay; h. 7⅞ in. (20.1 cm)
Acquired in 1971

Jomon, meaning "cord-marked," refers to the impressions left from rolling braided or twisted ropes across the surface of moist clay vessels in the Neolithic period in Japan, which is thus known as the Jomon period (c. 10,500–300 B.C.). At its height, this hunting and fishing culture developed a rich visual vocabulary to embellish its ceramic utensils. Early Jomon-period cooking vessels were plain, but over time a range of distinctive cord-marked and incised decorations and pinched, curvilinear rims were added. The mysterious masks, surging peaks, and undulating coils that decorate the Kimbell's Jomon jar are characteristic of Middle Jomon-period ceramics. A decorated vessel such as this was probably not made for daily use but for preparing food at special religious ceremonies.

Jomon clay figurines, called *dogu* (earthen idols), began to appear around 1500 B.C. Representing humans, usually female, and animals, they have in common with the pottery vessels the characteristic cord-marked decoration on their bodies and faces, and may have been used as protective charms or fertility symbols. Most were found deposited in pit dwellings, burial sites, or ritual shrines. The figurines exhibit a variety of abstract, humanoid shapes that are highly imaginative. The Kimbell's *Female Figurine* has a hollow, thin-walled body supported by short tubular legs and wide hips. The areas of smooth clay and contrasting bands of incised and cord-marked patterns on the face, hips, and chest, as well as the "goggle-eyes," are identifying features of the so-called Kamegaoka type of *dogu* figurine.

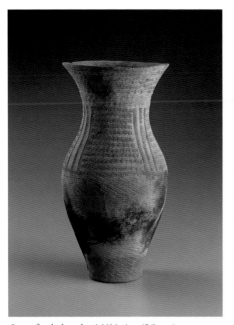

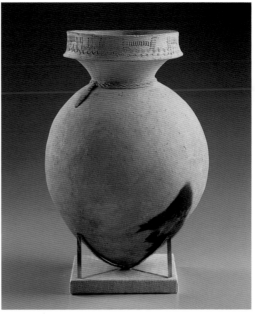

Low-fired clay; h. 11¹³⁄₁₆ in. (30 cm)
Acquired in 1985

Low-fired clay; h. 18⁷⁄₁₆ in. (46.8 cm)
Acquired in 1984

The Yayoi culture of central Japan marked the first identifiable influx of people from the Asian continent and witnessed the introduction of wet-rice cultivation and bronze and iron metallurgy from Korea. Named after the site in Tokyo where this type of buff-colored pottery was first discovered, the Yayoi period (300 B.C.–A.D. 300) also saw the beginnings of a settled, hierarchical society and a wealthy elite. Yayoi vessels reflect this society's dependence on the cultivation of rice and the widespread use of storage jars for stockpiling reserves. Sturdier, more functional vessels with symmetrical, taut profiles and restrained embellishment replace the irregular shapes and exuberant decoration of the preceding Jomon-period wares.

This graceful *Wide-Mouthed Jar* is decorated with a variety of incised patterns in three registers that accentuate the vessel's gently swelling shape. The wavy parallel lines on the mouth and neck, and the diagonal lines around the body, are characteristic of jars made in the Kanto region of eastern Japan.

The large *Ovoid Jar* is a particularly fine example of the fluid lines and uncluttered decoration that characterize the best of Yayoi pottery. The vessel was first shaped by hand and then finished on a wheel to produce thin, even walls and a balanced shape. The robust, swelling body, tapering to a point at its base; the simple, combed incisions on the lip; and the flat, braided cord around the neck are typical of the modest but bold decorative vocabulary of Yayoi potters.

Haniwa Seated Man
Hokota site, Kashima, Ibaraki prefecture, Japan; Kofun period, c. A.D. 500

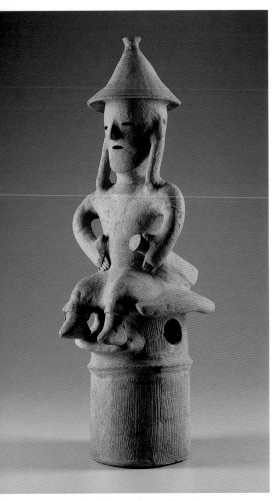

Low-fired clay with cinnabar pigment;
h. 30 in. (76 cm)
Acquired in 1972

Haniwa, which means "circle (or tube) of clay," is the term given to large numbers of hollow clay cylinders that were placed in and around the bases of large earthen mounds covering Japanese royal tombs. Their function is unknown, but it is thought that they were used to protect the sides of the mound from erosion or perhaps formed a symbolic barrier around the precincts of the dead, protecting the site from evil spirits. The majority of *haniwa* are unadorned, but a number of them are decorated with a variety of sculpted human figures, animals, and domestic or ceremonial objects, rendered with the typical simplification and abstraction that characterizes the Kimbell figure of a seated man. Seated on a platform, he has short legs and rounded, tubelike arms that are held in front in a somewhat formal pose. The body has no suggestion of clothing, but the masklike face, devoid of sculptural detail, is marked by triangles on the cheeks and chin, painted in red cinnabar. Although the status and function of the person represented are not known, his distinctive conical cap and the sword at his side suggest a low-ranking soldier. The majority of sculpted *haniwa* are from the Ibaraki prefecture, northeast of Tokyo.

The Kofun ("Old Tomb/Mound") period (A.D. 250–552) is characterized by the burial mounds built for the clan leaders of an emerging upper class, who would form the basis of imperial rule. The practice of building burial mounds and interring valuables with the dead was adopted in Japan from the Asian continent. During this period, great numbers of burial mounds of monumental proportion, such as the keyhole-shaped tomb of Emperor Nintoku (A.D. 313–399), near Osaka, symbolized the increasingly unified power of the governing class.

This Sue ware flask exemplifies a type of ceramic vessel produced in Japan in the sixth and seventh centuries A.D. for ritual use or for placement in tombs as offerings. Its technology reflects the contacts with Korea and China that accompanied the introduction of Buddhism and other aspects of continental culture to Japan in the Asuka period (A.D. 552–645).

The production of Sue wares signaled the beginning of a new phase of ceramic art in Japan. Earlier Jomon and Yayoi ceramics were built by hand in soft clay, and fired in open trenches at about 700 degrees Celsius. Sue wares are true stonewares, produced with the aid of a potter's wheel and fired in tunnel kilns at 1200 degrees Celsius.

Sue wares frequently exhibit unusual shapes that are sturdy and robust. The vigorous, swelling form of this flask is restricted to one side; the back is flat, its surface incised with thin lines. The fine clay of Sue wares, which were unglazed, fired to a metallic gray color. The spectacular splash of green glaze over one side of this vessel was accidental, created in the kiln by ashes that fell and fused on the surface of the pot during the firing process. This effect was especially prized by later Japanese potters, who consciously tried to reproduce it in their wares. Aside from their technical advancements, Sue wares are important for their anticipation of later developments in the ceramic arts of Japan.

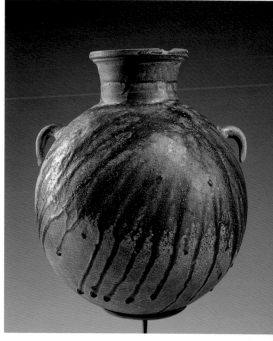

High-fired clay (Sue ware);
h. 12⅛ in. (31.4 cm)
Acquired in 1983

Hachiman in the Guise of a Buddhist Priest
Japan; Heian period, 11th century

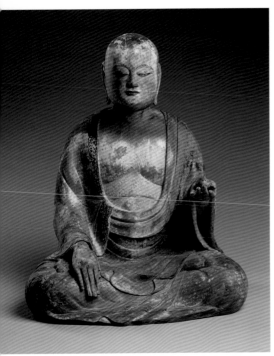

Polychromed wood; h. 19¼ in. (48.9 cm)
Acquired in 1981

The Shinto god Hachiman has enjoyed special prominence throughout Japanese history. He was originally a local military guardian, protecting an agricultural and mining community in Usa, northern Kyushu, which had ties to the Imperial house. Since his legendary birthplace in Japan was near south China, a possible source of military threats, Japanese rulers came to rely upon him for protection against that danger. In this role, Hachiman became known as the Shinto god of war.

The Kimbell's *Hachiman in the Guise of a Buddhist Priest* reflects a complex theological transformation that occurred when the Japanese sought to reconcile Buddhism, a foreign religion, with native Shinto beliefs. Shinto gods could symbolically enter the Buddhist priesthood, thereby acquiring a dual identity. In this image, Hachiman is dressed as a Buddhist priest. Seated in a meditative position, wearing a monk's robe, his head shaven, and carrying a jewel in his left hand, he resembles representations of the bodhisattva Kshitigarbha (in Japanese, Jizo), reflecting the fact that Shinto images shared the same stylistic features as Buddhist sculpture of the period. Carved from a solid block of wood, the figure's generously proportioned chest, shoulders, and legs impart a monumentality that belies the sculpture's relatively small size, while the slight tilt of the head imparts a touch of naturalism.

Shintoism is the native religion of Japan. The object of Shinto worship is the *kami*, which corresponds roughly to the term "spirit" or "god." *Kami* can include human ancestors, legendary heroes, or the personified forces of nature, such as the wind, the rain, a tree, or a rock. The development of Shinto sculpture and the representation of *kami* in human form reflect the Japanese attempt to reconcile their native religion with the powerful influence of Buddhism, which was imported from the Asian continent in the seventh century.

Kannon is the Japanese name for the Indian Buddhist deity Avalokitesh-vara, the bodhisattva of compassion. Because of the boundless love he offered to all beings, this was the most popular of all the Buddhist deities throughout Asia. The Nyoirin Kannon, a prominent deity in the Japanese Esoteric Buddhist pantheon, is one of the six "changed forms" of the bodhisattva Kannon especially associated with the granting of desires. The word *nyo-i* refers to the *cintamani*, the wish-granting jewel; the term *rin*, which means "wheel," refers to the turning of the wheel of the law. The Nyoirin Kannon was widely worshiped by those who hoped to gain riches and see their requests fulfilled.

This gracious image shows the deity seated in a pose of royal ease. Although drawings frequently depict this god as a bodhisattva with two arms, the six-armed form was also popular in Japan. As in this sculpture, one hand is often shown touching the cheek, with a left arm braced against the lotus pedestal (now missing). Of the other four arms, one of the right hands holds the jewel, and one of the left hands holds a lotus. The raised left arm would originally have had a wheel balanced on the upright finger, and the lowered right arm would have held a rosary.

Esoteric Buddhism first developed in India as a faith embracing both Buddhist and Hindu doctrines. The Esoteric sect worshipped a vast number of deities in an expanded pantheon of new forms. The multiple heads and arms seen in Esoteric

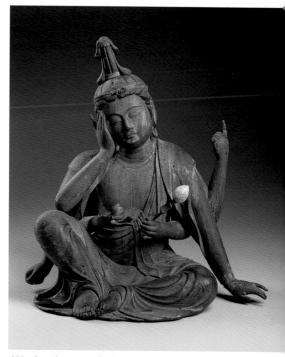

Wood with traces of gilt and pigment;
h. 19 in. (48.3 cm)
Acquired in 1985

Buddhist sculpture reflect the influence of Hinduism, symbolizing the numerous powers of the deity. Esoteric Buddhism was introduced into Japan in the ninth century by way of China, where missionaries had translated Esoteric texts from India and produced a new and varied religious iconography. The several forms of the bodhisattva Kannon reflect this complex theology.

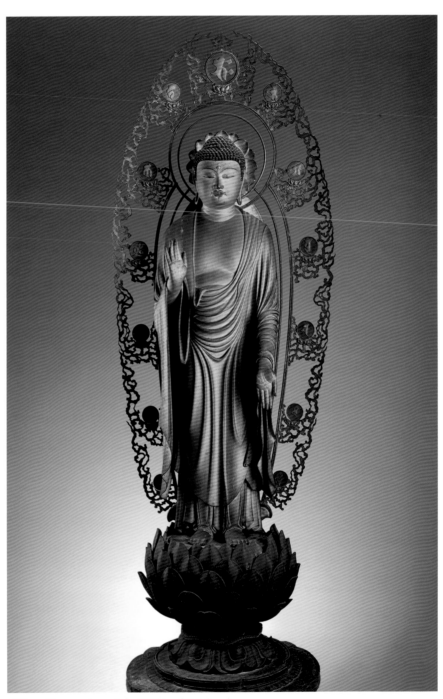

Gilt and lacquered wood; h. 54⅜ in. (138.2 cm)
Acquired in 1984

Kaikei, the great master sculptor of the Kamakura period (1185–1333), together with his slightly older contemporary Unkei (died 1223), established the primary school of sculpture that produced statuary for the major temples in Nara and Kyoto—the Kei school. They created a new, realistic style that revitalized Buddhist sculpture, which had become increasingly monotonous and stylized in the preceding century. Although the two artists worked on many projects together, Kaikei eventually developed an independent style that is more gracious and feminine than that of his colleague. Especially important among Kaikei sculptures is a distinctive style of refined, graceful Buddha, clothed in robes that are more deeply folded and decoratively draped than in the preceding Heian period.

Kaikei was a prolific artist; many Buddha statues by him, particularly of Amida (Amitabha), the Lord of the Western Paradise, are still extant. The Kimbell's sculpture is a rare image of the historical Buddha, Shaka (Shakyamuni), who is identified by the *abhayamudra* (gesture of reassurance, or granting of the "absence of fear") of the right hand. This gesture traditionally derives from the legend that Shakyamuni once stopped a rampaging, drunken elephant in his tracks by raising his right hand with the fingers close together and palm facing forward. His left foot advancing, the Buddha appears to move forward to greet the devotee with an expression of gentle and profound compassion. The beautifully proportioned figure is wrapped in an elegant robe that covers the body in rhythmical folds, rippling across the stomach and cascading over the arms. Entirely covered with gold lacquer, the robe is further embellished with a floral and geometric pattern of fine-cut gold leaf. Kaikei produced Buddha images continuously throughout his career, but his most beautiful works, including this, date to the first decade of the thirteenth century.

Shaka Buddha was of primary importance when Buddhism was established in Japan in the seventh century. However, his popularity was eclipsed during the Heian period (A.D. 794–1185), first by the magical rites and exotic gods of Esoteric Buddhism, and later by the promise of easy salvation and rebirth into the Western Paradise of the Amida Buddha. The Kamakura period saw a revival of the historical Buddha in a new type of image—as a divine savior who descends from heaven to meet the faithful. This image, called "Shaka *raigo*," is documented in paintings of the early thirteenth century that show the Buddha standing on a lotus pedestal atop a cloud, his hand raised in the gesture of fearlessness. The Kimbell statue is a rare example of this type in three-dimensional form, and one of only two known images of Shaka created by Kaikei.

Twenty-Five Bodhisattvas Descending from Heaven
Japan; Kamakura period, c. 1300

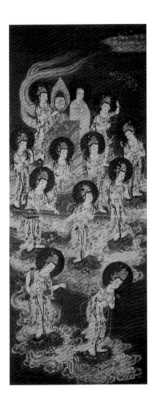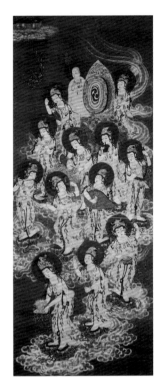

*Pair of hanging scrolls;
gold and mineral pigments
on silk; each 39 x 15¾ in.
(99 x 40 cm)
Acquired in 1986*

In this pair of paintings, twenty-five small music-making divinities, richly dressed in gold and jewels, float down from the heavens on diaphanous clouds. They are bodhisattva attendants to Amida Buddha, who inspired in his followers the hope of eternal life in his Western Paradise. The two groups are led on the right scroll by the bodhisattva Kannon, who holds a small lotus pedestal to receive the soul of the deceased, and on the left by Seishi, whose hands are held in the *anjalimudra*, the gesture of respect and salutation. The rest of the entourage play drums, a lute, koto, and other stringed instruments, and stand and dance on lotus pedestals as they float down on clouds, their long scarves and jewels swaying as they move. The figures' garments are executed in the painstaking *kirikane* technique of cut-and-pasted gold leaf.

The emergence of the cult of Amida Buddha was an important development of the late Heian period (897–1185), offering the easiest path to salvation. The devotee merely had to recite the *nembutsu*, a prayer repeatedly invoking the name of Amida Buddha, in order to gain entrance into the splendid Western Paradise. In the concept of *raigo*, Amida descends from paradise with a retinue of celestial beings to personally welcome the soul of the deceased believer into his heavenly realm. In Kamakura-period (1185–1333) *raigo* paintings, like the Kimbell's, the figures are shown standing in three-quarter view and bending slightly forward, as if rushing towards the devotee.

En no Gyoja was the legendary founder of the Shugendo sect, which emphasized the practice of religious austerities, and he thus came to represent the archetypical ascetic recluse. There is no clear documentation about his life, but he is said to have died in the early eighth century after living a hermetic life in the mountains. Because he shunned the established religious orders in the capital at Nara in favor of a solitary, itinerant life in the southern mountains, subsequent generations of clerics and laymen came to regard him as a model for those who wished to pursue religious devotion in a secular world. During the thirteenth and fourteenth centuries in particular the devotees of austere religious practices claimed En no Gyoja as the patriarch of Shugendo. Many images of him, both painted and sculpted, were commissioned by provincial temples and private believers.

This sculpture is one of a small number of posthumous portraits of En no Gyoja that survive. Since they were not produced until the Kamakura period (1185–1333), all such portraits are imaginary. This characteristic representation shows him as a bearded old man seated on a rocky ledge dressed in a monk's robe with a hood and cloak of leaves— references to his secluded life in the mountains—holding a staff and sutra scroll in his hands.

The Kamakura period, to which the Kimbell sculpture dates, experienced a renaissance in Japanese religious art. One of its hallmarks was a taste for vivid realism, evident in the lined, craggy face and expression of intense concentration of

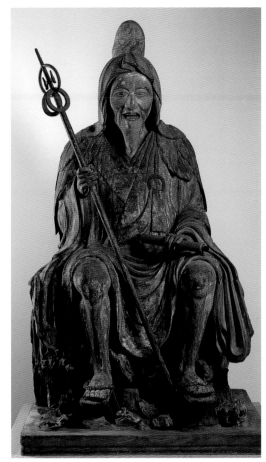

Polychromed wood; h. 55 in. (139.6 cm)
Acquired in 1984

this portrait. The eyes are fixed as if in a hypnotic gaze, and the mouth is open to expose the teeth and tongue, as if En no Gyoja were chanting the scriptures or delivering a lecture. Particular attention is paid to the signs of age and hardship in the priest's wizened body—the sinuous musculature, wrinkled joints, and bony knees, legs, and feet.

Shinto Mandala of Yuima
Japan; Nambokucho period, c. 1350

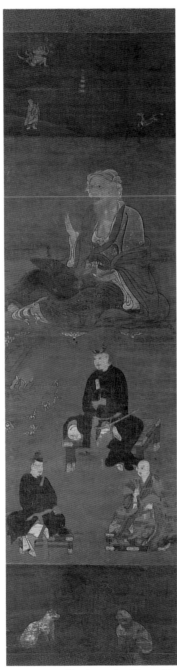

Hanging scroll; color and gold on silk;
35¼ x 9½ in. (89.5 x 24.1 cm)
Acquired in 1982

The upper and lower registers of this medieval Shinto mandala, characterized by their darker backgrounds, show (above) small figures of a thunder god, a Buddhist priest, a deer, and a pagoda; and (below) two lion-dogs facing each other. The large figure of a non-Japanese male dressed in secular costume in the second register is identified as an Indian, Vimalakirti, called Yuima in Japanese. Vimalakirti was a layman who is said to have lived in north central India during the lifetime of the historical Buddha, in the sixth century B.C. As a devotee of Buddhism, Vimalakirti reached the height of spiritual understanding, but he chose to remain a layman throughout his life. His insight and wisdom were such that, among all of the Buddha's disciples, only Manjushri, the bodhisattva of wisdom, felt confident enough to debate with him. Below him here are shown smaller-scale representations of a male in court robes flanked by a secondary nobleman and a Buddhist priest.

The combination of Buddhist and Shinto figures in the same scene is a not uncommon feature of Shinto mandalas. When native Shintoism reached an accommodation with Buddhism, a foreign religion, the two faiths united Buddhist deities with indigenous gods in a syncretic whole, merging the Japanese gods with their Buddhist counterparts. In this painting, the figure dressed in court robes below Yuima is thought to be his Shinto counterpart. The meaning of the apparently narrative motifs of the painting and the identities of the two smaller, seated figures of a nobleman and a priest are not known.

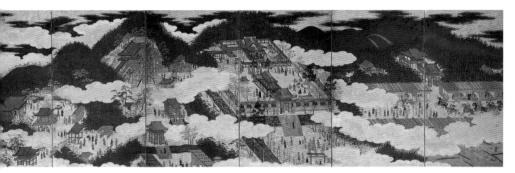

Six-fold screen; mineral pigments on gold; 35½ x 110 in. (90.2 x 279.5 cm)
Acquired in 1986

In the Momoyama (1573–1615) and early Edo (1615–1868) periods, Kyoto emerged as a large urban center with a newly wealthy merchant class that developed a taste for paintings reflecting their vibrant, affluent lifestyle. Called *rakuchu-rakugai* (literally, "in and out of Kyoto"), these colorfully painted screens depicted scenes in and around the capital, often illustrating famous scenic spots and important monuments or seasonal festivals. Also collected by visitors to the ancient capital, *rakuchu-rakugai* were usually painted as pairs of six-panel screens presenting bird's-eye panoramic views of the eastern and western sections of the city, with its major thoroughfares, architectural structures, and bustling scenes of daily life. They were painted with great attention to detail and accuracy, functioning much like photographs in recording the activity and landscape of the time. Most were produced by a professional school of *machi-eshi* (town painters), who were anonymous artisans working for commercial shops.

This meticulously detailed screen shows a portion of Higashiyama, the eastern hills that border the southern part of Kyoto. The site is easily recognizable by the inclusion of the still extant temple Kiyomizu-dera (second and third panels from the left), which is built high on a mountainside and supported by piers. The main focus of the painting is the structure in the center, which appears to be the shrine-temple complex called Hokoku Jinja, the Toyotomi family's mausoleum for the warlord Hideyoshi, built in 1599, the year after his death. The action of the painting moves from the right, with a procession of riders on horseback galloping through the shop-lined streets toward the complex in the center. Even among other examples of this meticulous style, the Kimbell screen is exceptional in its precise architectural details, lush landscape elements, and exact rendering of textile patterns on garments.

An Exiled Emperor on Okinoshima
Japan; Momoyama period, c. 1600

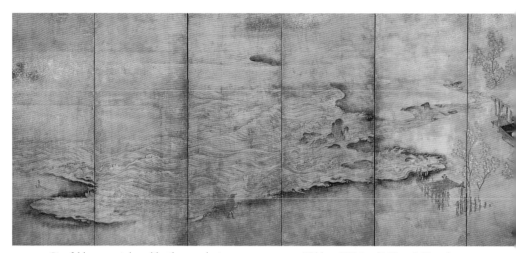

Six-fold screen; ink, gold, silver, and pigments on paper; 58¼ x 137 in. (148 x 348 cm)
Acquired in 1971

In this melancholy scene, the large sea of rough, billowing waves, the nobleman seated in the hut with only his books and koto as companions, and the dusky tones of ink and silver and gold, suggest the solitude of a distant island. A windblown visitor dressed in a straw cape, who appears to have arrived in a small boat moored at the left, trudges along the shore to the hut. The green of the tatami mats and the white and pink of the blossoming cherry trees (indicating springtime) provide the only brightness in an otherwise somber composition reflecting the sense of isolation and the forlorn state of mind of the nobleman.

The subject of the painting has not been conclusively identified, but is thought to represent the exile of a high-ranking nobleman, possibly an emperor.

Exile to a remote area of Japan or to a small offshore island was a common form of punishment for political crimes throughout Japanese history. Two emperors are known to have been exiled to the island of Okinoshima: retired emperor Gotoba-in (reigned 1184–98) and Godaigo (reigned 1318–39). Accounts of both exiles were recorded in the *Masukagami*, a historical work that covers the years 1180–1333. The account of Gotoba-in's exile, in a famous passage celebrated for its literary qualities, is the more likely to have been illustrated on an independent screen—although the scene depicted here could equally represent the events of Godaigo's exile when, after a year on the island, he escaped in springtime in a fishing boat brought by a loyal supporter, Takaoki Chidane.

KANO SHIGENOBU
Japanese, active c. 1620–1630
Wheat, Poppies, and Bamboo, early 17th century

This brilliant screen, originally one of a pair, depicts young wheat, blossoming poppies, and bamboo, all of the summer season. Boldly patterned with bright mineral colors on a gold ground, it exemplifies the exuberant decorative style of the Kano school. A heightened sense of realism is achieved with the use of the *moriage* technique, whereby parts of the composition are built up by the application of gesso to create raised designs on the painting surface.

The emerging elite of the Momoyama feudal system were the *daimyo* (feudal lords), who controlled extensive domains and served as advisors to the shogun (military overlords). The magnificent castles of the *daimyo* were embellished with colorful paintings on screens and sliding doors, often decorated with gold-leaf backgrounds, which served to brighten the huge, dark interiors. Among the retainers in the service of the *daimyo* lords were the painters of the Kano school, a family of secular artists who formed the most important school of decorative painting from the sixteenth to eighteenth century. The Kano masters followed what they considered a true Chinese, monochrome-ink painting tradition based on the art of the Chinese Southern-Song-dynasty court painters of the twelfth and thirteenth centuries. Eventually, the Kano painters added colorful and decorative elements to their work, developing a bold style well suited to these grand commissions. In particular, the Kano school painters of Kyoto popularized the *kimpeki* style of gold-ground screens painted in opaque mineral pigments.

The painting bears two abraded seals: the jar-shaped seal of the Kano school and that of the artist Shigenobu, whose biography has not survived, but who was known to be active in Kyoto in the 1620s.

Six-fold screen; ink, colors, and gofun on gold leaf paper; 59⅞ x 139¾ in. (152 x 357 cm)
Acquired in 1969

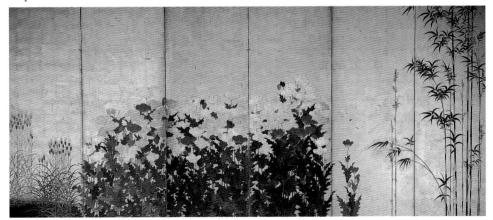

Sliding Door Panel with Design of Imperial Eagle, Plum Tree, and Camellia

Japan; Momoyama period, first half of 17th century

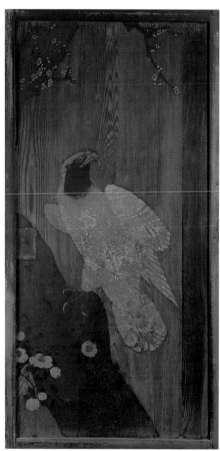

Cryptomeria wood, gesso with pigments; 62¾ x 32⅛ in. (159.4 x 81.6 cm)
Acquired in 1995

black, and some gold) to create a paste; this is applied in successive layers to the untreated panel, building up to create a design in low relief. The motif of the eagle, like the hawk, was most likely a symbol of the samurai (warrior) class in Japan. Both birds became recurrent themes in painting from about the fourteenth or fifteenth century. The eagle represented on this door has been identified as an imperial eagle, a species that originated on the east coast of China and was introduced to Japan as early as the fifteenth century. Plum blossoms are often paired with camellias to represent the rejuvenation that comes with the first signs of spring.

Beginning in the Momoyama period (1573–1615) and continuing into the Edo period (1615–1868), painted doors were commonly installed in the magnificent castle residences of the wealthy *daimyo* (feudal lord) and powerful shogun (military overlord) families. Constructed from wood and decorated with painted designs, sometimes with gilt backgrounds, these *sugito* served to brighten dark, damp castle interiors. They were enhanced with a variety of motifs ranging from landscapes, birds, and flowers, to historical, mythological, and allegorical scenes. As was the case in China, birds and flowers formed a special genre in Japanese decorative painting, each type and species having its own symbolic meaning. Birds of prey such as the eagle and the hawk were particularly popular subjects, represented in screens and on sliding doors, and were often paired with trees or flowers.

This sliding door panel, adorned with a majestic white eagle perched on a blossoming plum tree, is the right half of a two-panel *sugito* (cedar door). The plain wood surface of the door is decorated with gesso, a gluelike substance, mixed with pigments (primarily tones of white,

Negoro lacquerwares constitute a special group of simple food-serving utensils that are distinctive for their solid, cinnabar red finish and austere, functional forms. Although Negoro wares include objects with simple black lacquer finishes or painted designs, a deep, warm red is the most common color. The wares are especially admired when the plain red surface becomes almost translucent with age and is gently abraded from handling, allowing the black lacquer undercoat to show through.

The term Negoro comes from the name of the Negoro-dera temple in Wakayama prefecture. According to tradition, red lacquer vessels were first made at the temple in the thirteenth century for use by its own priests. Since the temple was destroyed during civil wars in 1585, no documentation survives to substantiate this tradition. Nevertheless, the term is now widely used for all red lacquer vessels that fall into the appropriate category of shapes.

The Kimbell's wine flask is a fine example of the simple, conservative, yet striking forms distinctive of Negoro lacquers. The broad, softly rounded shoulders curve to a sharp edge that sets off the extreme slope of the body to the narrow waist and broad, flat foot. The shape, called *heishi* in Japanese, derives from a Chinese pottery vessel type of the Tang period (A.D. 618–907) called *meiping*. *Heishi* is the term for a bottle used for offering sacred sake (Japanese rice wine) at the altar of a Buddhist temple. Sake was rarely poured in lacquered wooden bottles like this one, however, since they were intended mainly as ornaments.

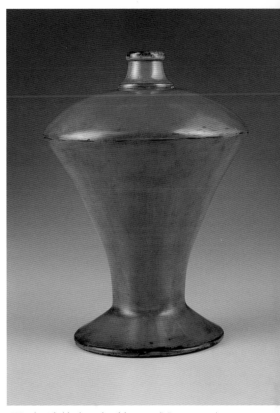

Wood with black and red lacquer (Negoro ware); h. 11¾ in. (29.9 cm)
Acquired in 1981

Storage Jar
Japan, Momoyama period, c. 1600

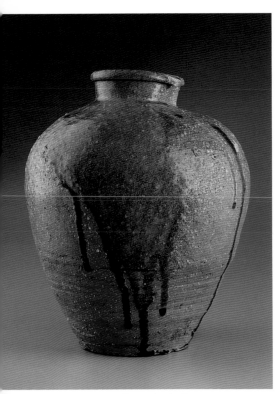

Stoneware with wood-ash glaze
(Shigaraki ware); h. 14 in. (35.6 cm)
Acquired in 1969

The distinct feature of Shigaraki ware is its bright green natural glaze, which appears over the burnt, reddish brown surface of the pots during the firing process. The local clay used for making Shigaraki bowls and jars is distinguished by a light sandy texture and a high proportion of feldspar granules that appear as glassy white spots on the surface of the fired vessel. Large storage jars like this one were coil-built in stages; they show horizontal registers where the potter stopped to let the pot dry enough to support the weight of the next rise of coils. The eye-catching natural green glaze flows from the mouth over the orange body of the jar. Connoisseurs of Japanese pottery have long admired the robust shapes and warm colors exhibited in such utilitarian vessels.

The Shigaraki kilns in Shiga prefecture have been an active pottery center since the Kamakura period (1185–1333) and continue to produce pottery up to the present day. Bizen, Tokoname, Tamba, Seto, Echizen, and Shigaraki are traditionally known as the Six Ancient Kilns, although additional medieval kiln sites have been discovered. Shigaraki potters used the *anagame*, the subterranean hillside kilns found at many medieval sites. These achieved higher temperatures and an oxidizing atmosphere, unlike the earlier Sue ware, reduction-fired kilns. The Shigaraki kilns initially produced functional wares to store seeds and tea. However, by the Momoyama period (1573–1615) the unassuming naturalness of the sturdy shapes, earthy colors, and rustic decoration of this domestic ware had come to be highly regarded by masters of the tea ceremony.

The rapid development and diversification of the Japanese porcelain industry in the seventeenth century was the result of many technically skilled potters being brought to Japan from Korea. Led by Ri Sampei (1579–1655), who discovered porcelain clays in northern Kyushu in 1616, Korean immigrant potters established a major porcelain production area in Arita, the town near these deposits. The Arita kilns initially produced white wares decorated with an underglaze cobalt blue. In the 1640s the techniques of polychrome overglaze enamels were introduced from China; eventually the Arita potters succeeded in manufacturing brilliant overglaze enamel colors that gleamed against a smooth, milky-white porcelain surface. Sakaida Kakiemon (1596–1666) is generally credited with the consequent development of applying polychrome enamels, predominantly red, blue, green, yellow, and purple, to fired vessels that were then refired at a lower temperature. Kakiemon is the name given to porcelains made by Sakaida and his descendents. This initiative eventually spawned a number of kilns in Arita with specialized decorative styles, including Kakiemon, Nabeshima, Imari, and Kutani.

The earliest Arita overglaze designs were mainly copies of Chinese wares, based on Chinese painting of the late Ming (1368–1644) and early Qing (1644–1911) dynasties. As time went on, however, designs became more thoroughly Japanese in flavor. The Kimbell's large and impressive Arita jar derives its form and certain elements of its design from

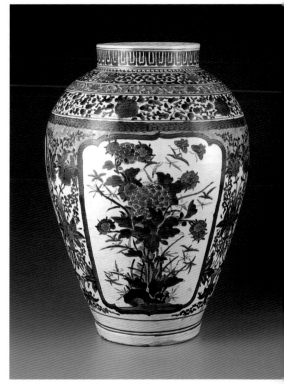

Porcelain with underglaze blue and overglaze colored enamels (Arita ware, Kakiemon type); h. 19¼ in. (48.9 cm)
Acquired in 1968

Chinese Ming-dynasty styles, notably in the upright leaf pattern on the rim, the floral scrolls on the shoulder, and the bordered panels on the body that enclose clumps of flowering plants. The free and imaginative execution of the blossoms and leaves has a distinctly Japanese flavor. The clear, milky-white color of the porcelain body suggests that this jar may date from the early period of overglaze porcelain production, sometime in the last quarter of the seventeenth century.

Handled Dish
Japan; Edo period, c. 1650

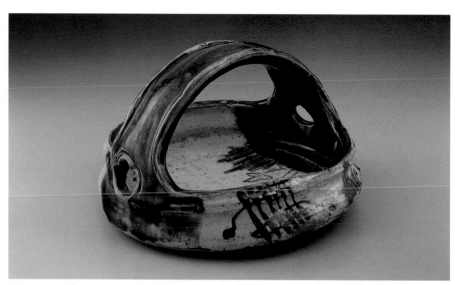

Stoneware with transparent glaze, iron oxide, and colored enamels (Oribe ware); h. 4⅞ in. (12.3 cm)
Acquired in 1983

Ceramics with copper green glazes were first fired at the Mino kilns around the middle of the sixteenth century, at the end of the Muromachi period (1392–1573). But it was not until the late Momoyama period, around 1600–1610, that the so-called Oribe ware, which is richly decorated with white slip, brown paint, and green glaze, came to be produced in quantity. The name of Oribe ware derives from the tea-ceremony practitioner and warrior of the Momoyama period, Furuta Oribe (1544–1615), the most devoted student of Sen no Riyku (1522–1591), one of the most famous tea-ceremony masters in Japan. Born in Mino, Oribe is believed to have guided production at some of the Mino kilns, near modern-day Nagoya city. Oribe favored bold, distorted shapes and imaginative new patterns in his teaware. Characteristically, the shapes combine geometric and curvilinear elements, and mechanical as well as organically derived features. At their best, Oribe wares are among the most innovative tea utensils made during the Momoyama period.

A wealth of shapes, surface designs, and painting styles characterizes Oribe ware production through the mid-seventeenth century. This irregularly shaped dish was used to serve sweets at a tea ceremony. It appears to have been started on a wheel and finished by hand to achieve the uneven shape. The handle was formed from clay drawn up from the sides of the dish; the trefoil-shaped open-work at each base of the handle makes the piece lighter in appearance. The contrast between the simple decoration of brown floral and geometric motifs and the eye-catching splash of bright green glaze over a finely crackled, cream-colored ground illustrates the special sense of design admired in Oribe wares.

Mukozuke Japan; Edo period, early 17th century	**Mizusashi** Japan; Edo period, c. 1700

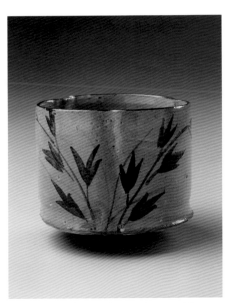 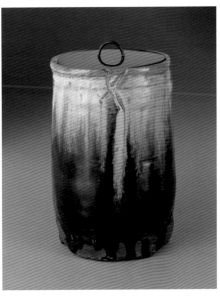

Stoneware with gray glaze and iron oxide
(e-karatsu ware); h. 3½ in. (8.9 cm)
Acquired in 1971

Stoneware with brownish black and creamy
white glazes (chosen-karatsu ware);
h. 7⅜ in. (18.5 cm)
Acquired in 1971

The main products of the Karatsu kilns on the island of Kyushu, which derived from Korean prototypes, were utensils for the tea ceremony. The *mukozuke* is a small, deep bowl used for serving side dishes in the traditional *kaiseki* meal that precedes the drinking of ceremonial tea. In the Kimbell *mukozuke*, a beautiful example of *e-karatsu* (painted Karatsu), the simple underglaze designs of leafy grass and curled vines are painted in iron oxide applied prior to glazing. The rim was shaped by hand to form petals before receiving its freely painted design. The distinctive lobed shape, graceful proportions, and warm, muted color of the bowl are qualities the tea connoisseur most admired in utensils from Karatsu.

A *mizusashi* is a jar with a lid used to hold fresh water for pouring into the *kama* (kettle) or for rinsing the tea bowls and tea whisk. The Kimbell's example is in the ware known as *chosen-karatsu* (in Korean, Karatsu), which is characterized by the bold combination of two different glazes—a white, straw-ash glaze and an iron oxide glaze that fires to a glossy dark brown—which streak and blur when they meet. Many pieces of *chosen-karatsu*, especially tall jars, were formed using the "patting method" *(tataki)*—coiling and paddling the clay vessel into shape—rather than on a wheel. The intentionally irregular contour of this jar and the incised X-shaped mark near the rim reflect the Japanese taste for pottery of a natural and often rustic authenticity, in which the direct touch of the potter's hand is not hidden but brought to the fore and prized.

OGATA KENZAN
Japanese, 1663–1743
Bowl with Bamboo Leaf Design,
early 18th century

OGATA KENZAN
Japanese, 1663–1743
Bowl with Pampas Grass Design,
early 18th century

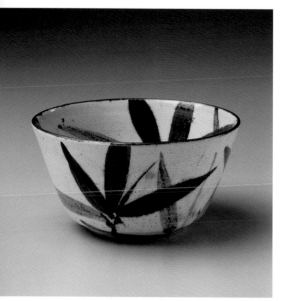

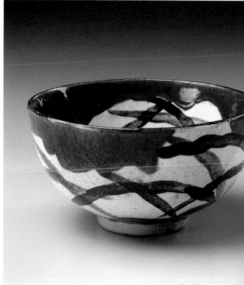

Stoneware with underglaze iron oxide and transparent glaze; h. 2⅜ in. (6.2 cm) Acquired in 1969

Stoneware with iron oxide, colored enamels, and transparent glaze; h. 3⅜ in. (8.5 cm) Acquired in 1971

Ogata Kenzan was one of the three great masters of painted ceramics in the Edo period (1615–1868). He developed an imaginative ceramic style characterized by a harmony between deftly painted designs and simple, sturdy ceramic forms. His workshop, based in Kyoto and later in Edo (Tokyo), also developed innovative uses of pigments and glazes. His distinctive style of freely brushed grasses, blossoms, and birds was employed especially for decorating tea ceramics.

Kenzan's early training as a painter is evident in the *Bowl with Bamboo Leaf Design*, where the thinness and tonal variations of the brushwork are evocative of ink painting. Both the intentionally asymmetrical shape, and the sharp-edged

leaves and contrasting colors and textures of the glazes, reflect the aesthetics of the tea ceremony, which were designed to appeal to different senses during the extended ritual of drinking. The bowl was originally part of a set of five or perhaps ten vessels that may have been made as *mukozuke* (side dishes) or *kumidashi chawan* (cups used for serving tea in a waiting room). Although the graceful design of the *Bowl with Pampas Grass Design* is just as carefully conceived, the end result appears more casual, with the bright green glaze dripping onto either side of the bowl. It was originally one of a larger set of *futa-chawan* (covered tea bowls) used for serving steamed food. The two-character signature *Kenzan* is brushed in brown paint on the bottom of both bowls.

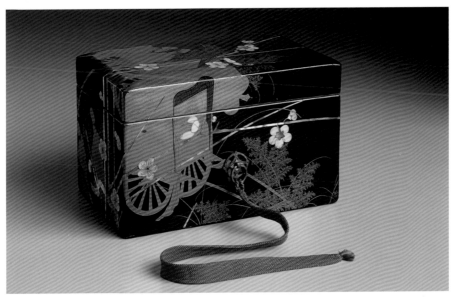

Black lacquer with gold and lead designs, mother-of-pearl and shell inlays; h. 5⅛ in. (13 cm)
Acquired in 1976

The decorative potential of lacquer has been exploited in Japan since the sixth century, in a variety of styles and techniques. Long admired for their durability and excellent finish, beautifully decorated lacquer objects were used as votive offerings in temples and as luxury items by the nobility. With the rise of a middle class in the Momoyama period (1573–1615), lacquer was put to new purposes. Among the new, practical lacquer items to appear were portable boxes in which the decoration continues from the lid and around the sides of the box, creating a harmony of form and decoration. In the Edo period (1615–1868), the working of lacquer reached new levels of artistic and technical refinement.

The decorative use of gold, lead, and mother-of-pearl and shell inlay in the scene of courtiers, carts, and blossoms on this box exemplifies the sophistication of design that Edo lacquerwares had attained. The scene depicted on the exterior of the box probably comes from the *Tale of Genji*, the famous Heian-period romantic novel written by Lady Murasaki Shikibu (c. 973– c. 1015). The specific subject is difficult to determine, but the prominence of the motif of bullock carts suggests that it might have been inspired by the episode *"Karuma arasoi"* (Battle of the Carts). On the inner face of the lid is a scene of two musicians and a dancer performing a *bugaku* dance. *Bugaku* dances, which derive from Chinese dances of the Tang period (A.D. 618–907), were adopted by the Japanese imperial court during the Heian period and performed at court ceremonies. Alternatively, this scene may allude to a chapter from the *Tale of Genji* such as the *"Momiji no ga"* (Festival of the Red Leaves).

Spring and Autumn Flowers, Fruits, and Grasses
Japan; Edo period, 18th century

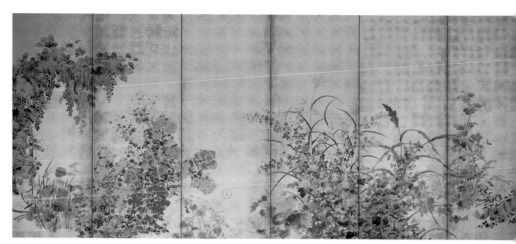

Pair of six-fold screens; mineral pigments on gold leaf;
left: 61⅛ x 142⅞ in. (155.9 x 362.9 cm); right: 61⅛ x 142⅝ in. (155.9 x 362.3 cm)
Acquired in 1983

The Rinpa school represents the fullest expression of the highly decorative approach to nature painting in Japan. This pair of six-fold screens depicts seasonal flowers, fruits, and grasses rendered in typically bright colors on a brilliant gold background. The wisteria, hydrangea, morning glories, and hollyhocks on the right represent spring and the transition to summer, while the millet, eggplant, bush clover, chrysanthemums, and grapes on the left suggest late summer and autumn. The rich, glowing mineral colors and the subtleties of a technique called *tarashikomi*, which mixes ink with pigments to produce a puddled effect, heighten the elegant decorativeness that gives these screens their distinctive character.

Rinpa is an artistic tradition that was founded in the Momoyama period by the calligrapher Hon'ami Koetsu (1558–1637) and the designer-painter Tawaraya Sotatsu (died c. 1640), and was perpetuated in the Edo period by Ogata Korin (1658–1716), his brother Kenzan (1663–1743), and various followers. The name Rinpa derives

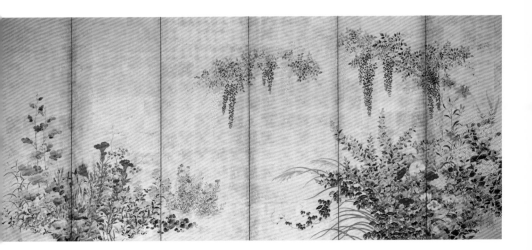

from the second syllable of the name "Korin" and the character for "school" *(pa)*. The Rinpa school was not literally a school but an artistic tradition based on the common aspirations of its followers. Rinpa was characterized by vivid colors and bold, decorative patterning that derived from a revival of the native *yamato-e* tradition of pictures and themes drawn from classical literature and poetry. Other popular Rinpa subjects included birds and flowers of the four seasons. Rinpa clients were drawn from both the court and the wealthy merchant classes of Kyoto and Edo (Tokyo).

The artist of these screens has not been identified. Each screen bears a circular seal carved in the style of Rinpa Inen seals, but the characters have not been deciphered. The soft and luscious quality of the brushwork, the sense of depth created by color, and the judicious placement of foliage groupings suggest a date in the middle of the Edo period.

TORII KIYONOBU
Japanese, 1664–1729
Beauty in a Black Kimono, c. 1710–20

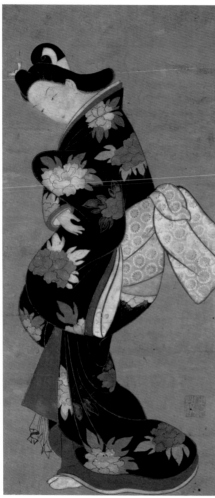

*Hanging scroll; ink, colors, and gold on paper;
23⅞ x 10⅞ in. (60.7 x 27.7 cm)
Acquired in 1988*

The urban culture of the Edo period (1615–1868) was dominated by a newly affluent merchant class that soon began to influence artistic production through its interest in the colorful world of the pleasure quarters, a walled-off section of the city containing brothels, teahouses, and the theater district. Here men would go to be in the company of beautiful courtesans who were schooled in poetry, painting, calligraphy, and the refinements of the tea ceremony. Idealized depictions of these famous courtesans, their clients, and well-known male actors became increasingly popular, giving rise to a new type of art called *ukiyo-e*— pictures of the ever-changing "floating world" of the fashionable and cultured pleasure district. The decorative *ukiyo-e* school dominated both genre painting and prints throughout the Edo period, continually representing the most current styles and trends that appealed to the urbane inhabitants of Edo (Tokyo), Kyoto, and Osaka.

This painting of a young woman dressed in an eye-catching, boldly patterned black kimono is a rare work by the early *ukiyo-e* artist Torii Kiyonobu, the son of a kabuki actor and theatrical design painter. Kiyonobu, the founder of the Torii school of painting and print-making, was very successful with works that focused on the theater and the denizens of the pleasure quarters. Here, the demure pose and coquettish expression of an elegantly dressed woman capture the seductive qualities popular among patrons of the pleasure quarters. As is typical of fashionable portraits of ladies produced at this time, the hair and facial features are stylized, the artist focusing attention on the garments. The kimono is decorated with a checker-board-pattern, jacquard weave over which are painted peonies in red, ocher, and blue. Gold outlines around the flowers and the edges of the garment further enhance the richness of the fabric and liveliness of the pattern.

The Edo period (1615–1868) school of *ukiyo-e* (pictures of the floating world) focused on genre scenes and stylized portraits of the famous courtesans, samurai, and kabuki actors who inhabited the pleasure districts of the great urban centers of Edo (Tokyo), Kyoto, and Osaka. Genre painting had became popular during the Momoyama period (1573–1615), with the execution of large, detailed screen paintings of cityscapes, seasonal festivals, and the general populace. In the seventeenth century, *ukiyo-e* artists began treating less extensive subjects, scenes that would have been small sections of the large Momoyama screens, illustrating daily life and the lively activities of the theater and pleasure quarters, in both paintings and woodblock prints.

Single figure studies became increasingly popular, the background and setting fading from the picture as attention was focused on pose and costume. In this painting, a stylish young man pauses under a blossoming plum tree as he surveys the scene around him. He wears an eye-catching striped kimono worn over a red undergarment and a brown sash. His accessories—a peaked straw hat, wooden clogs, flute in his sash, and *kesa*, or square apron that is part of a priest's costume—indicate that he is affecting the look of a *komuso*, or mendicant flute player.

Miyagawa Choshun was one of the great *ukiyo-e* artists of the first half of the eighteenth century. Trained in the Tosa school of traditional Japanese painting, Choshun is one of the few *ukiyo-e* artists of his day who did not design the popular woodblock prints but painted exclusively on paper and silk. He was a painter

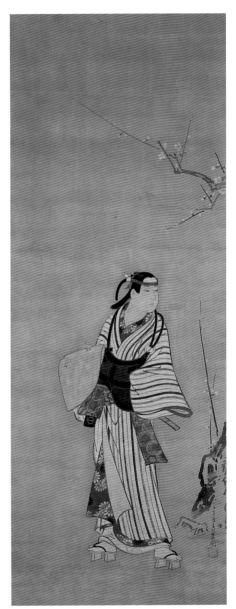

Hanging scroll; ink and light colors on paper; 37¾ x 14⅛ in. (95.9 x 35.9 cm) Acquired in 1984

of great delicacy and a skilled colorist, as is evident in this elegant painting of a fashionable youth.

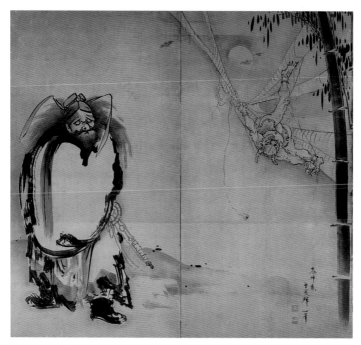

Two-fold screen;
ink on paper;
62½ x 68 in.
(158.7 x 172.8 cm)
Acquired in 1987

Soga Shohaku was one of the Three Eccentrics of the Edo period (1615–1868). During his lifetime he dominated the art world of Kyoto, although many of his contemporaries considered him mad. Accounts of Shohaku's life are full of anecdotes about his bizarre behavior, and stories about him took on a legendary character. He enjoyed immense popularity in Japan during his lifetime, and his paintings were appreciated for their unconventional approach to classical subject matter.

Shoki, the subject of this painting, is the Japanese name of a Chinese popular hero, Zhong Kui, who lived in the seventh century, during the early Tang dynasty (A.D. 618–907). Trained as a physician, Zhong Kui was unjustly defrauded of a first-rank grade in his civil examinations. Overcome with shame,

he committed suicide on the steps of the imperial palace. The emperor then ordered that he be buried with high honors in a green robe reserved for the imperial family. Out of gratitude, Zhong Kui's spirit dedicated itself to protecting the empire from demons.

The conventional "portrait" image of Zhong Kui was said to have been created in China by the celebrated eighth-century artist Wu Daozi, who was noted for his bold calligraphic style. Shoki the Demon Queller became a popular subject of Japanese painting in the Edo period, and Shohaku painted it in many versions, always with humor and imagination. Though executed in ink with strong and forceful strokes, his paintings are never extreme in their exaggerations but marked by a refinement of brushwork that lies at the core of his achievement.

The *nanga* (southern painting) school, also called *bunjinga* (literati painting), was one of the two most dynamic schools of Japanese painting during the eighteenth and first half of the nineteenth century. In contrast to the sensuous school of native decorative art, called *ukiyo-e* (pictures of the floating world), the *nanga* school was the last manifestation of the centuries-old Japanese preoccupation with China. It was based on the monochrome-ink landscape styles of Chinese literati painters, adopted and modified according to Japanese taste, and was patronized principally by the cultivated upper strata of Japanese society living in Kyoto.

Yosa Buson was one of the two greatest painters of the *nanga* school. He was also one of the most famous poets of the Edo period (1615–1868). It is believed that his serious career as an artist began in 1751, when he finally settled in Kyoto after a ten-year period of wandering. The signature *Sha-in* on the Kimbell's painting is one that Buson used from 1778 until his death. This period is regarded as his most successful, when he best expresses his feeling for poetry through his painting.

This scroll depicts a landscape with a narrow road winding upward through the mountains. A solitary traveler wrapped in a green cloak crosses a footbridge constructed over a swollen, rushing stream. Inscribed on the scroll is the last line of a poem by the Chinese Tang-period poet Han Yu (768–824): *A single path in cold mountains through the myriad streams.* Using this as his theme, Buson evokes the sense of cold through the pale green and gray coloring, the leafless trees, and the traveler's cloak.

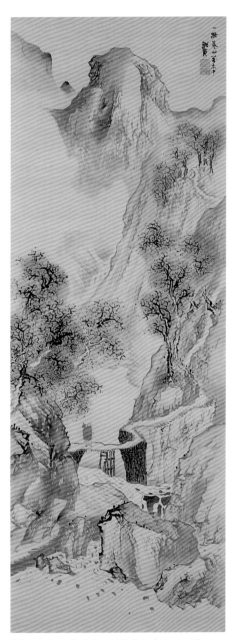

Hanging scroll; ink and light colors on silk; 40 x 14⅛ in. (101.5 x 36.4 cm) Acquired in 1981

ITO JAKUCHU
Japanese, 1713–1800
Fukurojin, the God of Longevity and Wisdom, c. 1790

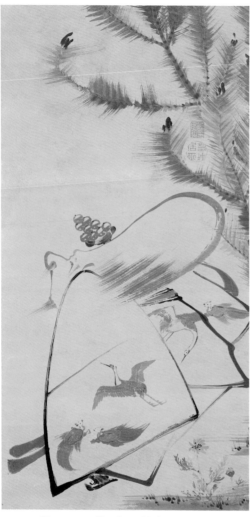

Hanging scroll; ink and light colors on paper;
45⅝ x 22¼ in. (115.9 x 56.5 cm)
Acquired in 1986

Jakuchu, one of the Three Eccentrics of the Edo period (1615–1868), was a remarkable individualist whose paintings defy easy classification. Born in Kyoto, he was the eldest son of a wealthy green-grocer. Although he inherited the family business, he left the running of the shop to his brother and devoted his entire life to painting. Jakuchu is believed to have studied initially with a minor master of the Kano school, but eventually rebelled against this discipline in favor of a more individual style. Jakuchu's oeuvre is extensive and broad in scope. His style ranges from colorful, decorative works on silk to daring compositions in ink; his subjects include elegant depictions of flowers and barnyard fowl, as well as major Buddhist icons and narrative themes.

This humorous image depicts Fukuro-jin, one of a group of Chinese divinities called the "Seven Household Gods," who were also popular folk deities in Japan. Fukurojin, an old man, is always distin-guished in this group by an exaggerated, tall forehead, which is taken to be indica-tive of his superhuman intelligence and wisdom. He stands under a pine tree with branches that are softly brushed to create the sense of long, thick pine needles, and is dressed in a voluminous robe decorated with cranes and long-tailed turtles. In Asian mythology these three motifs—pine, crane, and turtle—are symbols of longevity. In this freely brushed and seemingly spontaneous work, Jakuchu has employed his unique technique of making a single, wet stroke of ink stand out from the next by a rim of paler ink spread by absorption at its edges. This method effectively adds depth and texture to a largely monochromatic work.

ISODA KORYUSAI
Japanese, active c. 1764–1788
Courtesan Playing the Samisen, c. 1785

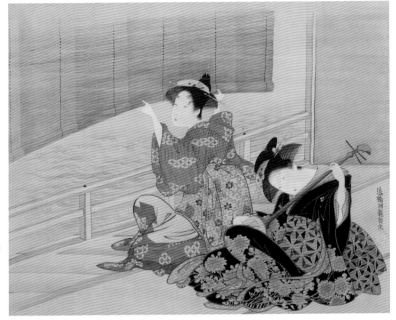

*Hanging scroll; ink
and gold on silk;
15½ x 19½ in.
(39.4 x 49.5 cm)
Acquired in 1984*

This painting is a late masterwork by Isoda Koryusai, who was an important and prolific *ukiyo-e* painter and print-maker in the last quarter of the eighteenth century, a time when Koryusai and other artists showed a keen fascination with the natural world. In the Kimbell's painting, the intimate scene of a courtesan and her attendant in a teahouse overlooking a river subtly suggests the elegance and entertainment of the pleasure quarters. The bamboo shade that is being rolled up by the young attendant indicates that the weather is warm, while the chrysanthemums decorating the kimono of the courtesan signal the end of summer and the approach of autumn. The wind gently blows ripples across the water. Reflecting the most current modes, the two women wear a popular hairstyle of the period, in which the side locks billowed out, taking on the abstract form of a lantern top or open fan. The richly patterned textiles and the strong diagonal formed by the railing of the verandah make this monochromatic painting a work of unusual sophistication and visual appeal.

Koryusai is believed to have been born a samurai (warrior) and to have relinquished his rank in order to move to the capital city of Edo (Tokyo) to become an artist. His early training is unclear, but his style was strongly influenced by the *ukiyo-e* master Suzuki Harunobu (1725–1770). In 1781 Koryusai received the honorary title *hokkyo* from the Japanese government in recognition of his artistic talent and productivity. He gave up print designing in the 1780s to devote himself entirely to painting, although few of his painted works have survived.

REKISENTEI EIRI
Japanese, active c. 1790–1800
Beauty in a White Kimono, c. 1800

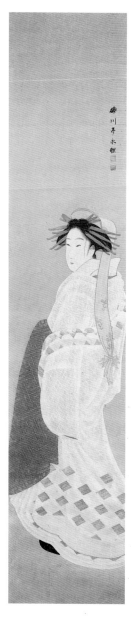

*Hanging scroll;
ink and mineral
pigments on paper;
48⅞ x 10⅜ in.
(124 x 26.3 cm)
Acquired in 1981*

and outer cloak, which are designed in a variety of delicate geometric patterns. The snowflake pattern of the kimono is produced by a tie-dying technique, while the outer robe is brocaded with a pattern of quadruple lozenges evocative of ice crystals. The red sash that ties in front features a diaper pattern in gold, called *sayagata*, and indicates the figure's youth and high rank as a courtesan. A thin strand of hair dangling against the courtesan's cheek is an informal touch that contrasts gently with the perfect formality of her dress and adds to the seductive appeal of the painting.

Paintings of courtesans displayed the latest styles of dress among the fashion-conscious ladies of the pleasure quarters, and they sometimes refer to specific events or special festival days. The all-white costume in this painting was worn only in Edo (Tokyo) on *hassaku*, the first day of the eighth lunar month, which was known as the "eighth-month snow" or "fall snow." The courtesans of the Yoshi-wara district in Edo wore white on that day to commemorate the first time, in 1590, that the Generalissimo Tokugawa Ieyasu (died 1616) entered Edo. Ieyasu, who was later appointed shogun (military overlord) of all Japan, was responsible for making Edo the administrative and cultural capital of Japan.

The *ukiyo-e* artist Rekisentei Eiri painted a celebrated portrait of the famous Edo-period novelist Santo Kyoden (active c. 1790), as well as a number of splendid pictures of courtesans. His identity is often confused with two other painters who are known to have used the name Eiri for brief times in their careers.

This decorative hanging scroll shows a courtesan, who pauses to glance seductively over her left shoulder, proudly displaying her magnificent white kimono

Shibata Zeshin was the outstanding Japanese lacquer artist and painter of the nineteenth century. A strong proponent of traditional Japanese culture at a time when younger artists were being overwhelmed by new influences from the West, he effectively demonstrated in his work that innovation could coincide with tradition. The son of a sculptor, he was apprenticed to a lacquer maker and showed exceptional talent in that medium from an early age. His subsequent painting instruction in the naturalistic Shijo style was intended to improve the design of his lacquer work. An energetic and prolific artist, he earned distinction during his lifetime for paintings that showed unusual creativity, including works painted in a special technique using lacquer.

Zeshin painted several works showing animals mimicking human behavior, a subject that appears in Japanese art as far back as the Heian period (A.D. 794–1185). By demonstrating the apparent humanity of the animals, Zeshin creates a kinship between viewer and subject; and because monkeys naturally resemble man in their actions, they were a frequent choice of subject for works of this kind.

Painted during Zeshin's artistic maturity, *Waterfall and Monkeys* is exceptional for its monumentality of scale and concept. While both waterfalls and monkeys are popular as singular subjects in Japanese painting, this imaginative and humorous combination is unique. Zeshin creates a lively scene of a troop of young monkeys with their beleaguered mother, crawling about the craggy rocks at the base of a fast-flowing waterfall. The naturalness and variety of the monkeys' poses

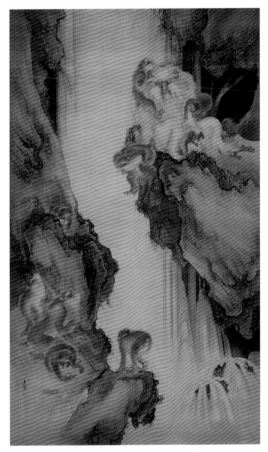

Hanging scroll; ink and light colors on silk; 73⅞ x 44¾ in. (187.7 x 113.7 cm) Acquired in 1984

and expressions suggest that Zeshin observed simian behavior firsthand. His interest in realism is further apparent in the delicate rendering of the monkeys' fur, from the soft washes and short, fine lines that define the youngsters' coats, to the longer, fluid strokes of the mother's thick hair. A large and ambitious painting, *Waterfall and Monkeys* demonstrates Zeshin's sure sense of space and compositional balance.

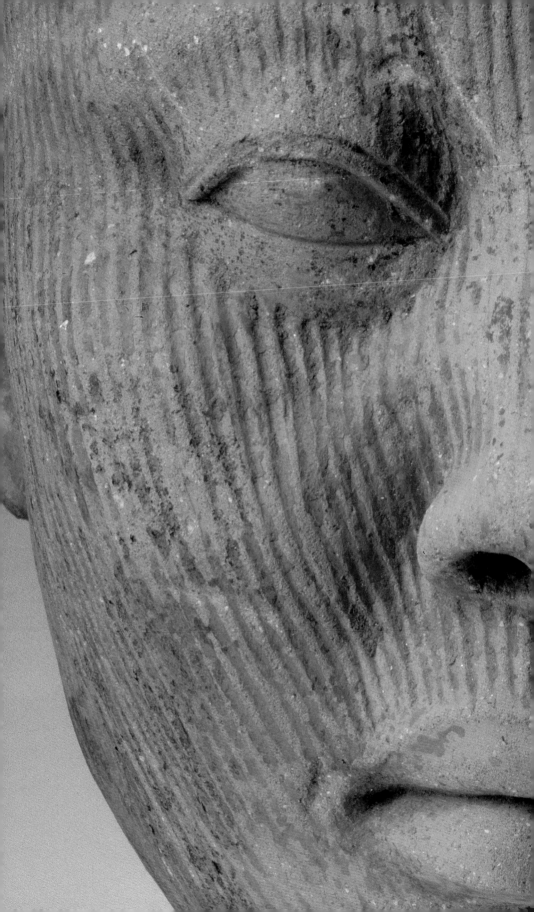

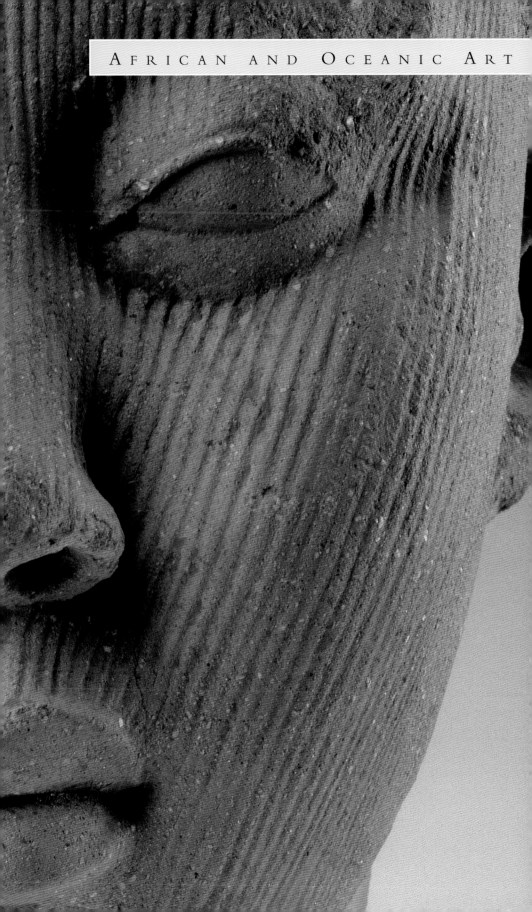

Male Figure
Nok culture; northern Nigeria, Africa; c. 195 B.C.–A.D. 205

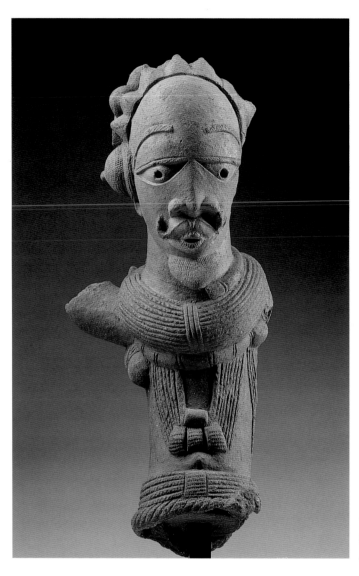

Terra-cotta;
h. 19½ in. (49.5 cm)
Acquired in 1996

Nok terra-cottas are the earliest known sculptures from ancient Nigeria, dating from about 500 B.C. to about A.D. 500. Sculptures of this kind were first discovered in 1943 by Bernard Fagg near the small northern Nigerian village of Nok, after which the culture that produced them was named. Among the characteristic features of the Nok style are the treatment of the eyes, which form a segment of a circle or triangle, with the arched eyebrow balancing the sweep of the lower lid; the piercing of the eyes, nostrils, mouth, and ears; and the sometimes unanatomical placement (or absence) of the ears. The distribution of such sculpture over an area of three hundred square miles suggests that Nok culture was hierarchically structured, with a unified political or religious power base.

In their finest works, including the two Kimbell sculptures, the highly skilled Nok artisans created images of great power, beauty, and sophistication. With its expressively modeled head, finely detailed features—especially the lips, mouth, beard, and coiffure—and carefully defined costume, the commanding *Male Figure* represents the fully developed Nok style. The complex hairstyle is composed of three rows of seven conical buns, with larger hemispherical caps over the ears. The importance of jewelry in Nok culture is illustrated by the elaborate costume, which is lavishly adorned with meticulously rendered necklaces and beaded chains. The horn, shown slung over the back of the shoulders, may identify the figure as a shaman. The sculpture is broken at the waistline, but may originally have been kneeling.

The unadorned *Head* represents a more restrained tradition within Nok art, and was perhaps produced in another area. Sculpted in the round, it was most likely broken at the neck from a full figure. The simple features delineated in the smooth surface of the head are noticeably flatter than those of the *Male Figure*. The uniform, caplike coiffure reaches from ear to ear, covering them completely.

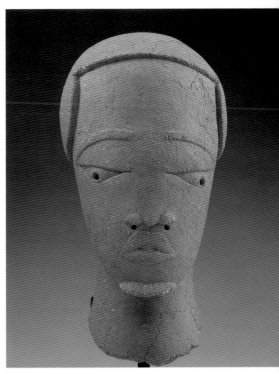

Terra-cotta; h. 12¾ in. (32.4 cm)
Acquired in 1996

The eyes, nostrils, and a spot beneath the covered ears are pierced; the flat, wide unpierced lips are slightly parted to show clenched teeth. There is no mustache, but the standard small beard projects from the bottom of the chin. The eyes, of typical triangular shape, are surmounted by thin eyebrows decorated with cross-hatching. Altogether, the restrained articulation of the facial features—a minimalist conception that resonates with much modernist European art—endows this head with a quietly regal composure.

Head, Possibly a King
Ife culture; southwestern Nigeria, Africa, 12th–14th century

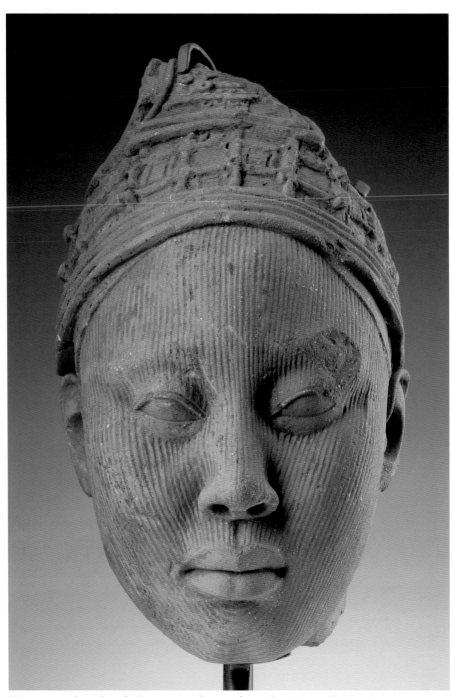

Terra-cotta with residue of red pigment and traces of mica; h. 10½ in. (26.7 cm)
Acquired in 1994

The art of Ife, which flourished in the area of southwestern Nigeria occupied by the Yoruba peoples from the twelfth to the fifteenth century, is unique in Africa in representing human beings with a high degree of naturalism. Ife art developed first in terra-cotta and was later translated into metal, its subject matter centering around royal figures and their attendants, reflecting the political structure of a city-state ruled over by a divine king, the Oni of Ife. Sculpted heads (either freestanding or as part of a full figure) were buried in the ground at the foot of giant trees and later exhumed to be used ritually as offerings or sacrifices, sometimes on an annual basis. Ife bronzes and terra-cottas have been recovered from groves containing sacred shrines, from crossroads, and from older sections of the palace compound.

The Kimbell's exquisitely modeled head is in the naturalistic style typical of the Ife classical period (twelfth to fourteenth century). When originally modeled in raw clay, it must have been fully life-size, but the drying and firing of the clay have made it slightly smaller. The physiognomy of the face has been modeled with extraordinary subtlety, and the striations, which may represent scarification patterns, incised with great delicacy. The cool, detached expression is typical of Ife work at its best. The slight bulge of the central part of the forehead, together with the pronounced upward and outward tilt of the eyes, are characteristic of the hand of one of the greatest Ife artists. The square crown, formed of four rectangular aprons overlying a conical form, and embellished with a network of intersecting beads, is so far unparalleled in Ife art. The two holes above the temples, which are also unique to this piece, were perhaps intended to hold feathers during the ceremonies for which the figure was originally made. Like the majority of Ife heads in terra-cotta, the Kimbell example seems to have been broken from a full-length figure. The serene and dignified countenance as well as the elaborate crown suggest that this head represents an Oni, who is to this day the paramount religious leader of traditional Yoruba peoples. The sensitive realism of this head marks it as one of the masterpieces of Ife art, and confirms the status of Ife among the supreme high points of African artistic achievement.

Standing Oba
Kingdom of Benin; Benin City, southern Nigeria, Africa; late 18th century

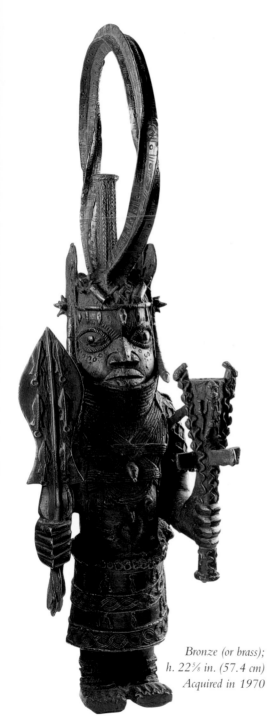

Bronze (or brass);
h. 22⅜ in. (57.4 cm)
Acquired in 1970

One of West Africa's greatest kingdoms, Benin flourished for over five centuries in the forest of southern Nigeria. European travelers had periodic contact with the Edo people of this region, and from the early seventeenth century onward there are accounts of the extensive use of cast metal (actually brass) relief panels and other objects in architecture. The art of Benin first became known in Europe and America in 1897 after a British punitive expedition conquered the kingdom's capital, now called Benin City.

The king, known as the Oba, is the central figure in the Benin kingdom and a frequent subject of Benin royal art. The Oba's ancestors were gods, and it is believed that he controls the forces that affect the well-being of the entire kingdom. The Kimbell sculpture portrays an Oba dressed in full ceremonial regalia. The beads which made up his chest covering, his high neckpiece, and the net-form headdress were actually made of coral; the gong-shaped proclamation staff in his left hand was made either of brass or ivory, while the ceremonial sword in his right hand—with which the Oba would dance to honor his divine ancestors—was of brass. In this work his power is reiterated by the relief of six small swords on the blade of the large one, and the alternating images of a sword and stylized heads of Portuguese soldiers on the Oba's kilt. As the Portuguese arrived in Benin by sea, the inclusion of Portuguese heads in the regalia of the Oba symbolized the wealth he gained through foreign trade and his affiliation with Olokun, god of the sea.

In Central Africa the role of chief is often linked with that of hunter. For the Chokwe people, the importance of the hunter stems from the myth of their founding hero, Chibinda Ilunga. According to legend, Chibinda Ilunga, the son of a great Luba chief and a passionate huntsman, journeyed into Lunda territory and wooed Lweji, a Lunda chieftainess, with his sophisticated hunting weapons and gifts of game. They eventually married, founding the Lunda empire and establishing within that tribe the concept of divine kingship. Chibinda Ilunga also taught the Lunda the art of hunting, introducing his superior weapons—the bow, arrow, hatchet, lance, and use of charms. From the union of Chibinda Ilunga and Lweji, if rather indirectly, came the Mwata Yamvo rulers of the Lunda, to whom the Chokwe paid tribute and regularly furnished sculptors, who produced many kinds of court art almost up to the present day. By association, Chibinda Ilunga became a culture hero and model for Chokwe chiefs. His figure came to represent the archetypal chief who maintains the well-being of his people, and served as a role model for men in Chokwe society generally.

As in much African art, the representation of the coiffure, headdress, and other ornaments serve to emphasize the figure's status and identity. Chibinda Ilunga wears elaborate headgear with rolled side elements as a sign of his royal rank. He holds a wanderer's staff in his right hand and a carved antelope horn in his left. The horn is a container for substances that supernaturally assist the hunt. The absence of a gun from his weapons

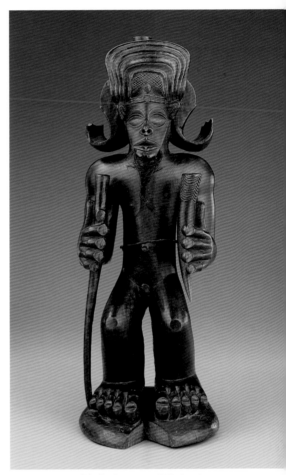

Wood, hair, and hide; h. 16 in. (40.6 cm)
Acquired in 1978

suggests that the Kimbell figure repeats an earlier archetype of the hunter hero, before the introduction of firearms in the seventeenth century. The greatly enlarged hands and feet emphasize his physical strength and endurance, while the beard conveys his wisdom as an elder and ancestor. Since the hunter chief was the most sacred subject portrayed by the Chokwe, such figures were attempted only by the most skilled artists.

Warrior Ancestor Figure
Hemba people; area of Lualaba, Luika, and Lukuga rivers, Democratic Republic of the Congo, Africa; 19th century

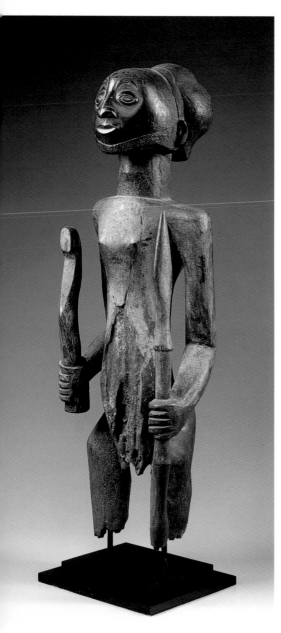

Wood; h. 33⅛ in. (84.1 cm)
Acquired in 1979

This dignified figure of a Hemba warrior, with his upright posture and lofty, outward gaze, would have served as the focus for ancestor veneration among one of the Hemba peoples of the central and eastern Congo. Each clan possessed an ancestral effigy that was revered as the image of a founder, both actual and ideal. For clan leaders, an effigy figure signified the origin and legitimacy of their rule. As a receptacle for the ancestor's spirit, the figure is both conceptually and stylistically universalized; it is not concerned with the specific or momentary. Embodying inner moral and ethical values as well as outer signs of power and leadership, these sculptures served as forceful examples to the ancestor's living descendants. Such figures were preserved in funerary houses or chiefs' houses and expressed the continuing relationship between the living and the dead.

Reflecting the cult of the warrior assimilated from the Luba people, the Kimbell ancestor figure holds a large parade knife in his right hand and a lance in his left. As extensions of his arms, his weapons symbolize courage and masculine physical prowess. These emblems of power, along with the carefully trimmed beard and the characteristic, cruciform headdress, probably allude to the office of war chief. Retaining overall the columnar stability of the living tree from which he carved the work, the sculptor has structured the image from bold spherical and cylindrical forms, enlivened by the interplay of forceful diagonals and stabilizing horizontals. The focus of energy remains the noble head, the dwelling place of spirit and wisdom.

Diviner's Mask
Yombe people; Democratic Republic of the Congo and
Angola, Africa; early 20th century

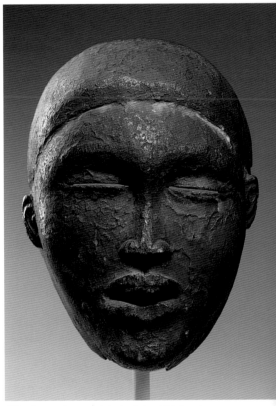

Among the Yombe people, masks
were used in divination ceremonies,
through which past or future events were
revealed. This example was worn by a
nganga diphomba, a divination specialist
devoted primarily to the detection of
members of the community responsible
for various crimes, accidents, and other
disasters. The *diphomba* prosecuted anti-
social acts, and during a ritual trial functioned as the vehicle for the verdict of
the ancestral spirit. Yombe masks are
generally regarded as idealized representations of the diviners who wore them, but
the closed eyes, parted lips, and overall
expression of intense concentration on
the Kimbell mask lend it a sense of
heightened realism.

The mask's crusted, black surface is the
result of its having been stored in the
rafters of a building where it was exposed
to the oils and smokes of cooking. The
black color of the mask is also associated
with judgment and divination. Had it
been reused, it would almost certainly
have been cleaned and repainted as a part
of its preparation for receiving the spirit.

In African art, the mask is the primary
component of any form of transformation
by impersonation. It neutralizes the identity of the wearer and provides a material
residence for the inhabiting spirit. Little is
known about the use and meaning of
many masks in African cultures, where to
reveal their secrets is to destroy their
reason for being—in effect to kill them.
Some masks have relatively blank counte-
nances and depend upon costume and
context—dance, chant, and even speech—
to create personality. Others, such as this
Yombe mask, seem aglow with character.

Wood, organic materials; h. 9 in. (22.8 cm)
Acquired in 1979

Kneeling Mother and Child
Makonde people; Tanzania-Mozambique border area, Africa; late 19th century

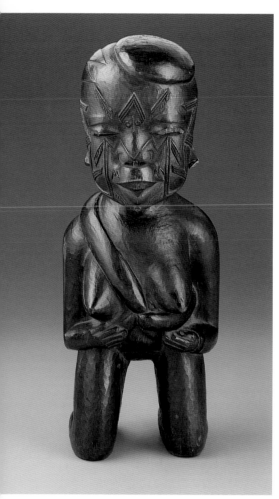

Wood; h. 14½ in. (36.8 cm)
Acquired in 1979

Among the few East African peoples who make sculpture in any quantity, the Makonde are notable for their unusually naturalistic figures. A strong sensuality in the representation of the body is complemented by the attention given to intricate detailing, which often centers on an elaborate coiffure or tribal markings. In this work the coiffure would have been achieved by shaving away part of the hair and sculpting the rest into a raised design. Typically, the facial scarification is also described with a high degree of particularity. Such hair and skin decorations are viewed by the Makonde people as indications of rank, status, and identity—Makonde females are scarified as they pass into adulthood. Makonde scarifications are more elaborate than those of any other group in Mozambique, comprising complex designs of chevrons, angles, zig-zags, and straight lines, as well as circles, diamonds, or dots.

Most African mother-and-child sculptures are intended to ensure fertility, but this piece is concerned also with the high position of the female in Makonde society, which is matrilineal by succession, inheritance, and marriage. Women are also accorded a high status in Makonde mythology, religion, and art. Perhaps intended to represent the primeval matriarch who founded the Makonde tribe, the figure is remarkable for its vigorously carved forms and sensitively articulated detail—the mother's hooded eyes, her fingers holding the sling in which the baby straddles her back, its tiny feet and hands extended. The ears and upper lip are pierced and hold ornaments, which are symbols of leadership in this region of East Africa.

Standing Ancestor Figure
Maori culture, possibly Rongowhakaata people; New Zealand;
Te Huringa period I, c. 1800–1840

The Maori tribes of New Zealand excelled in the decoration of their timber buildings with elaborate relief carvings and sculptures. This powerfully conceived, freestanding figure may have functioned either as a *tekoteko*—a carved figure placed on the gable peak of an assembly house, food storehouse, or chief's dwelling—or as a *poutokomanawa*, the center post that holds up the ridge-pole of a large house such as that of a chieftain. Symbolically, the ridgepole is the backbone of the ancestor who is represented by the house. The figure represents either a god or a recently deceased male ancestor who, in Maori culture, looks after the welfare of his descendants.

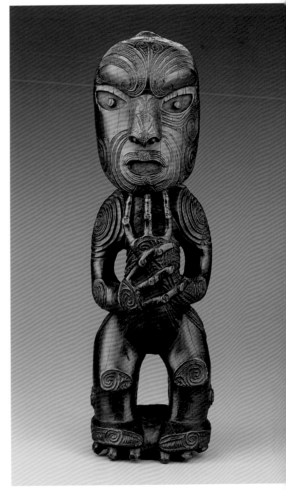

Wood; h. 17⅝ in. (44.8 cm)
Acquired in 1989

The form of the figure—the large head, narrow torso, bent knees, and knobby three-fingered hands placed over the chest and stomach—is a familiar type in Maori sculptures of gods and ancestors. As is common with these statues, the face is carved with an intricate curvilinear pattern reproducing the tattoos *(moko)* that decorate the faces of Maori chieftains. The carvings on the arms are not the same tattoos as on the face, but specific patterns that are either unique to a particular family *(whanau)*, or have an individual significance for that sculpture. Spirals mark the joints of the figure at the shoulders, elbows, wrists, knees, and hips; the rough edges indicate that these were cut with stone tools, before the introduction of steel knives in the early nine-

teenth century. The style of carving is characteristic of works made by the Rongowhakaata tribe in the area around Gisborne, on the east coast of the north island of New Zealand.

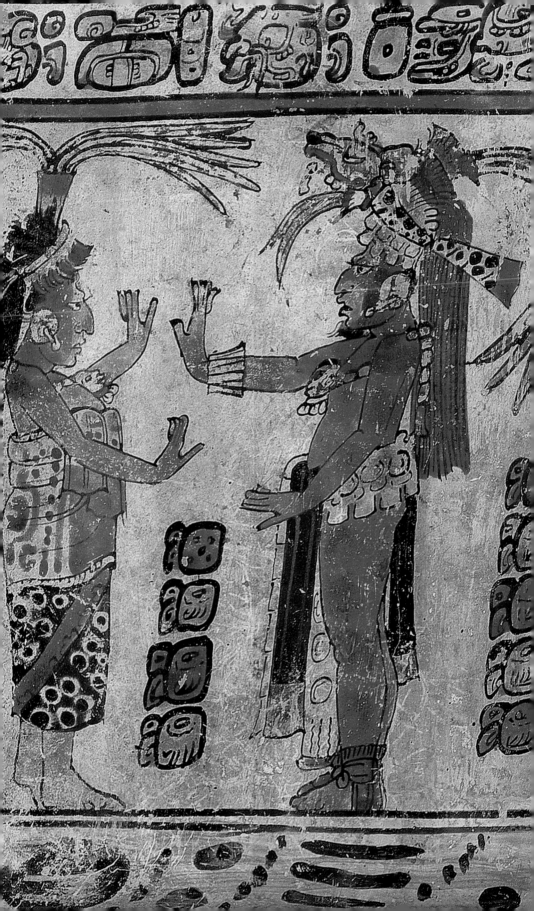

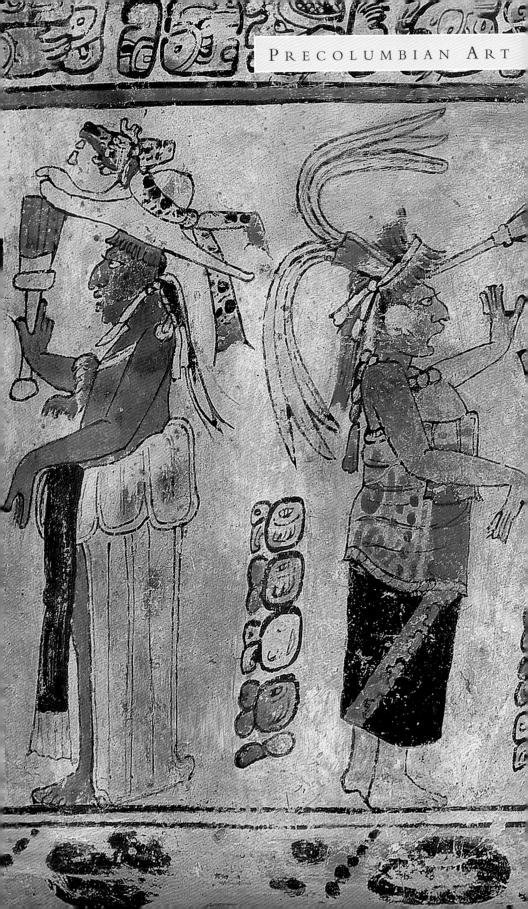

Standing Figure
Olmec culture; Mexico; c. 900–400 B.C.

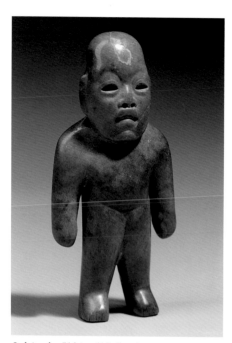

Jadeite; h. 5½ in. (13.9 cm)
Acquired in 1981

As the earliest complex culture of Mesoamerica, the Olmecs of modern Veracruz and Tabasco occupy a preeminent position in the emergence and early development of Precolumbian civilization. The Olmec culture flourished from about 1500 B.C. to 400 B.C., and during this period many of the recurrent elements of later Mesoamerican iconography, art, religion, and ritual first became apparent. Their settlements saw the establishment of the first sacred centers composed of plazas, mounds, and pyramids; and the ceremonial centers contained colossal basalt sculptured heads that portrayed secular leaders as well as deities. Representations of deities include human-animal composites of jaguars, harpy eagles, snakes, and crocodiles. Olmec artistic style, with its focus on jade, ceramic, and stone sculpture, continued for centuries without radical variation, and formed the basis of Maya, and much other Mesoamerican, art. The human forms are generous, with substantial masses defined by simplified, boldly flowing contours. Details are generally limited to those essential for image and content recognition. Figures and facial types tend towards the androgynous; heads are large, probably to emphasize their importance, bodies more short and stocky.

About 900 B.C., jadeite and other varieties of greenstone acquired a special significance for the Olmec elite and replaced clay as the preferred material for precious, small-scale objects. Rare and challenging to carve, jade was a precious material that seems to have been reserved primarily for ritual uses. Its translucent green color was venerated together with water as a symbol of life and fertility. The jade *Standing Figure* represents one of the most recurrent types in Olmec jadework. Despite its small size, it is unusually monumental in impact. The lifelike proportions and subtle musculature of the figure epitomize the extraordinary craftsmanship and sensitivity of Olmec jade carving at its finest. The subject appears to be human rather than divine, and may represent a venerated ancestor. Although their function and purpose are not clear, the numerous extant examples of this kind of figure suggest they had an important ceremonial function in Olmec ritual.

The hollow ceramic *Seated Figure* of a child, with snarling expression, plump babyish proportions, and incised headdress, belongs to a type found throughout

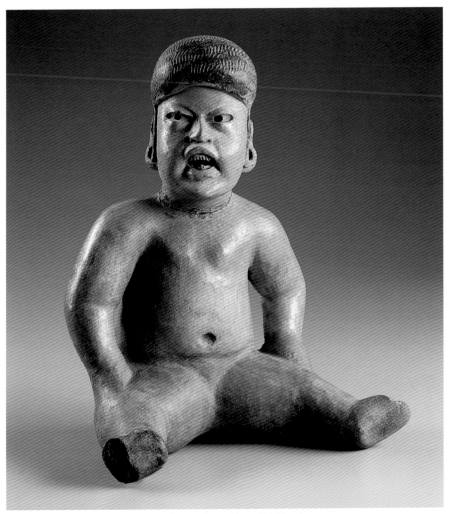

Ceramic with white slip and traces of paint; h. 10⅞ in. (27.7 cm)
Acquired in 1971

Olmec territory. These so-called "hollow baby" figures, either white-slipped or in white kaolin clay, are typical of the earliest Olmec sites. They depict asexual infantile figures with plump bodies, and have been variously interpreted as jaguar-human hybrids (the "were-jaguar"), as children with deformities that mark them as having supernatural powers, as images of rain gods, or simply as well-fed infants. They vary in appearance from near-jaguar to predominantly human. Highly humanized variants, like this one, are most frequently found near Veracruz and westward to the Central Highlands. Its rounded, simplified forms and smooth finish are traits shared with the finest Olmec works in jade and basalt.

Seated Woman
Xochipala culture; Guerrero, Mexico; c. 1500–1200 B.C.

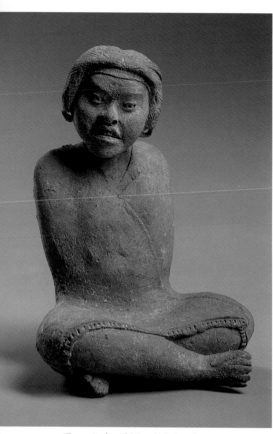

Ceramic; h. 4⅜ in. (11.1 cm)
Acquired in 1971

During the Preclassic period (1500 B.C.–A.D. 150) in Mexico, largely contemporaneous with the Olmec civilization on the Gulf Coast, a number of independent, agriculturally based regional cultures were being established in central and West Mexico. These cultures produced an astonishing quantity and variety of non-Olmec-style clay pottery and figurines, the latter providing vivid images of these peoples, their costumes, and lifestyles. The figurines seem to have been planted in the ground with seeds as magical receptacles for the transfer from a living body of harmful or overly powerful forces; they may also have served as spirit companions, or as vehicles placed in burials to carry the dead on their journey to the afterlife.

Among these early cultures, the most inventive tradition of terra-cotta figurine-making was located at Xochipala, a remote West Mexican village in the state of Guerrero, near which all the known examples in this style have been found. The Xochipala style, dating to the pre-Olmec period, is characterized by a sophisticated naturalism applied to a wide range of everyday subjects, producing some of the finest and most expressive ceramic sculpture in Mesoamerica. Anatomical details are rendered with consummate skill: fully modeled eyeballs with pierced pupils, parted lips revealing two rows of teeth, finely worked feet with fanned toes, and delicately incised hair fashioned into stylized arrangements. The Kimbell figure of a *Seated Woman*, though small in size, is modeled with remarkable subtlety, especially in the intent facial expression, articulated coiffure, and delicately fringed shawl, all accentuated by the extreme simplicity of the dress. Its success in capturing the spirit and physical presence of an actual woman inevitably raises the question of whether it was intended, in some sense, as a portrait.

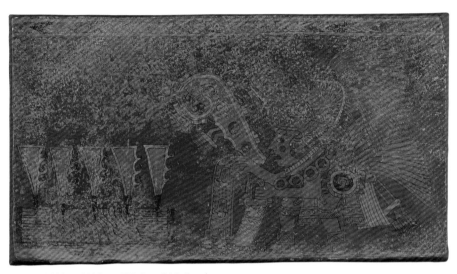

Fresco; 23¾ x 43½ in. (60.2 x 110.5 cm)
Acquired in 1972

In this richly symbolic mural fragment from Teotihuacán, a priest or god costumed in an elaborately plumed head-dress performs a ceremony involving the scattering of incense while singing. Orderly sequences of such ritual images, painted in true fresco on damp plaster, once formed part of the decoration of Teotihuacán residential and temple complexes. They appear to represent cere-monies in which specific favors were sought from the gods. Here, the object of the ceremony seems to center on the glyphlike symbol to the left, depicting five maguey spines thrust into a stack of reeds. In all likelihood this is a place name. The officiating figure holds an incense bag in his left hand, while flower-decorated water streams from his right. Proceeding from his mouth is a large speech scroll edged with vegetation (probably meaning "flowery song"); the hearts, jade, and other symbols in the scroll may stand for the song's content.

The city of Teotihuacán, in the Central Highland Valley of Mexico, was the capital of the first classical civilization of Mesoamerica, dating from around the first to the seventh century A.D. Located about thirty miles northeast of Mexico City, Teotihuacán was an urban and ritual complex eight miles long with a number of buildings on the main avenue, including the second largest pyramid in Meso-america. Both the residential and ceremo-nial structures were characterized by "slope-and-panel" profiles on their plat-forms and terraces, as well as elaborate polychrome wall frescoes. Around A.D. 600, internal factional struggles led to the city of Teotihuacán being burned and aban-doned. Over seven hundred years later, the great ruins of Teotihuacán were venerated by the Aztecs as the "City of the Gods."

Urn in the Form of Cociyo, God of Lightning and Rain
Zapotec culture; Monte Albán IIIa, Oaxaca, Mexico; c. A.D. 400–500

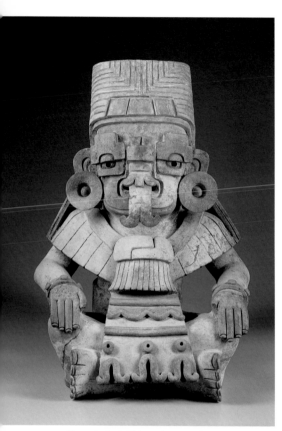

Ceramic; h. 28½ in. (72.4 cm)
Acquired in 1985

The Zapotec civilization developed over a period of more than one thousand years in relative geographic isolation in the modern state of Oaxaca, in southern Mexico. The primary capital of Zapotec culture was the ceremonial site of Monte Albán, constructed on an artificially flattened mountaintop. The Zapotecs used the buildings at Monte Albán to worship a complex pantheon of nature gods who were similar to those of other Mesoameri-can peoples. Archaeologists have divided Zapotec culture into four stages, each associated with the style of gray-ware effigy urns they placed with their honored dead. The urns depict both gods and important human beings, some in ritual garb impersonating gods. This urn repre-sents Cociyo, the Zapotec name for the Mesoamerican god of lightning and rain. In his Zapotec manifestation, this rain god is identified by an amalgam of facial elements forming a powerfully sculptural mask. The stepped, two-part forms enclos-ing the eyes represent clouds and, by extension, the precious water needed to grow crops. The doubly plugged nasal extension is a development from earlier snouted deity elements that combine jaguar and snake allusions—the roar of the jaguar with the reverberation of thun-der. The three fangs that protrude from this snout cover a bifurcated tongue, the almost invisibly flashing tongue of a snake, the symbol of the lightning bolt. The broad mouth with drawn-back lips can be traced back to the earliest Zapotec-area images, which are derived from Olmec prototypes, among which would have been images of the baby rain god.

The rest of the dress is as much that of a priest as of a deity, with the large disk-shaped earplugs and the knotted collar of high rank. The striations of the cape may be intended to represent feathers. The kilt is decorated with a wavelike pattern, with three attached tassels at the bottom. The ensemble thus echoes the various natural phenomena of a tropical mountain thunderstorm.

Small ceramic sculpture flourished in a
number of distinctive and original
forms among the Precolumbian cultures
of central Mexico. Hollow modeled
figures from the Veracruz area of the Gulf
Coast, such as this Kimbell example, are
noted for their typical smiling expressions
and the great care given to details of
ornament and attire. The animated open
mouth, softly modeled cheeks, and
broadly flattened head of this exceptionally well-preserved piece are characteristic
of the finest small ceramics of the Totonac
culture, which flourished in central
Veracruz during the time of the Maya
and Teotihuacán. In style it resembles
figures from Nopiloa, which likewise
contrast smooth mold-made areas with
enlivening hand-modeled details, filed
front teeth, lively smiles, and broadly
sculpted costumes. Particularly noteworthy are the meticulous rendering of the
eyes, teeth, earrings, hands, and jewelry.

Smiling Girl wears an elaborate headdress, with a swag of seeds draped across
the front. Her dress is decorated with
painted geometric motifs, now rather
worn. She eagerly offers a basket of rolled
tortillas in her left hand, while extending
her right in a way that displays her long
tapering fingers and rings.

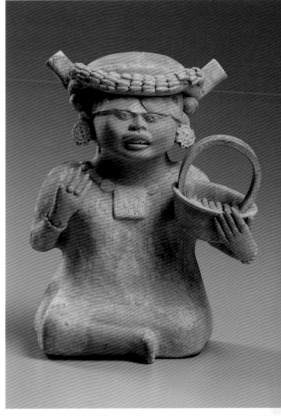

Ceramic with white slip and traces of paint;
h. 7⅝ in. (19.2 cm)
Acquired in 1978

Conch Shell Trumpet
Maya culture; Guatemala; c. A.D. 250–400

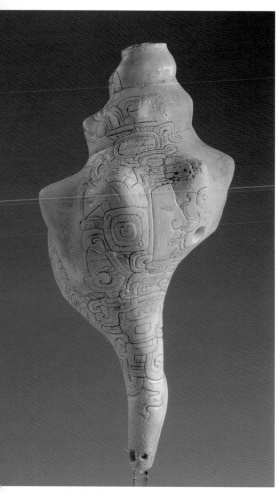

Shell with traces of cinnabar;
h. 11⅞₆ in. (29.3 cm)
Acquired in 1984

This elaborately decorated conch shell bears the face of a Maya king, carefully incised following the undulations in the shell's surface, and a column of glyphs to the side recording the name of its royal owner. The king's chin strap and the knots above and below his ear ornament are all personified, a device that indicates the accrued power and force in the object. The primary headdress element is a jaguar deity, which seems to be topped by the glyph for "heaven." The portrait is probably of the ancestor who was recalled when the trumpet was used in a bloodletting rite.

The holes at the top of the shell and along the side edges indicate that it was intended as a ritual trumpet. From representations of their use on Maya painted vessels, it is known that conch shell trumpets were sounded by hunters returning with slain deer. Other vessel representations suggest that the deer obtained in these hunts were intended for special sacrificial uses. Such a sacrificial context for the use of trumpets would fit with conquest-period accounts that describe the frightening music of trumpets and drums that accompanied ritual human sacrifice. Conch shells, both plain and carved, are generally found in tombs, where, as natural underwater objects, they became symbols of death and the watery Maya underworld, Xibalba.

Tripod Vessel
Maya culture; Mexico or Guatemala;
c. A.D. 300–900

Rounded Bowl
Maya culture; Mexico or Guatemala;
c. A.D. 300–900

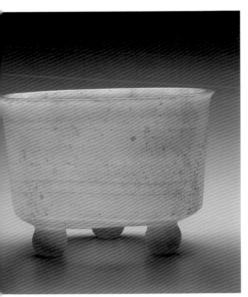

Travertine marble; h. 9⅜ in. (23.9 cm)
Acquired in 1994

These Maya limestone vessels are unusual for their beautiful material and simple forms. The *Tripod Vessel* of travertine limestone is crafted from a single piece of stone into a cylindrical vase with straight flaring sides ending in a slightly everted lip. At the base are three supports of rounded "tear-drop" form. The expertly ground walls are so thin as to be translucent, making the piece surprisingly lightweight for its size. The cylindrical shape of the vessel copies that of Teotihuacán ceramics, but the spherical tripod feet suggest that it may date from the Late, rather than the Early, Classic period. The small *Rounded Bowl* has the same everted lip and a flattened base. Made of limestone, the walls are not as thin or translucent as the tripod vessel, giving it a whiter, milkier appearance.

The main corpus of Maya art is noted for its dense and complex pictorial decoration. Like Maya pottery, the surfaces of limestone and other white stone vessels were often carved or painted. In the case of these vessels, however, the absence of decoration only enhances the appeal of their pure, elegant forms.

The vessels were probably manufactured in central Guerrero, Puebla, or Oaxaca. While their specific findspot is unknown, they were discovered in Maya territory, where they had probably been brought by *pochteca*, a special class of traders from the highlands, who were allowed to travel throughout Mesoamerica and beyond bearing cacao, cloth, skins, jade, and pottery. The superior quality of the workmanship suggests that these bowls were intended for a wealthy Maya clientele, probably as funerary offerings.

Limestone; h. 3⁹⁄₁₆ in. (9.1 cm)
Acquired in 1994

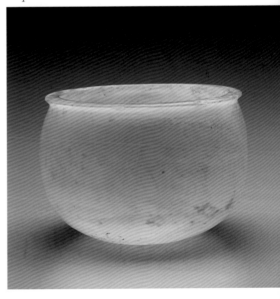

Tripod Vessel with Lid
Maya culture; Guatemala; c. A.D. 400–500

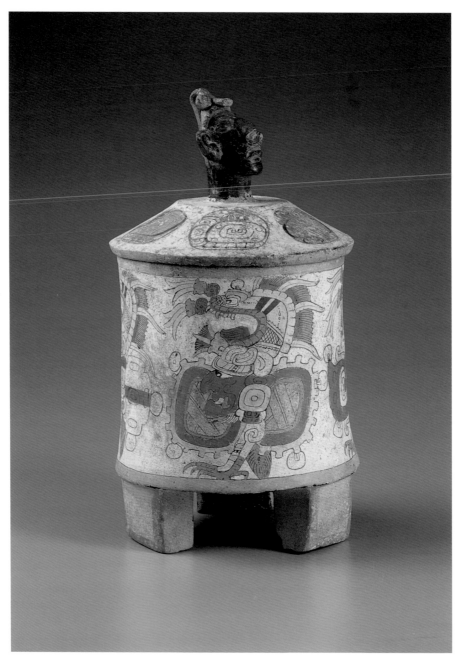

Ceramic with stucco and polychrome pigments; h. 11 in. (27.9 cm)
Acquired in 1997

The art of the Maya is principally the art of the ruling elite. Vessels were made to honor and commemorate once-living rulers and to venerate their gods and ancestors; these objects, laden with power and symbolism, were then buried in tombs alongside their royal or noble owners. Much of the pottery found in Maya tombs was made especially to accompany the soul on its journey through the Underworld, Xibalba, a watery world that could be entered only by sinking beneath water or by passing through a maw in the surface of the earth. Funerary vessels of the Early Classic period (A.D. 250–600) often represented the watery surface of that Underworld and its inhabitants, shown either in narrative scenes or in processions.

The stuccoed body of this vessel is delicately painted with images of four chimerical creatures, each with a feathered, snakelike neck and head, a body containing the head of an aged divinity that may be Pawahtun (the god of the end of the year, and bearer of the sky and earth), spondylus shells for "wings," and bird feet. Each figure is distinguished from the others by a different form of decorative "wing" and by colors that indicate its directional orientation. The cover is adorned with

a small sculpted head, Maya in profile, having distinctive ear and nose plugs and an elaborate coiffure. The six glyphs on the cover represent a standard dedicatory verse found on ritual drinking vessels.

In the Early Classic period, architecture, royal burial offerings, sculpture, and ceramics show the results of powerful waves of influence from the large metropolis of Teotihuacán in central Mexico, whose representatives established colonies and effective control in the Maya areas of southern Guatemala and the Yucatán. The ceramic hallmark of the Teotihuacán civilization was the cylindrical vessel with a cover and three slab feet. Maya potters borrowed this classical tripod shape and decorated it with reliefs, engravings, and brilliant paintings on a stucco background. The Kimbell's extraordinarily well-preserved vase represents a hybrid of Teotihuacán shape and purely Maya decoration. Following Teotihuacán practice, it is reasonable to suppose that such vessels were used as beverage containers in daily life, and for the deceased. The iconography, inscription, and very high quality of this vase all suggest that it was a ritual vessel containing the Maya chocolate drink, to be placed in the tomb of a nobleman.

Stela with a Ruler
Maya culture; El Perú, Petén region, Guatemala; A.D. 692

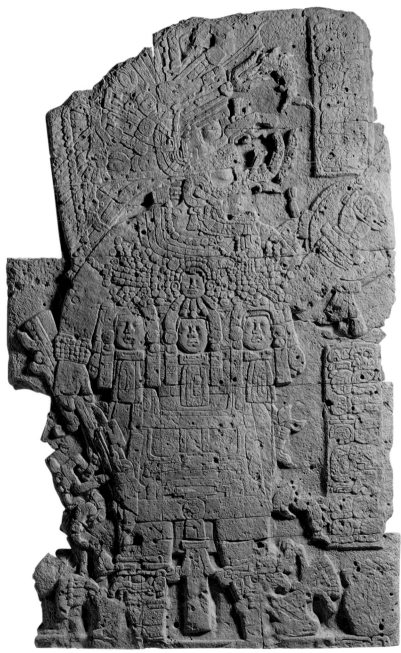

Limestone; 107⅜ x 68⅜ in. (272.7 x 173.7 cm)
Acquired in 1970

Many of the principal characteristics of Maya culture were in place by the Late Preclassic period (300 B.C.–A.D. 150). These elements, drawing on the cultural inheritance of the Olmecs and Teotihuacán, gave rise to a series of regional principalities with imposing monumental architecture, a complex religion, advanced calendrics, hieroglyphic writing, and a sophisticated art style expressed most spectacularly in polychrome pottery, bas-reliefs, and wall paintings.

The Maya were prolific makers of carved stone-slab monuments, or stelae, which were normally set up within architectural complexes and most often portray specific, named individuals who were members of the hereditary dynasties that ruled Maya city-states. The imposing figure in *Stela with a Ruler* is identified by the accompanying inscriptions as K'inich B'alam (Sun-Faced Jaguar), ruler of El Perú, a Late Classic period (A.D. 600–900) Maya site in the Petén region of Guatemala. The Kimbell stela was once part of a sculptural ensemble of three stelae displayed in a plaza at El Perú. The central monument, now in the Cleveland Museum of Art, represents on the same scale an equally intimidating woman, who holds in her left hand a shield and in her right the same ritual assemblage as is held by the ruler here. She has been identified by the inscriptions as Na Kan Ajaw (Royal Woman of the Snake Polity) and may represent K'inich B'alam's wife. The Cleveland stela was flanked on either side by the Kimbell stela and another stela (still in situ) portraying an unidentified male figure, both males facing Na Kan Ajaw. The principal event commemorated by the Kimbell and Cleveland stelae is the ending in A.D. 692 of a *k'atun*, or twenty-year period, a date of special importance in the structure of Maya rulership.

The primary elements of costume in *Stela with a Ruler* were intended to situate the Maya ruler not just locally and in his historic role but, more importantly, in his relation to the gods and the cosmos. The main headdress element, repeated in the ruler's anklets, is the head of the Water-lily Snake, a deity symbolizing standing bodies of water and the earth's abundance, and patron god of the number thirteen. The several representations of fish leaping toward water-lily blossoms—at the top of the headdress and, less recognizably, at the back of the headdress and at either knee—reinforce this symbolism. Through these devices the ruler is shown as guarantor of agricultural success. The ruler's mosaic mask represents a jeweled serpent. Like his female counterpart on the Cleveland stela, he grasps a round shield in his left hand, emphasizing the war role of Maya rulers (and possibly of their wives); the ritual object held by both in their right hands has not been identified. Partly hidden by the king's left thigh is a deified perforator, used by the ruler at important period endings like this one to shed blood from his penis as an offering to the gods.

Vessel with Ceremonial Scene

Maya culture, Chocholá style; Campeche, reputedly from Jaina Island, Mexico; c. A.D. 690–750

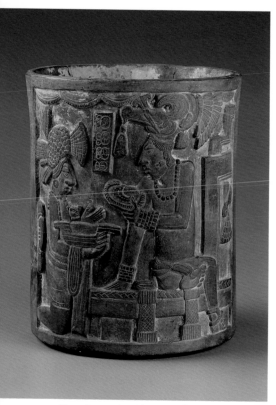

Carved ceramic with traces of pigment;
h. 8⅛ in. (20.7 cm)
Acquired in 1974

The scene on this vessel appears to depict a ritual that is being enacted in a sumptuous palace interior, indicated by the swagged curtain framing the top of the scene. A lord seated on a mat-topped throne hands over a fringed object, which may be a decorated mirror, to a kneeling attendant who is holding a bowl or basket. The lord wears an elaborate bird headdress that is pierced through the nostril with a sting-ray spine, the ancient instrument of ritual bloodletting. The boldly incised text on the reverse of the vessel is a Primary Standard Sequence, describing this as a vase for a certain kind of chocolate drink, and ending with the patron's name, which includes the hieroglyph *muyal*, "cloud."

Several Late Classic period (A.D. 600–900) sites near Chocholá, Maxcanú, and Xcalumkín, in the northern Yucatán, have yielded vessels carved in this distinctive style known as Chocholá. Shapes include cups, straight cylinders with slightly flaring rims, and cylinders with rounded bottoms. The decoration is carved into the clay before firing; some also have postfiring pigment applied to the surface. Many bear carved imagery in a single scene on one side only, with text on the other side, often in a slanted column. Vessels in this style have been recovered from as far as Jaina Island, but must have been manufactured in the Chocholá area.

The elaborate mythological scene on this vessel, carved in low relief in the leather-hard clay before firing, achieves at a smaller scale much the same effect as the Maya stone relief carvings. On either side of an inverted L-shaped panel of five glyphs, the Water-lily Jaguar and Chak face one another, paired as actors in a sacrificial death dance. Chak, the god of rain and lightning, is identified by shell earflares and a shell diadem, his long hair gathered together and tied, and by his thunderbolt axe. He is seated before the so-called Kawak Monster, the head of a creature covered in reptilian scales, with half-closed eyes and a huge tongue that drops to the ground from its gaping mouth. This is actually the iconic form of *witz*, "mountain," and it seems as if the rain god, who dwells in mountain caves, has just emerged from his home. The Water-lily Jaguar is identified by a water-lily blossom or leaf on his head, death-eye cuffs and collar, and a pattern of spots on his body. While he is a jaguar, his motions and postures are in most representations those of a human.

The scene represented is part of a now-lost mythic cycle in which the Water-lily Jaguar—sometimes in infantile form and usually lying on top of the

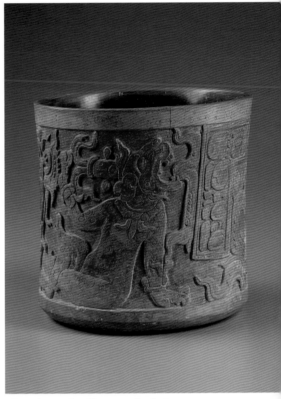

Carved ceramic with traces of red pigment;
h. 6⅝ in. (16.8 cm)
Acquired in 1980

mountain glyph—is sacrificed by the axe-wielding Chak. Since this episode does not occur in the *Popol Vuh*, the great Maya religious epic, its meaning still eludes us.

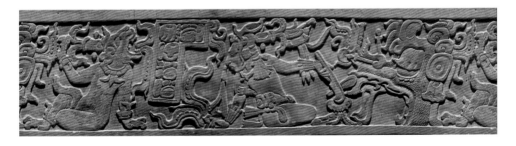

Vessel with Five Figures

Maya culture; Usumacinta River Valley, Chiapas, Mexico; c. A.D. 750–800

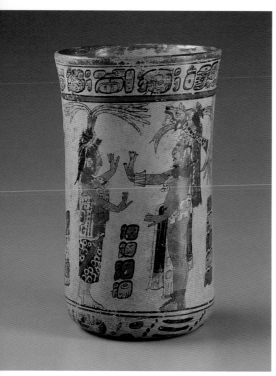

Polychromed ceramic; h. 10¼ in. (25.8 cm)
Acquired in 1979

The painted vessels of the Maya rank conspicuously among their most impressive artistic achievements. The finest vessels, intended for the Maya elite, were elaborately decorated with sophisticated pictorial imagery. The wide range of subject matter includes scenes of Maya nobility performing public and private rituals, victories in battle or the ritual ball game, the natural environment, images of supernatural characters and mythical deities, and depictions of the Maya Underworld, called Xibalba, and its occupants. Many of these vessels ultimately were filled with the Maya chocolate drink and placed in tombs to accompany the soul and provide nourishment on its journey through Xibalba.

Maya pictorial vessels are preponderantly of a simple, cylindrical form. After applying a slip to the surface, a fine brush was used to delineate the forms in a variety of pigments. Pictorial vessels provide an idea in miniature of the richness of Maya mural painting, most of which was painted

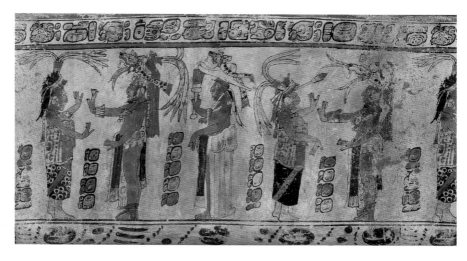

on perishable materials and no longer survives.

Three of the four Kimbell painted vases depict processional scenes, a common mode of representation on Maya vessels. On each side of the *Vessel with Five Figures*, a noble lord prepares to dance with a lady. While the two women are clearly differentiated in dress and facial expression, the opposing male figure of a lord may in fact be the same individual, as the facial profiles with goatee beards are identical. The lord's headdress features a band of jaguar pelt crowned by an animal head. The second male, standing between the two pairs of figures, is possibly an attendant. He holds a baton of a type that appears also in war scenes, here perhaps indicating his status. Just below the rim is the Primary Standard Sequence, a formulaic text that here describes the vessel as a vase for the chocolate drink; following it are the name glyphs of the vase's royal owner or patron. The vertical texts are repetitions of the same glyph, perhaps meaningless.

The *Vessel with a Procession of Warriors* is one of three known pots that may be assigned to the same hand; the Kimbell vessel shows the outcome of a battle

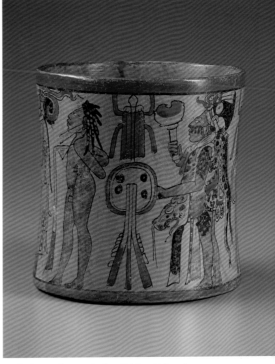

Polychromed ceramic; h. 6⅜ in. (16 cm)
Acquired in 1976

depicted on the other two pots. The naked figure with arms bound behind his back is a captive who is being led by an elaborately dressed warrior for sacrificial display. The leader of the party may be the figure

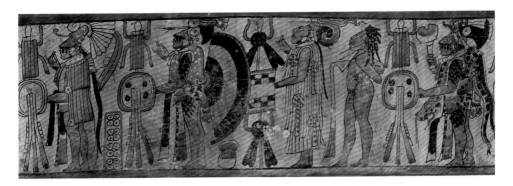

Vessel with a Ball Game Scene
Maya culture; Mexico or Guatemala; c. 700–800

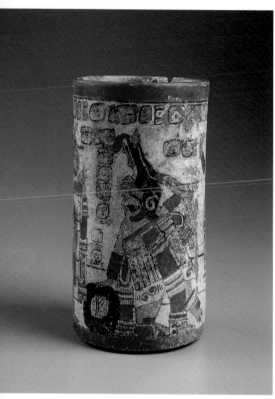

Polychromed ceramic; h. 8¾ in. (22.2 cm)
Acquired in 1989

wearing a full jaguar pelt and wielding a bloody weapon. The person in front of the captive wears a costume of cloth and paper strips studded with bloodied medallions; he has a spiny bloodletter in his headdress and may be responsible for carrying out the bloodletting rituals. The fourth person wears a feathered cape and the petal cap characteristic of secondary figures.

The figures on *Vessel with a Ball Game Scene* are engaged in a ritual ball game commonly played in Late Classic period (A.D. 600–900) Maya cities. The protective ball game equipment includes a heavy wood-and-leather belt and knee pad. The figure with his hand on the ball is wearing a deer headdress, often worn by victorious ballplayers. The glyphic text in front of his head gives his name and describes him as a prince (*chok*). The background shows the pyramid steps upon which spectators would have watched the game.

Far more complex in composition and spatial arrangement, *Vessel of the Ik' Dancer*

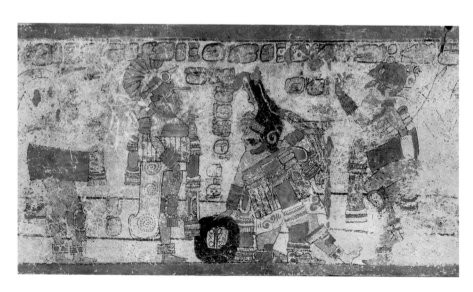

is one of a series of vessels depicting
events in the life of a lord nicknamed the
Fat Cacique, ruler of the Ik' polity. The
action of the scene is divided between the
interior and exterior of a palace building
raised on a low platform with two steps.
Inside the building, Fat Cacique is seated
on a bench with a huge pillow, both
covered with jaguar pelts. On either side
of the lord is an attendant, partly obscured
by the door jambs that frame this scene; a
dwarf sits on the first step below. Three
dancers stand in front of Fat Cacique
before the blank outer wall of the building performing a ritual bloodletting
dance. Their white loincloths are spattered
with blood from this ceremony in which
they would perforate their genitals, and, as
they whirl, blood would be drawn into
the paper panels extending from their
groins. The Maya elite routinely practiced
such bloodletting as an offering to the
gods, who had shed their own blood to
create humanity. The blood of captives was
also often shed to give to the gods.

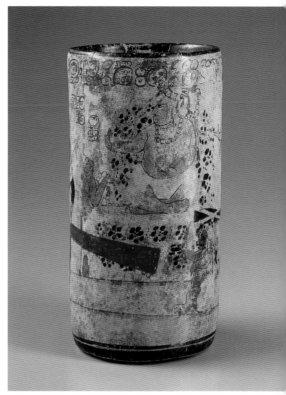

Polychromed ceramic; h. 8¾ in. (22.3 cm)
Acquired in 1985

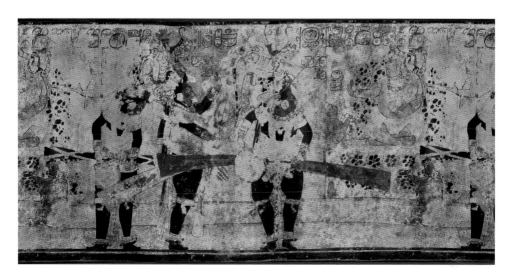

Vessel with an Enthroned Lord and Seated Figure
Maya culture; Xcalumkín, Campeche, Mexico; A.D. 765

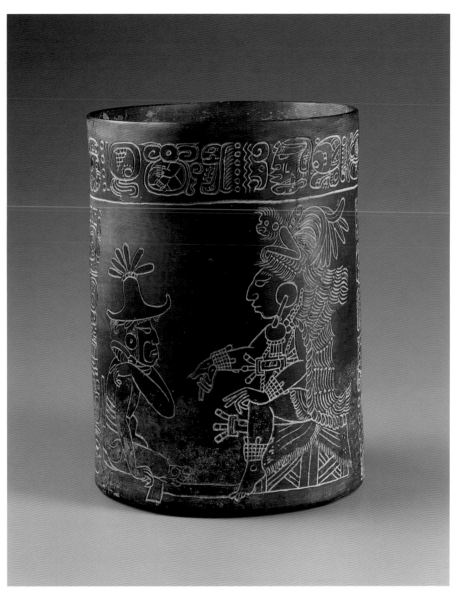

Incised ceramic with traces of red pigment; h. 9 in. (22.9 cm)
Acquired in 2000

While most Maya pottery is painted, some regions also produced vessels bearing carved or incised designs with detail as fine as any of the painted scenes. One of the most prominent of these schools emerged during the Late Classic period (A.D. 600–900) around the city of Xcalumkín, in the Puuc region of northern Campeche, Yucatán peninsula.

The finest surviving example of the

Xcalumkín style is this superbly incised vessel, which depicts a young lord seated upon a low wooden basketry throne draped with a fringed jaguar skin. He is elaborately dressed in a luxurious fur or feather cape and wears a feathered head-dress inside of which perches a stuffed monkey. The lord gestures with both hands toward the figure seated cross-legged before him on the floor, who is more simply clad in a loincloth with a broad sash, a scarf tied around his neck, and a brimmed hat topped with six feath-ers. The seated figure's left arm crosses over his right shoulder in a gesture of loyalty, obedience, and submission to the lord. The glyphs in a horizontal register below the rim and in vertical bands on either side of the two figures define the "interior" space in which the meeting is taking place, most likely a palace. Around some of the figures (notably the monkey's face) and glyphs can be seen more lightly scratched "sketches" for the final design made by the artist to guide him in executing the final incisions. Evidence of such *pentimenti* in Maya art is very rare, the known examples being confined to this and other incised ceramics of the Chocholá-Xcalumkín area.

The hieroglyphic text to the left of the figures gives the year the vase was dedi-cated, A.D. 765, and, along the rim, the names of the vessel's owner, ah-ma-t'zu, and the reigning king, aj-sa-wa-[?]. In the column to the right of the figures are two more names: aj-pa-sa-hi-na, or aj-pashiin, the carver of the vase, who may also be the king; and AH-u-[?]-lu, possibly a second carver. As with much Precolumbian art, the detailed interpreta-tion of the iconography remains a matter of scholarly debate. According to one interpretation, the scene represents a young lord, the son of the reigning king, who, as the inscription suggests, was also the artist/scribe who made the vase. The same scribal signature appears on Lintel 1 from the Initial Series Building at Xcalumkín, which would indicate that this king was the ruler of Xcalumkín. The secondary figure is identified by his plumed sombrero as a *sahal* (military chief, usually a close relative of the ruler), to whom the young lord is giving instructions.

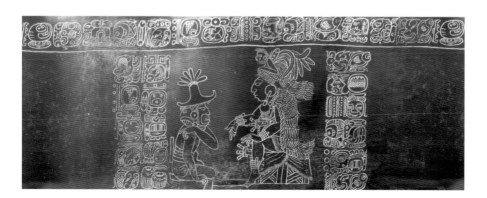

Standing Ruler
Maya culture; Guatemala; c. A.D. 600–800

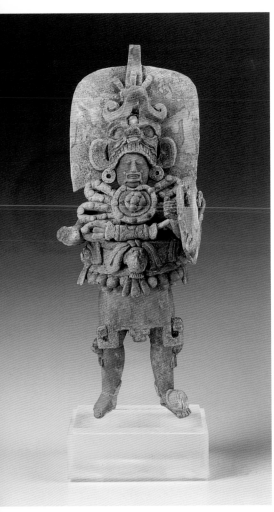

Ceramic with traces of paint;
h. 9⅜ in. (23.8 cm)
Acquired in 1984

among the most fully realized of Maya sculptures in the round. The Kimbell's *Standing Ruler* represents a Maya lord costumed to impersonate a dynastic ancestor. The rectangular device over the mouth, along with the shield in one hand and the now-missing spear in the other, closely resemble the accoutrements of the nine ancestral figures in the sarcophagus chamber of Palenque's Temple of the Inscriptions. His wide belt once supported a rack of feathers across his back, and his knee-length apron is marked with a symbol of the World Tree, the central axis of the Maya world. Elements of the complex costume below the headdress recur in other portrayals of Maya rulers; these seem to define and reiterate his rank, and his position in the cosmos. As a complete three-dimensional representation of a figure type more familiar in low-relief stelae, this figurine is extremely rare.

Most known Maya figurines come from the cemetery island of Jaina, off the coast of Campeche, but high-quality examples have also been recovered from Palenque, in Mexico, and Río Azul, in Guatemala. In their extreme sensitivity and realism these exquisitely detailed figurines represent the apogee of Maya ceramic sculpture. Their role in Maya belief and ritual is not clear, but their common appearance in Maya burials suggests a ritual function of some importance. Here the royal associations of the subject may indicate a rite performed by the king and commemorated through the making of this figurine.

A mong the greatest achievements of Maya art are their small-scale ceramic sculptures, including a well-known group of exquisite figurines typically only a few inches high. Despite their diminutive scale, these are also

This carved and painted relief panel shows the presentation of captives in a palace throne room indicated by swag curtains at the top. The five figures are the king of Yaxchilan, Itzamnaaj Balam III, seated at top left; his *sahal* (a military chief), Aj Chak Maax, at the right; and three bound captives in the lower left corner. The glyphic text, which gives a date of 23 August 783, records the capture of a lord named Balam-Ahau by Aj Chak Maax, and a sacrificial blood-letting three days later under the auspices of the ruler. The three bound prisoners may be scribes from a captured city, as the one seated in front holds a "stick bundle" normally associated with depictions of Maya scribes, and all three wear head-dresses with *hun* (book) knots. All but the leftmost captive are identified by name. The inscription on the throne front beneath the seated lord is carved with the king's name and titles, but the glyphs are inscribed in reverse order, from right to left.

The name of the artist responsible for sculpting this relief appears on the vertical panel of four glyphs under the *sahal*'s outstretched arm, perhaps indicating that the *sahal* was himself also the creator of this work. Signed works of Maya art are rare, and the signature on this relief suggests that it was considered of great value in its time.

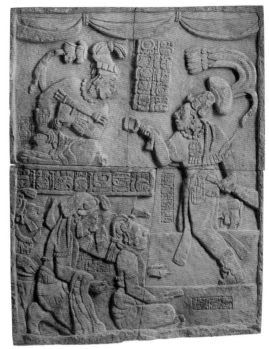

Limestone with traces of paint;
45⅜ x 35 in. (115.3 x 88.9 cm)
Acquired in 1971

The Kimbell relief, which comes from an unidentified site named Laxtunich, probably served as a wall panel inside a Maya building or as a lintel over an entrance. Lintels as large as this often recorded important dynastic events. It is assumed that their placement at points of transition between the outside, secular world and an inside, more sacred realm was of primary importance.

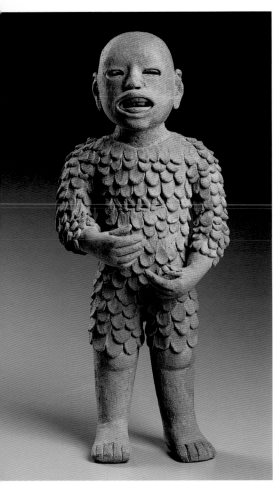

Ceramic; h. 15¾ in. (40 cm)
Acquired in 1979

Xipe Totec, the Aztec god of spring and regeneration, figures in many Mesoamerican cults. A fertility deity, Xipe Totec vividly conveys the concept of death and rebirth by wearing the flayed skin of a sacrificial victim. Meaning literally "our lord, the flayed one," Xipe Totec is also associated with the arrival of spring, when the earth covers itself with a new coat of vegetation and exchanges its dead skin for a new one. During the corn-planting festival, Xipe Totec was worshipped by a priest who, dressed in the skin of a flayed victim, ritually enacted the death-and-renewal cycle of the earth. Xipe Totec was the divine embodiment of life emerging from the dead land and of the new plant sprouting from the seed.

In this sculpture, the face of a living being is seen behind the mouth and eye openings of the sacrificial victim, whose skin is laced together by cords at the back of the wearer's skull. Similar lacing is also seen on the chest, amid the vigorously articulated body covering. This work closely resembles Aztec stone figures in the smooth modeling, sturdy body, and rounded lips and eyes. Clay sculptures of Xipe are also common in the pre-Aztec art found in Nahua areas such as the Valley of Mexico and southern Veracruz, where figures in a similar red orange clay have been discovered.

The Mixtec culture came to prominence between 1200 and 1400 in northern Oaxaca, as the neighboring Zapotec culture gradually waned in power and influence. Mixtec culture is noted for its extraordinarily skilled arts and crafts, including lavishly polychromed pottery, intricate stone mosaics, fine metal jewelry, and elaborate manuscript painting. Outside the area of direct Mixtec control, works in a broadly Mixtec style were made from West Mexico to the Gulf Coast and into the Maya regions. Mixtec and Mixtec-influenced art is generally two-dimensional in form and is noted for its dense and brilliantly colored patterns. Sculpted figures are relatively rare, in contrast to the earlier West Mexico cultures of Colima, Jalisco, and Nayarit, which produced distinctive, vigorously modeled and painted figures. The complexity of the three-dimensional form and elaborately painted and incised surface of this vessel reflect a brilliant conjunction of West Mexican and Mixtec stylistic traits.

The *Rain God Vessel* represents an important aspect of Mesoamerican religious practice—deity impersonation—by which the gods were brought directly into the world of experience. The disguise portrayed in this piece, however, is a double one of both warrior and rain god. In the ancient shamanic traditions of West Mexico, this crouching figure is a shaman warrior, positioned as if ready to leap. He holds a club in his right hand and

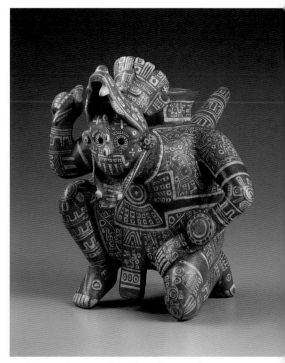

Polychromed ceramic; h. 9¾ in. (24.7 cm)
Acquired in 1974

has a shield attached to his left wrist; his entire head is engulfed in an animal-head helmet resembling a coyote. These are all appurtenances of the warrior, yet the small size of the weapon and shield suggest a fight more symbolic than real. The mask covering the face is the other element in the double disguise, and relates directly to deity impersonation. The ringed eyes, long fangs, and mustache markings are traits of the rain god, worshiped widely throughout Mesoamerica from Olmec times onward.

Seated Man, Possibly Huehueteotl
Aztec culture; Mexico; c. 1500

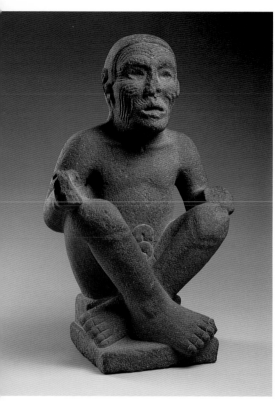

Basalt; h. 25¼ in. (64.1 cm)
Acquired in 1969

The Aztecs first came to the central Valley of Mexico as a nomadic group in approximately 1300 from the northwest desert of Mexico, and eventually settled on the shores of Lake Texcoco. Around 1337 they occupied an island in the middle of the lake and named it Tenochtitlan (modern-day Mexico City) after their chief, Tenoch. Aztec society was militaristic and regimented, and their art and culture show a pervasive interest in ritual and the symbolism of death. Guided by a sense of divine destiny, and a complex religion that included the practice of blood-sacrifice to ensure the daily reappearance of the sun and the survival of their people, the Aztec established themselves as masters over much of Mesoamerica north of the Maya area until the conquest by the Spanish in 1521.

The Aztec pantheon included a vast number of gods who encapsulated almost every function of time and life. Many of these deities were borrowed from other cultures of Mexico and given a distinctively Aztec cast that reflected their political and social structures. The Kimbell's *Seated Man* was probably a local cult image and may have served as a guardian figure for the stairway of an Aztec temple platform. On ceremonial occasions he may have held a banner staff in his right hand and perhaps wore a special costume. His sturdy body and coarse features indicate that he is an old *macehualli*, or man of the people. The bold facial scarification and more subtle, abstract patterns on the kneecaps, shoulder blades, and vertebrae suggest that he also represents the "Old God," Huehueteotl, the Aztec patron of fire, and lord of the center of the Universe. At its most successful, Aztec sculptures, such as this, have a striking and monumental directness that sets them apart from their Maya and other Mesoamerican predecessors.

Pendant: Twin Warriors
Conte style; Azuero Peninsula, Panama;
c. 700–1200

Pendant: Two Deer Heads
Conte style; Azuero Peninsula, Panama,
c. 700–1200

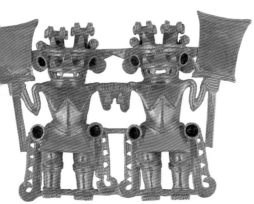

*Gold; 3¼ x 4⅞ x 1 in.
(8.2 x 12.2 x 2.5 cm)
Acquired in 1979*

The art of casting elaborate designs in gold had emerged in Panama by the middle of the first millennium A.D., regional schools excelling in the techniques of cast and beaten gold. Gold became the primary prestige material in this region, and high-status individuals wore numerous ornaments in this material, which were later placed in quantity in their burials.

One of the most distinctive regional styles of Panama is that of the Conte group. In the *Two Deer Heads* pendant, what may initially appear as merely decorative elaboration above the deer heads is in fact an artful stylization—a pair of outward-facing profile heads of an important deity, a crested saurian. The long, many-toothed snout of the crocodile is topped by a notched "crest" that alludes to the skin texture of the crocodile and

other lizards. The eyes of all four heads were once inset with bone, amber, or hardstone. The pendant may have had a talismanic function, invoking saurian or other animal spirits that were believed to have a special protective relationship to the wearer.

The subject of the *Twin Warriors* pendant is one of the most central to the Conte style, rendered here with exceptional technical and sculptural skill. A pair of standing bat-human figures hold paddle-shaped clubs in their outer hands. Each has a crested saurian head hanging from either side of its waistband. Their batlike heads are surmounted by what may be a pair of frontal birds, with simplified profile bird-heads at either side doubling as ear ornaments. These figures may represent warrior chiefs who were intermediaries between the earthly and cosmic realms. Pendants of this type probably functioned as emblems of status or as amulets.

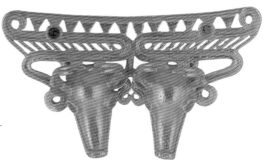

*Gold; 2⅞ x 4¾ x 1 in. (7.2 x 11.9 x 2.5 cm)
Acquired in 1979*

Standing Dignitary
Huari empire; South Coast, Peru; c. A.D. 600–1000

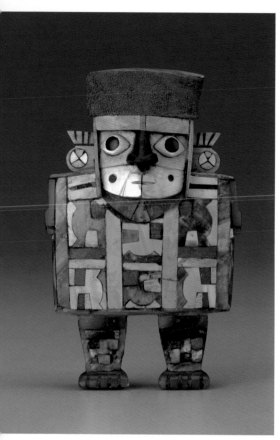

Wood with shell-and-stone inlay and silver;
h. 4 in. (10.2 cm)
Acquired in 2002

This rare Huari freestanding figurine is composed of intricate and densely patterned inlays of mother-of-pearl, purple and orange spondylus shell, mussel shell, turquoise, pyrite, greenstone, lapis lazuli, and silver (for the headdress) on a wood matrix. The torso is cloaked in a long ceremonial tunic decorated in an interlocking tapestry weave with three rows of a simplified and abstracted zoomorphic motif, which can be read as feline (jaguar or puma) heads, or as standing llamas. The wearing of a court tapestry tunic identified one's rank in the Huari empire, and the emphasis on the elaborateness of this costume suggests that the figure represented was a dignitary of some status. In life, tunics were worn as ceremonial garb, and in death they were placed over the wearer's mummy bale. In shell-and-stone inlay, the complex textile patterns of the tunic are inevitably simplified.

The corpus of Huari inlaid material is very small. This is the only published example of a freestanding figurine entirely covered in the inlaid shell technique, which is here particularly finely conceived and executed. The high-level craftsmanship and wide range of materials used in its manufacture indicate the presence in Huari society of an elite that could afford and appreciate such a luxury item, which probably served to convey the social status of the owner.

The city of Huari, near present-day Ayacucho in Peru, was the capital of a northern empire. The capital of a southern empire was at Tihuanaco on Lake Titicaca, in present-day Bolivia. Tihuanaco was a ceremonial and religious center and home to several magnificent stone structures. One of the most famous, the Gateway of the Sun, features a large, standing, frontal deity. The prominent enlarged head of the Kimbell's figure is similar to that of the deity on the Gateway of the Sun, but it is more naturalistic.

ACKNOWLEDGMENTS

The text of this *Handbook* has been written by current and former staff of the Kimbell Art Museum, assisted by a number of specialists who reviewed and updated selected areas of the collection.

Contributing Kimbell Art Museum staff (current and former)

Nancy E. Edwards (European art)
Timothy Potts (Ancient art)
Jennifer Casler Price (Asian, African, Oceanic, and Precolumbian art)
Charles F. Stuckey (Eighteenth- to twentieth-century European art)
Ruth Wilkins Sullivan (Ancient and European art to 1550)
Malcolm Warner (Eighteenth- to twentieth-century European art)

Contributing specialist advisors/editors

Colin B. Bailey (Eighteenth-century French art)
Michael D. Coe (Precolumbian art)
Helen I. Jessup (Southeast Asian art)
William B. Jordan (Spanish art)
Arielle P. Kozloff (Egyptian art)
Janice Leoshko (Indian and Nepalese art)
John Lunsford (African and Oceanic art)
Carolyn C. Wilson (Italian Renaissance art)

The text was edited by Timothy Potts, assisted by Nancy E. Edwards and Malcolm Warner. The *Handbook* was designed by Tom Dawson, museum designer, and copyedited by Wendy P. Gottlieb, manager of publications, assisted by Anna Lazarus.

INDEX OF ARTISTS AND TITLES

PHOTOGRAPH CREDITS